ROUGH
GUIDES

T0082328

POCKET **ROUGH GUIDE**
PARIS

...ten and researched by
...CHEL IFANS

CONTENTS

PARIS

A trip to Paris, famous as the most romantic of destinations, is one of those lifetime musts. Long the beating heart of European civilization, it remains one of the world's most refined yet passionate cities. The very fabric of the place is exquisite, with its magnificent avenues and atmospheric little backstreets, its grand formal gardens and intimate neighbourhood squares. And for all the famed pride and hauteur of its citizens, the city seems to be opening itself up to visitors even more, as it pedestrianizes an increasing number of riverbanks and squares and makes more of its splendid monuments accessible.

Pont Alexandre III

Passage Verdeau

The city is divided into twenty arrondissements in a spiral, centred on the Louvre. The inner hub comprises arrondissements 1ᵉʳ to 6ᵉ, and it's here that most of the major sights and museums are to be found. Through the heart of the city flows the Seine, skirting the pair of islands where Paris was founded. The historic pillars of the city, the church of Notre-Dame and the royal palace of the Louvre, stand on the riverbank along with one of the world's most distinctive landmarks – the Eiffel Tower. The Louvre has one of the world's truly outstanding museums, while the art collections of the Musée d'Orsay and Centre Pompidou are unrivalled.

Yet, Paris is a city that manages to feel both global and local. There is a host of smaller museums, and alongside the great civic monuments lie distinct *quartiers* that make Paris feel more a collection of sophisticated villages than a modern-day metropolis. Communities still revolve around well-loved cafés and restaurants, and the student, LGBTQ+ and immigrant quarters are, by and large, lively and well-defined. So too

When to visit

Spring is the classic time to visit Paris; the weather is mild (average daily 6–20°C), and plentiful bright sunny days are balanced by occasional freshening rain showers. Autumn, similarly mild, and winter (1–7°C) can be very rewarding, but on overcast days the city can feel melancholic and cold winds can really cut down the boulevards; winter sun, however, is the city's most flattering light, and hotels and restaurants are relatively uncrowded in this season. Paris in high summer (15–25°C) is not the best time to go: large numbers of Parisians desert the capital between July 15 and the end of August for the beach or mountains, and many restaurants and shops close down for much of this period.

Best places for a Parisian picnic

Picnicking on the grass is rarely allowed in central Paris – except on the elegant place des Vosges. But public benches, bridges and riverbanks make civilized alternatives: try the pedestrian bridge, the Pont des Arts; the Parc Rives de Seine; the lime-tree-shaded square Jean XXIII, behind Notre-Dame; the intimate Jardin du Palais Royal; or the splendid Jardin du Luxembourg. Further out, the parks of Buttes-Chaumont and André-Citroën offer idyllic spots for lounging on the grass.

are the wealthier districts, with their exclusive boutiques and restaurants. Neighbourhoods such as the elegant Marais, St-Germain and romantic Montmartre are ideal for shopping, sitting in cafés and aimless wandering, while throughout the city you can find peaceful green spaces, ranging from formal gardens and avant-garde municipal parks to ancient cemeteries. The capital has put much focus on sustainability in recent years and there are 1,000km of cycle paths around the city. It entered the Top 30 Global Sustainable Destinations list in 2023 and plans to become Europe's greenest city by 2030.

Above all, Paris is a city defined by its food. Few cities can compete with the thousand-and-one cafés, brasseries, *bistrots*, restaurants, bakeries, food shops and markets that line the boulevards and back alleys alike. You'll find anything from ultra-modern fashion temples to traditional mirrored palaces, tiny neighbourhood *bistrots* and crowded Vietnamese diners. Parisian nightlife is scarcely less renowned: its theatres and concert halls pull in artists of the highest calibre, while tiny venues hosting jazz gigs, art events and Parisian *chanson* nights offer a taste of a more local, avant-garde scene. The café-bars and clubs of Pigalle, the northeastern districts and the Left Bank fill with the young and style-conscious from all over.

Le Comptoir Général

Where to...

Eat

There's a real buzz about the current Paris dining scene, as talented young chefs open up new *bistrots* and rework French classics or experiment with unusual ingredients. A new wave of wine bars, or *caves à manger*, are also coming up with interesting cuisine, often in the form of sharing plates, focusing on well-sourced fresh ingredients paired with natural or organic wines. For more traditional French cuisine, you don't have to look far: every *quartier* has its own local *bistrot*, serving staples such as *steak au poivre*. For a really authentic experience, go for a classic brasserie, where you can dine amid splendid original decor. You can almost always eat more cheaply at lunchtime, when most places offer set menus from around €15. Even some of the haute cuisine restaurants become just about affordable at lunch.

OUR FAVOURITES: Le 5ème Cru see page 96, Abri see page 131, Le Square Gardette see page 141.

Drink

It's easy to go drinking in Paris. Most cafés stay open late and serve alcoholic drinks as well as coffee; old-fashioned wine bars and English-style 'pubs' can be found everywhere, while a new breed of hipster cocktail bars with a speakeasy vibe are currently very popular. The best areas for late-night drinking include Bastille, SoPi (South Pigalle), the Haut Marais and Oberkampf, with numerous youthful venues and many doubling as clubs. On the Left Bank, the Quartier Latin has lots of postage stamp-sized student dives, while St-Germain is the place for cheery posh partying.

OUR FAVOURITES: Le Comptoir Général see page 142, Candelaria see page 79, Moonshiner see page 89.

Shop

One of the most appealing shopping areas is St-Germain, with its wide variety of clothes shops and gourmet food stores. Designer wear and haute couture are concentrated around the Champs-Elysées and on rue du Faubourg-St-Honoré, while more alternative fashion boutiques can be found in the Marais, especially around rue Charlot, and in Montmartre, in particular on rue des Martyrs. For quirky one-off buys and curios, head for the atmospheric *passages* (nineteenth-century shopping arcades), just off the Grands Boulevards.

OUR FAVOURITES: Le Bon Marché see page 106, Merci see page 76, Astier de Villatte see page 57.

Go out

The Paris club scene is lively, with a variety of cool promoters offering eclectic, mixed programmes in a variety of venues from superclubs to refitted theatres and riverboats – check out the boats moored beside the Bibliothèque Nationale. Where the city truly excels though, is in its array of live music, from world music and rock to jazz and *chanson*. Montmartre is home to some iconic venues, as is the Rue des Lombards.

OUR FAVOURITES: Batofar see page 121, Le Sunside see page 67, L'International see page 143.

Paris at a glance

The Champs-Elysées and Tuileries p.34.
Sweeping avenues and impressive vistas – this is Paris at its grandest.

Montmartre and northern Paris p.122.
Famed for its artists, hilly Montmartre still clings to its countercultural identity.

WAGRAM

The Bois de Boulogne and western Paris p.144.
Lakes, gardens and an adventure playground.

Parc Monceau

Musée Jacquemart-André

Gare St-Laz

BOULEVARD HAUSSMANN

Print

N

AVENUE FOCH

AVENUE DE FRIEDLAND

Arc de Triomphe

AVENUE DES CHAMPS-ELYSÉES

AVENUE D'IENA

AVENUE MARCEAU

BLVD MALESHERBES

AVENUE FRANKLIN D. ROOSEVELT

8e

BOIT

16e

AVENUE MONTAIGNE

AVENUE DES CHAMPS-ELYSÉES

Colonne Ver

RUE ROYALE

CHAILLOT

AVENUE DU PRESIDENT WILSON

Grand Palais

Petit Palais

Ja

AVE GEORGES MANDEL

QUAI D'ORSAY

QUAI D'ORSAY

QUAI ANATOLE

QUAI DE

AVE PAUL DOUMER

Palais de Chaillot

AVENUE DE NEW YORK

QUAI BRANLY

River Seine

INVALIDES

BOULEVARD DE LA TOUR

BOULEVARD SAINT-

SAINT-GERMAIN

M d'O

RUE RAINOUARD

QUAI BRANLY

Musée du Quai Branly

RUE SAINT-DOMINIQUE

Tour Eiffel

AVENUE BOSQUET

Parc du Champs de Mars

Hôtel des Invalides

7e

BOULEVARD DE GRENELLE

AVENUE DE SUFFREN

AVENUE DE TOURVILLE

AVENUE DE BRETEUIL

GRENELLE

Ecole Militaire

AVENUE DE SUFFREN

AVENUE DE SÉGUR

AVENUE DE SAXE

RUE DE SÈVRES

BOULEVARD DE GRENELLE

AVENUE EMILE ZOLA

RUE DE SÈVRES

BLVD

DU MONTPARNASSE

The Eiffel Tower area p.42.
The tower soars above this refined district.

RUE DE VAUGIRARD

Tour Montpa

◁ **Day-trips** p.150.
Versailles, Chantilly and Giverny are easily accessible from Paris.

St-Germain p.100.
The Left Bank hosts myriad shops and cafés.

JAVEL

15e

MONTPARNASSE

14

0	metres	500
0	yards	500

Montparnasse and southern Paris p.110.
Head south for recherché sights and the city's most authentically local cafés and restaurant

e Grands Boulevards p.52.
d *passages*
 city's main shopping area,
 grand department stores
 elegant arcades.

Beaubourg and Les Halles p.62.
"Beaubourg", or the Pompidou Centre,
still wows visitors, while nearby
Les Halles is the city's largest
shopping centre.

LA VILLETTE

e Louvre p.30.
 of the world's
atest art museums.

Northeastern Paris p.134.
The vibrant districts of
northeastern Paris boast
some of the city's best nightlife.

Gare
du Nord

Parc des
Buttes
Chaumont

RUE DU
FAUBOURG MONTMARTRE

RUE LA FAYETTE

BLVD DE

MAGENTA

RUE DU FAUBOURG ST-MARTIN

BLVD DE STRASBOURG

Gare
de l'Est

BOULEVARD DE LA VILLETTE

9e

es
te
RUE LA FAYETTE
HAUSSMANN

BOULEVARD POISSONNIERE

Palais
Brongniart

RUE MONTMARTRE

2e

RUE REAUMUR

L'Hôpital
St-Louis

10e

RUE DU FAUBOURG DU TEMPLE

BELLEVILLE

h
Palais
Royal

1er

RUE ST-MARTIN

BLVD DE SEBASTOPOL

3e

The Marais p.68.
Arguably the city's most beguiling
quartier, with its handsome
Renaissance buildings.

RE RIVOLI

Forum des **Centre**
Halles **Pompidou**

BLVD DE

Musée
Picasso

BOULEVARD VOLTAIRE

usée du
ouvre
LOUVRE

RUE DE RIVOLI

QUAI DE LA MEGISSERIE

4e

Hôtel de
Ville

MARAIS

BOULEVARD BEAUMARCHAIS

BOULEVARD RICHARD LENOIR

11e

ALADAMS

Ile de
la Cité

QUAI DE L'HOTEL DE VILLE

RUE ST-ANTOINE

St-Germain-
des-Prés
AINT-GERMAIN

RUE DE LA CITE

Notre-
Dame

RUE DE LA TOURNELLE

Ile St-Louis

BLVD HENRI IV

BLVD
MORLAND

BOULEVARD BOURDON

BOULEVARD DE LA BASTILLE

RUE DU FAUBOURG ST-ANTOINE

-GERMAIN

Q. DE LA TOURNELLE

QUAI HENRI

RUE DE LYON

Opéra
Bastille

AVENUE DAUMESNIL

ulpice

6e

Palais du
Luxembourg
n du Luxembourg

RUE SAINT JACQUES

BOULEVARD SAINT MICHEL

QUARTIER
LATIN

QUAI SAINT BERNARD

River Seine

AVE LEDRU-ROLLIN

Promenade
Plantée

e du
bourg

RUE SAINT MICHEL

Universités
Paris VI et
Paris VII

BOULEVARD DIDEROT

Gare de Lyon

BOULEVARD SAINT MICHEL

Panthéon

5e

Jardin des
Plantes

BERCY

12e

ée
ne

The Islands p.24.
At the heart of Paris lie
two charming islands.

Gare
d'Austerlitz

13e

he Quartier Latin p.90.
he historic student quarter
reserves a flavour of both
edieval and bohemian Paris.

Bastille and Bercy p.82.
The Bastille quarter is full of lively bars,
restaurants and chic boutiques, while
the old warehouse district of Bercy
has been imaginatively renovated.

15

Things not to miss

It's not possible to see everything Paris has to offer in one trip – and we don't suggest you try. What follows is a selective taste of the city's highlights.

> Eiffel Tower
See page 42
It may seem familiar from afar, but close up the Eiffel Tower is still an excitingly improbable structure; ascending to the top is an unforgettable experience.

< Notre-Dame
See page 26
Rising from an island in the middle of the Seine, the majestic early Gothic cathedral of Notre-Dame is at the very core of Paris.

∨ Parc Rives de Seine
See page 101
Join the joggers and cyclists, have a picnic, or just soak up the wonderful views along this scenic riverside loop that takes in both the Right and Left banks.

< Place des Vosges
See page 72
A superb architectural ensemble lined with arcaded seventeenth-century buildings.

∨ Sainte-Chapelle
See page 24
Sainte-Chapelle's stunning stained-glass windows are among the greatest achievements of French High Gothic.

< **Musée Picasso**
See page 69
A fabulously restored Marais mansion is the setting for this unrivalled collection of Picasso's paintings, sculptures, drawings and ceramics.

∨ **Musée d'Orsay**
See page 100
France's greatest collection of Impressionist (and pre- and post-Impressionist) art, housed in a beautiful converted railway station.

∧ Centre Pompidou
See page 62

The Pompidou's radical "inside-out" architecture looks just as groundbreaking as it did when it first opened in the 1970s, and its modern art museum is a knockout.

‹ Jardin du Luxembourg
See page 105

These delightful formal gardens are the city's most appealing; people relax on green metal chairs, children sail toy yachts around the pond, and old men play chess under the chestnut trees.

∧ **Père-Lachaise**
See page 138
Not only is this one of the world's most famous cemeteries, where Oscar Wilde, Edith Piaf and Frederic Chopin lie buried, it's also one of the most hauntingly beautiful, full of towering trees and ivy-covered statuary.

∨ **Musée Rodin**
See page 49
Rodin's finest works are shown off to their best advantage in the sculptor's elegant eighteenth-century mansion and garden.

∧ Louvre

See page 30

You could easily spend a whole day (and more) exploring the Louvre's world-class collections, including famous Italian Renaissance paintings and ancient Greek and Roman sculpture.

∧ Haut Marais

See page 75

This little enclave near the revamped place de la République buzzes with creativity as ever more design boutiques, art galleries, hip cocktail bars and lifestyle hotels set up here.

< **Fondation Louis Vuitton**
See page 145
Frank Gehry's astonishing "cloud of glass" in the Bois de Boulogne holds an inspiring collection of contemporary art.

∨ **Passages**
See page 54
These atmospheric nineteenth-century shopping arcades have an air of nostalgia about them, with their shops selling secondhand books, antique prints, vintage film posters and old stamps, coins and postcards.

THINGS NOT TO MISS

Day One in Paris

Ile de la Cité See page 24. Paris was founded on this tiny island, which rises out of the River Seine.

Notre-Dame See page 26. The magnificent Gothic cathedral of Notre-Dame is the uplifting, historic heart of the city.

Sainte-Chapelle See page 24. This chapel is an exquisite jewel box, walled in medieval stained glass.

Pont-Neuf See page 24. The riverbank quays lead west to the Pont-Neuf, the oldest bridge in the city, and beyond to the square du Vert Galant, where you can sit and watch the Seine flow by.

Pont Neuf

🍴 **Lunch** See page 108. Head away from the tourist bustle, south into St-Germain, for lunch at contemporary *bistrot*, *L'Epi Dupin*.

Jardin du Luxembourg See page 105. These gardens are filled with people playing tennis or chess and couples strolling round the elegant lawns.

Pont des Arts See page 100. This handsome pedestrian bridge runs from St-Germain to the Louvre; you can pick up the Batobus beside it and head downriver.

Musée d'Orsay See page 100. This grand old railway station houses some of the most beguiling Impressionist works ever painted.

Musée d'Orsay

Eiffel Tower See page 42. Continue on the Batobus or stroll along the waterside Parc Rives de Seine to this world-famous structure, ever more thrilling the closer you get to it.

🍴 **Dinner** See page 120. Head over to Montparnasse for a meal at small but perfect *bistrot*, *Le Timbre*.

Batobus Eiffel tower

Day Two in Paris

Centre Pompidou See page 62. Begin the day with a crash course in modern art – the Musée National d'Art Moderne has an unbeatable collection of Matisses, Picassos, and more.

The Marais See page 68. Amble through the delightful Marais quarter, abounding in fascinating museums, inviting cafés and quirky boutiques.

Lunch See page 77. Stop off at the *Marché des Enfants Rouges*, known for its street food; sit at one of the communal tables or grab a takeaway and picnic in the nearby Square du Temple.

Galerie Vivienne See page 54. Head over to the Grands Boulevards and explore the enchanting passages, nineteenth-century shopping arcades. The Galerie Vivienne is probably the finest, with its lofty glass ceiling, floor mosaics and Grecian motifs.

Palais-Royal See page 53. The handsome arcaded buildings of the Palais Royal enclose peaceful gardens and shelter some quirky antique shops selling pipes, Légion d'Honneur medals and lead soldiers.

Jardin des Tuileries See page 38. Saunter along the chestnut tree-lined alleys of the Jardin des Tuileries, admiring its grand vistas, formal flower beds and fountains.

Place de la Concorde See page 37. An impressive piece of town planning, with a gold-tipped obelisk at its centre, broad avenues radiating off it, and grand monuments, such as the Arc de Triomphe, in every direction.

Dinner See page 40. Eat out on the terrace or in the classy dining room of *Loulou*, the restaurant of Les Arts Décoratifs.

Le Marais

Jardin des Tuileries

Place de la Concorde

Riverside Paris

The elegant riverbanks and bridges of the Seine provide some of Paris's finest vistas. Spend a day strolling along the riverside and enjoying the views.

Boat trip See page 172. The classic way to enjoy the Seine is from the water. Take a bâteau mouche from the Pont de l'Alma or hop on the Batobus.

Parc Rives de Seine See page 101. Check out what's happening on this landscaped riverfront promenade; there are frequent events, food festivals and activities, and it's a great place to simply linger.

🍴 **Lunch** See page 142. Enjoy a drink, tapas or half-dozen oysters at the quirky floating barge Rosa Bonheur sur Seine.

Pont des Arts See page 100. The pedestrian Pont des Arts enjoys classic views of the Ile de la Cité and the Louvre.

River islands See pages 24 and 28. The graceful Pont-Neuf will take you across to the Ile de la Cite and the Ile Saint Louis, with its leafy riverside quais. Further south, the slender Ile aux Cygnes offers a tranquil promenade that culminates at a mini statue of Liberty.

🍴 **Dinner** See page 51. Drink in wonderful views of the Seine and the Eiffel Tower from the terrace of Monsieur Bleu, an elegant restaurant within the Palais de Tokyo contemporary art gallery.

The Batobus

Ile aux Cygnes

Monsieur Bleu

Budget Paris

Despite Paris's reputation as an expensive city, there are many treats to be enjoyed for free, plus plenty of good-value deals to be had at restaurants.

Petit Palais See page 36. The Petit Palais regularly hosts chamber concerts during the day, many free of charge. Its intriguing collection of artworks is also free to visit.

Musée d'Art Moderne de la Ville de Paris See page 46. This free art gallery celebrates Paris's Modernists; there's a stunning mural by Matisse and great views across the Seine.

Buses See page 171. Touring by bus is enjoyable and inexpensive; hop on the #63 near the Pont de l'Alma and take a sightseeing ride along the Left Bank, passing Les Invalides and the Musée d'Orsay.

Petit Palais

🍴 Lunch See page 99. Alight at Maubert-Mutualité and seek out Les Trublions, a contemporary bistrot where you can get an excellent two-course lunch for €14.90.

Hôtel de Ville See page 75. Head back to the Right Bank and check out the latest free exhibition at the Hôtel de Ville; they're usually on a Parisian theme and very worthwhile.

Centre Pompidou See page 62. The Pompidou Centre's Galerie de Photographies stages free photography exhibitions taken from its extensive archives, particularly strong on the 1920s and 30s and including works by Man Ray and Brassaï.

Hôtel de Ville

🍴 Dinner See page 87. The French cuisine at charming restaurant L'Encrier is excellent value, with set menus from €22.

Centre Pompidou

PLACES

Quintessential Paris scene at sunset

The Islands

There's no better place to start a tour of Paris than its two river islands, Ile de la Cité, the city's ancient core, and charming, village-like Ile St-Louis. The Ile de la Cité is where Paris began. It was settled in around 300 BC by a Celtic tribe, the *Parisii*, and in 52 BC was overrun by the Romans who built a palace-fortress at the western end of the island. In the tenth century the Frankish kings transformed this fortress into a splendid palace, of which the Sainte-Chapelle and the Conciergerie prison survive today, while at the other end of the island they erected the great cathedral of Notre-Dame. The maze of medieval streets that grew up around these monuments was largely erased in the nineteenth century by Baron Haussmann, Napoléon III's Préfet de la Seine, and replaced with imposing public buildings, housing the police and law courts – though nowadays most of the activity has shifted to more modern offices in the 17e and the buildings lie more or less empty, possibly to be opened up to the public and turned into museums at some point in the future.

Pont-Neuf

MAP P.26, POCKET MAP C16
Ⓜ Pont Neuf.

Despite its name, the **Pont-Neuf** is Paris's oldest surviving bridge, built in 1607 by Henri IV, one of the city's first great town planners. A handsome stone construction with twelve arches, the bridge links the western tip of the Ile de la Cité with both banks of the river. It was the first in Paris to be made of stone rather than wood, hence the name. Henri is commemorated with a stately equestrian statue.

Square du Vert-Galant

MAP P.26, POCKET MAP C16
Ⓜ Pont Neuf.

Enclosed within the triangular "stern" of the island, the **square du Vert-Galant** is a tranquil, tree-lined garden and popular lovers' haunt. The square takes its name (a "Vert-Galant" is a "green" or "lusty" gentleman) from the nickname given to Henri IV, whose amorous exploits were legendary.

Place Dauphine

MAP P.26, POCKET MAP C16
Ⓜ Cité.

Red-brick seventeenth-century houses flank the entrance to **place Dauphine**, one of the city's most secluded and attractive squares, lined with venerable townhouses. The noise of traffic recedes here, likely to be replaced by nothing more intrusive than the gentle tap of boules being played in the shade of the chestnuts.

Sainte-Chapelle

MAP P.26, POCKET MAP D16
4 bd du Palais Ⓜ Cité. Ⓦ sainte-chapelle.fr.
Charge, plus option to combine ticket with the Conciergerie.

The slender spire of the **Sainte-Chapelle** soars high above the Palais de Justice (law courts). Though damaged in the Revolution, it was sensitively restored in the mid-nineteenth century and remains one of the finest achievements of French High

Gothic, renowned for its exquisite stained-glass windows.

The building was constructed by Louis IX between 1242 and 1248 to house a collection of holy relics, including Christ's crown of thorns and a fragment of the True Cross, bought from the bankrupt empire of Byzantium. First you enter the lower chapel, where servants would have worshipped; very simply decorated, it gives no clue as to the splendour that lies ahead in the upper chapel. Here you're greeted by a truly dazzling sight – a vast, almost uninterrupted expanse of magnificent stained glass, supported by deceptively fragile-looking stone columns. When the sun streams through, the glowing blues and reds of the stained glass dapple the interior and it feels as if you're surrounded by myriad brilliant butterflies. The windows, two-thirds of which are original (the others are from the nineteenth-century restoration), tell virtually the entire story of the Bible, beginning on the north side with Genesis and various other books of the Old Testament, continuing with the Passion of Christ (east end), and ending with the Apocalypse in the rose window.

Conciergerie

MAP P.26, POCKET MAP D16

2 bd du Palais Ⓜ Cité. Ⓦ paris-conciergerie.fr. Charge, plus option to combine ticket with Sainte-Chapelle.

Located within the Palais de Justice complex, the **Conciergerie** is Paris's oldest prison, where Marie-Antoinette and, in their turn, the leading figures of the Revolution were incarcerated before execution. It was turned into a prison – and put in the charge of a "concierge", or steward – after Etienne Marcel's uprising in 1358 led Charles V to decamp to the greater security of the Louvre. One of its towers, on the corner of the quai de l'Horloge, bears Paris's first public clock, built in 1370.

Inside are several splendidly vaulted Gothic halls, among the few surviving vestiges of the original Capetian palace. Elsewhere a number of rooms and prisoners' cells, including Marie-Antoinette's, have been reconstructed to show what they might have been like at the time of the French Revolution.

Interior of Sainte-Chapelle

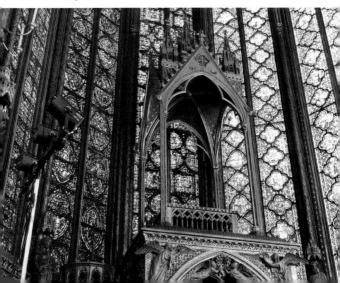

Cathédrale de Notre-Dame

Cathédrale de Notre-Dame

MAP P.26, POCKET MAP E17

Ⓜ Cité & Ⓜ RER St-Michel.
Ⓦ notredamedeparis.fr. Cathedral; free.
Towers: Ⓦ tours-notre-dame-de-paris.
fr; Charge, but under-18s and EU
residents under 26 free. Free guided
tours in English on certain days; meet at
welcome desk.

One of the masterpieces of the
Gothic age, the **Cathédrale de
Notre-Dame** rears up from the
Ile de la Cité like a ship moored
by huge flying buttresses. It was
among the first of the great Gothic
cathedrals built in northern France
and one of the most ambitious, its
nave reaching an unprecedented
33m. It was begun in 1160 and
completed around 1345. In
the seventeenth and eighteenth
centuries it fell into decline,
suffering its worst depredations
during the Revolution. In the
1820s that the cathedral was
at last given a much-needed
restoration, a task entrusted to the
great architect-restorer Viollet-le-
Duc, who carried out a thorough
renovation, remaking much of the
statuary on the facade (the originals
can be seen in the Musée National
du Moyen Age) and adding

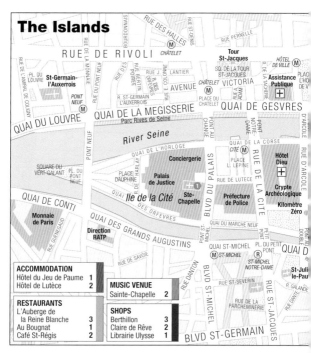

the steeple and baleful-looking gargoyles, which you can see close up if you climb the towers.

On April 15th 2019, a huge fire took hold of the cathedral, and the world watched as firefighters attacked the blaze. Most damage was done to the upper part of the cathedral, notably the spire. Since the fire, the cathedral has been partially shut for repairs but is due to reopen in December 2024. Until then, the parvis and the archaeological crypt remain open. Redevelopment of the forecourt is scheduled for 2027. Incidentally, treasures salvaged from the fire are part of an exhibition which opened in the Louvre in 2023.

The cathedral's facade is one of its most impressive exterior features; the Romanesque influence is still visible, not least in its solid H-shape, but the overriding impression is one of lightness and grace, created in part by the delicate filigree work of the central rose window and the gallery above.

Inside, you're struck by the dramatic contrast between the darkness of the nave and the light falling on the first great clustered pillars of the choir. It is the end walls of the transepts which admit all this light, being nearly two-thirds glass, including two magnificent rose windows coloured in imperial purple. These, together with the vaulting and the soaring shafts reaching to the springs of the vaults, are all definite Gothic elements, while there remains a strong sense of Romanesque in the stout round pillars of the nave and the general sense of four-squareness.

Kilométre Zéro

MAP P.26, POCKET MAP D17
Ⓜ Cité.

On the pavement by the west door of Notre-Dame is a spot,

Ile St-Louis

marked by a bronze star, known as **Kilométre Zéro**, from which all main-road distances in France are calculated.

Crypte Archéologique

MAP P.26, POCKET MAP D17
Parvis-Notre-Dame ⓂCité & ⓂRER St-Michel. Ⓦcrypte.paris.fr. Charge.
The well-presented **Crypte Archéologique** is a large, excavated area under the place du Parvis revealing the remains of the original cathedral, as well as vestiges of the streets and houses that once clustered around Notre-Dame: most are medieval, but some date as far back as Gallo-Roman times.

Le Mémorial de la Déportation

MAP P.26, POCKET MAP E17
ⓂCité. Free.
Scarcely visible above ground, the stark and moving **Mémorial de la Déportation** is the symbolic tomb of the 200,000 French who died in Nazi concentration camps during World War II – among them Jews, Resistance fighters and forced labourers. Stairs barely shoulder-wide descend into a space like a prison yard and then into a crypt, off which is a long, narrow, stifling corridor, its walls covered in thousands of points of light representing the dead. Above the exit are the words "Pardonne, n'oublie pas" ("Forgive; do not forget").

Ile St-Louis

MAP P.26, POCKET MAP E17–F18
ⓂPont-Marie.
The smaller of the two islands, **Ile St-Louis**, is prime strolling territory. Unlike its larger neighbour, it has no big sights; rather, the island's allure lies in its handsome ensemble of austerely beautiful seventeenth-century houses, tree-lined *quais* and narrow streets, crammed with restaurants, art galleries and gift shops. For centuries the Ile St-Louis was nothing but swampy pastureland, a haunt of lovers, duellists and miscreants on the run, until in the seventeenth century the real estate developer, Christophe Marie, filled it with elegant mansions.

Shops

Berthillon

MAP P.26, POCKET MAP F17
31 rue St-Louis-en-l'Île Ⓜ Pont-Marie.
Ⓦ berthillon.fr.
Long queues form for Berthillon's exquisite ice creams that come in unusual flavours, such as rhubarb and Earl Grey tea.

Claire de Reve

MAP P.26, POCKET MAP F17
35 rue St-Louis-en-l'Île Ⓜ Pont-Marie.
Ⓦ clairedereve.com.
This is the shop of your childhood dreams, stuffed with exquisite wind-up toys and handmade puppets on strings, such as The Three Musketeers, Puss in Boots and other fairy-tale characters – many of them one-offs.

Librairie Ulysse

MAP P.26, POCKET MAP F17
26 rue St-Louis-en-l'Île Ⓜ Pont-Marie.
A tiny bookshop, piled from floor to ceiling with new and secondhand travel books.

Restaurants

L'Auberge de la Reine Blanche

MAP P.26, POCKET MAP J9
30 rue St-Louis-en-l'Île Ⓜ Pont-Marie.
Ⓦ aubergedelareineblanche.fr.
This long-established little restaurant creates a homely atmosphere with its warm welcome, bistro-style chairs and tables, and copper pans hanging from the wood-beamed ceiling. Expect classics such as *soupe à l'oignon*, *coq au vin* and *tarte tatin*, as well as more creative dishes – perhaps honey-spiced duck. €

Au Bougnat

MAP P.26, POCKET MAP H9
26 rue Chanoinesse ⓂSt-Michel/Cité.
Ⓦ aubougnat.com.

Set in one the few remaining seventeenth-century houses on the island, this traditional *bistrot* with its attractive wood-panelled interior, draws in regulars and tourists for its reliable French cuisine.

Café St-Régis

MAP P.26, POCKET MAP E17
6 rue Jean du Bellay Ⓜ Pont-Marie.
Ⓦ lesaintregis-paris.com.
A buzzy café-restaurant, ideally situated for people-watching. Come for a morning coffee or the good-value happy hour. Tasty French and American snacks and dishes.

Classical Music

Sainte-Chapelle

MAP P.26, POCKET MAP D16
4 bd du Palais Ⓜ Cité.
Ⓦ classictic.com.
Classical music concerts are held in the splendid surroundings of the chapel more or less daily.

Berthillon

The Louvre

The Louvre is one of the world's truly great museums. Opened in 1793, during the Revolution, it soon acquired the largest art collection on earth, thanks to Napoleon's conquests. Today, it houses paintings, sculpture and precious art objects, from Ancient Egyptian jewellery to the beginnings of Impressionism. Separate from the Louvre proper but within the palace is the museum Les Arts Décoratifs, dedicated to fashion and textiles, decorative arts and advertising.

The palace

MAP P.32, POCKET MAP B15–C15

The site of the French court for centuries, the palace was originally little more than a feudal fortress begun by Philippe-Auguste in 1200. It wasn't until the reign of François I that the foundations of the present-day building were laid, and from then on almost every sovereign added to the Louvre, leaving the **palace** a surprisingly harmonious building. Even with the addition in 1989 of the initially controversial glass **Pyramide** in the Cour Napoléon – an extraordinary leap of imagination conceived by architect I.M. Pei – the overall effect of the Louvre is of a quintessentially French grandeur and symmetry.

Painting

The largest of the museum's collections is its **paintings**. The early **Italians** are perhaps the most interesting, among them Leonardo da Vinci's *Mona Lisa*. If you want to get near her, go during one of the evening openings or first thing in the day. Other highlights of the Italian collection include two Botticelli frescoes and Fra Angelico's

Musée du Louvre and La Pyramide

Visiting the Louvre

Ⓜ Louvre Rivoli/Palais Royal-Musée du Louvre, Ⓦ louvre.fr. Charge to enter, but free to under-18s and under-26s who are resident in EEA on Fri after 6pm & everyone on the first Sat of each month between 6–9.45pm.

You can buy tickets in advance online. The main entrance is via the Pyramide, but you'll find shorter queues at the entrance directly under the Arc du Carrousel (also accessible from 99 rue de Rivoli and from the Palais Royal-Musée du Louvre métro stop). You can join the fast-track queue at the Pyramide if you've pre-booked or have a museum pass (see page 174).

The museum has numerous cafés, notably the elegantly modern *Café Richelieu* (first floor, Richelieu) with its wonderful summer-only terrace offering a view of the Pyramide; *Café Mollien* (first floor, Denon), which is the busiest but also has a summer terrace; and the cosy and classy *Café Denon* (lower ground floor, Denon).

Coronation of the Virgin. Fifteenth- to seventeenth-century Italian paintings line the Grande Galerie, including Leonardo's *Virgin and Child with St Anne* and *Virgin of the Rocks*. Epic-scale nineteenth-century French works are displayed in the parallel suite of rooms, among them the *Coronation of Napoleon I* by David, Ingres' languorous nude *La Grande Odalisque*, and Géricault's harrowing *Raft of the Medusa*.

A good point to start a circuit of **French paintings** is with the master of French Classicism, Poussin; his profound themes, taken from antiquity, the Bible and mythology, were to influence generations of artists. You'll need a healthy appetite for Classicism in the next suite of rooms, but there are some arresting portraits. When you move into the less severe eighteenth century, the more intimate paintings of Watteau come as a relief, as do Chardin's intense still lifes. In the later part of the collection, the chilly wind of Neoclassicism blows through the paintings of Gros, Gérard, Prud'hon, David and Ingres, contrasting with the more sentimental style that begins with Greuze and continues into the Romanticism of Géricault and Delacroix. The final rooms take in Corot and the Barbizon school, the precursors of Impressionism. The Louvre's collection of French painting stops at 1848, a date picked up by the Musée d'Orsay (see page 100).

Antiquities

The **Near Eastern Antiquities** category covers the Mesopotamian, Sumerian, Babylonian, Assyrian and Phoenician civilizations, and the art of ancient Persia. One of the collection's most important exhibits is the Code of Hammurabi, a basalt stele from around 1800 BC, covered in Akkadian script setting down King Hammurabi's rules of conduct for his subjects.

The **Egyptian Antiquities** collection starts with the atmospheric crypt of the Sphinx. Everyday life is illustrated through cooking utensils, jewellery, the principles of hieroglyphics, sarcophagi and a host of mummified cats. The collection continues with the development of Egyptian art.

In 2023, a new exhibition opened which includes relics, pieces of gold and silverware, and illuminated manuscripts that survived the fire in Notre Dame Cathedral. At the time of writing, it is planned to remain for a couple of years.

The biggest crowd-pullers after the *Mona Lisa* are found in the **Greek and Roman Antiquities** section: the *Winged Victory of Samothrace*, and the late second-century-BC *Venus de Milo*, striking a classic model's pose.

section and continues through 81 relentlessly superb rooms to a salon decorated in the style of Louis-Philippe, the last king of France. Walking through the complete chronology gives a powerful sense of the evolution of aesthetic taste at its most refined and opulent. The circuit also passes through the breathtaking apartments of Napoléon III's minister of state.

Sculpture

The **Sculpture** section covers the development of the art in France from the Romanesque to Rodin in the Richelieu wing, and Italian and northern European sculpture in the Denon wing, including Michelangelo's *Slaves*, designed for the tomb of Pope Julius II. The huge glass-covered courtyards of the Richelieu wing – the cour Marly with the Marly Horses, which once graced place de la Concorde, and the cour Puget with

Egyptian art in the Louvre

Objets d'Art

The vast **Objets d'Art** section presents the finest tapestries, ceramics, jewellery and furniture commissioned by France's wealthiest patrons. It begins with the rather pious Middle Ages

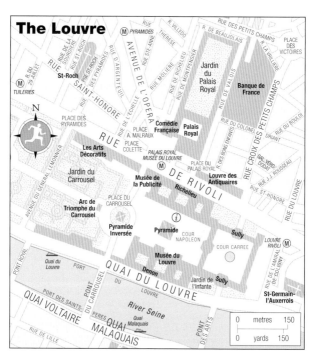

Puget's *Milon de Crotone* as the centrepiece – are very impressive.

Islamic Art

The **Islamic Art** collection was opened in 2012 in the central cour Visconti. The courtyard is covered by an undulating, gold-filigree glass roof – supported by just eight slender columns – that seems to float in mid-air. Suggestive for some of the shimmering wings of an insect, for others a flying carpet or sand dunes, the roof is a fittingly stunning 'crown' to the beautiful artworks below. Some 3,000 objects are on display, many never before seen by the public, ranging from early Islamic inscriptions to intricate Moorish ivories, and from ninth-century Iraqi moulded glass to exquisite miniature paintings from the courts of Mughal India.

Les Arts Décoratifs

MAP P.32, POCKET MAP B14
107 rue de Rivoli, Ⓦ madparis.fr. Charge, includes audioguide.

Separate from the rest of the Louvre, **Les Arts Décoratifs** is devoted to design and the applied arts, including fashion, textiles and graphic art. The core of its collection is furnishings, arranged chronologically and starting with the medieval and Renaissance rooms, displaying curiously shaped and beautifully carved pieces, religious paintings, tapestries and Venetian glass.

The Art Nouveau and Art Deco rooms include a 1903 bedroom by Hector Guimard – the Art Nouveau designer behind the original Paris métro stations. Individual designers of the 1980s and 90s, such as **Philippe Starck,** are also represented.

The museum stages regular exhibitions on designers such as Christian Dior and on themes as diverse as jewellery, Barbie-doll fashion and hairstyles. Its extensive collection of advertising posters, including Toulouse-Lautrec's posters of Montmartre nightlife, is also the subject of frequent, engaging exhibitions. The museum ticket is valid all day, so you could, for example, break up a visit with lunch at the elegant ground-floor restaurant, Loulou (Ⓦ loulou-paris. com; see page 40), which has seating outside in the Tuileries gardens in the summer.

Maria Grazia Chiuri's designs for Christian Dior in Musée des Arts Décoratifs

The Champs-Elysées and Tuileries

The breathtakingly ambitious Champs-Elysées is part of a grand, nine-kilometre axis, often referred to as the "Voie Triomphale", or Triumphal Way, that extends from the Louvre at the heart of the city to the Défense business district in the west. Combining imperial pomp and supreme elegance, it offers impressive vistas along its entire length and incorporates some of the city's most famous landmarks: the place de la Concorde, Tuileries gardens and the Arc de Triomphe. The whole ensemble is so regular and geometrical it looks as though it might have been laid out by a single town planner rather than successive kings, emperors and presidents, all keen to add their stamp and promote French power and prestige.

The Champs-Elysées

MAP P.36, POCKET MAP B5–E6

The celebrated avenue **des Champs-Elysées**, a popular rallying point at times of national celebration (and crisis)

Colossal Arc de Triomphe

and the scene of big military parades on Bastille Day, sweeps down from the Arc de Triomphe towards the place de la Concorde. Its heyday was during the Second Empire, when members of the haute bourgeoisie built themselves splendid mansions along its length and fashionable society frequented the avenue's cafés and theatres. Nowadays this broad, tree-lined avenue is still an impressive sight, especially when viewed from the place de la Concorde, and although fast-food outlets and chain stores tend to predominate, it has been steadily regaining some of its former cachet as a chic address. A number of exclusive designers, such as Louis Vuitton, and major fashion brands including H&M and Abercrombie & Fitch, have moved in, along with a major branch of the Galeries Lafayette department store. Remnants of the avenue's glitzy past live on at the *Lido* cabaret, *Fouquet's*

The Grand Palais

café-restaurant, the perfumier Guerlain's shop (occupying an exquisite 1913 building), and the former *Claridges* hotel, now a swanky shopping arcade.

Arc de Triomphe

MAP P.36, POCKET MAP B5

Ⓜ Charles-de-Gaulle. Ⓦ paris-arc-de-triomphe.fr. Charge.

Crowning the Champs-Elysées, the **Arc de Triomphe** sits imposingly in the middle of place Charles de Gaulle, also known as l'Etoile ("star") on account of the twelve avenues radiating from it. Modelled on the ancient Roman triumphal arches, this imperial behemoth was built by Napoleon as a homage to the armies of France and is engraved with the names of 660 generals and numerous French battles. The best of the exterior reliefs is François Rude's *Marseillaise*, in which an Amazon-type figure personifying the Revolution charges forward with a sword, her face contorted in a fierce rallying cry. A quiet reminder of the less glorious side of war is the tomb of the unknown soldier, placed beneath the arch and marked by an eternal flame that is stoked every evening by war veterans. The climb up to the top is well worth it for the panoramic views.

Grand Palais

MAP P.36, POCKET MAP D6

Ⓜ Champs-Elysées-Clemenceau. Ⓦ grandpalais.fr. Charge.

At the lower end of the Champs-Elysées is the **Grand Palais**, a grandiose Neoclassical building with a fine glass and ironwork cupola, created for the 1900 Exposition Universelle. The cupola forms the centrepiece of the *nef* (nave), a huge, impressive exhibition space, used for large-scale installations, fashion shows and trade fairs. In the north wing of the building is the Galeries nationales, Paris's prime venue for major art retrospectives.

The Grand Palais' western wing houses the Palais de la Découverte (Ⓦ palais-decouverte.fr; charge), Paris's original science museum dating from the late 1930s, with interactive exhibits, an excellent

The Petit Palais

MAP P.36, POCKET MAP D6–7
Av Winston Churchill Ⓜ Champs-Elysées-
Clemenceau. Ⓦ petitpalais.paris.fr. Free.
The **Petit Palais** houses the
Musée des Beaux Arts. Built
at the same time as its larger
neighbour the Grand Palais, the
building is hardly "petit" but
certainly palatial, with beautiful
spiral wrought-iron staircases
and a grand gallery on the lines
of Versailles' Hall of Mirrors.
The museum has an extensive
collection of paintings, sculpture
and decorative artworks, ranging
from the ancient Greek and
Roman period up to the early
twentieth century. At first sight
it looks like it's mopped up the
leftovers after the city's other
galleries have taken their pick,
but there are some real gems
here, such as Monet's *Sunset
at Lavacourt* and Courbet's
provocative *Young Ladies on*

Musée de l'Orangerie

planetarium and engaging
exhibitions on subjects as diverse
as dinosaurs, clay and climate
change. Due to reopen in 2024
following renovation.

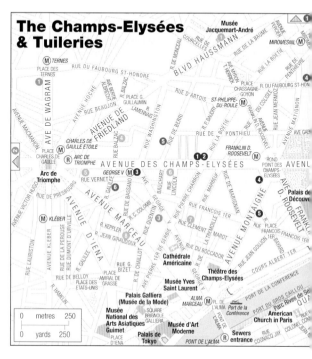

The Champs-Elysées & Tuileries

the Bank of the Seine. There's also fantasy jewellery of the Art Nouveau period, a fine collection of seventeenth-century Dutch landscape painting, Russian icons and effete eighteenth-century furniture and porcelain. A stylish café opens out onto the interior garden, and lunchtime concerts are often held on Thursdays.

Musée Jacquemart-André

MAP P.36, POCKET MAP D5

158 bd Haussmann Ⓜ Miromesnil/St-Philippe-du-Roule. Ⓦ musee-jacquemart-andre.com. Charge.

The **Musée Jacquemart-André** is set in a magnificent nineteenth-century *hôtel particulier* (mansion), hung with the superb artworks accumulated on the travels of banker Edouard André and his wife, former society portraitist Nélie Jacquemart. A stunning distillation of fifteenth-

and sixteenth-century Italian genius, including works by Tiepolo, Botticelli, Donatello, Mantegna and Uccello, forms the core of the collection. Almost as compelling as the splendid interior and collection of paintings is the insight gleaned into a grand nineteenth-century lifestyle.

Place de la Concorde

MAP P.36, POCKET MAP E6–7

Ⓜ Concorde.

The vast **place de la Concorde** has a much less peaceful history than its name suggests. Between 1793 and 1795, some 1,300 people died here beneath the Revolutionary guillotine – Louis XVI, Marie-Antoinette and Robespierre among them. Today, constantly circumnavigated by traffic, the centrepiece of the place is a gold-tipped obelisk from the temple of Ramses at Luxor,

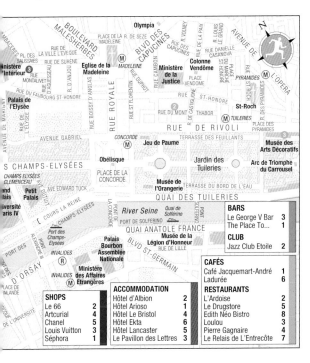

offered as a favour-currying gesture by the viceroy of Egypt in 1829.

Jardin des Tuileries

MAP P.36, POCKET MAP E7–F7
Ⓜ Concorde/Tuileries.

The **Jardin des Tuileries**, the formal French garden par excellence, dates back to the 1570s, when Catherine de Médicis cleared the site of the medieval warren of tile makers (*tuileries*) to make way for a palace and grounds. One hundred years later, Louis XIV commissioned André Le Nôtre to redesign them, and the results are largely what you see today: straight avenues, formal flower beds and splendid vistas. The central alley is lined with clipped chestnuts and manicured lawns, and framed at each end by ornamental pools, surrounded by an impressive gallery of copies of statues by the likes of Rodin. Much loved by children are the trampolines on the rue de Rivoli side and the funfair that sets up here in the summer.

Musée de l'Orangerie

MAP P.36, POCKET MAP E7
Jardin des Tuileries Ⓜ Concorde. Ⓦ musee-orangerie.fr. Charge.

The Jardin des Tuileries' **Orangerie**, an elegant Neoclassical-style building designed to protect the garden's orange trees, now houses a private collection of late nineteenth-century art, including eight of Monet's giant water lily paintings. Highlights from the rest of the collection include sensuous nudes by Renoir and a number of Cézanne still lifes. Book online in advance to avoid long queues.

Jeu de Paume

MAP P.36, POCKET MAP E6–7
Jardin des Tuileries Ⓜ Concorde. Ⓦ jeudepaume.org. Charge.

The Neoclassical **Jeu de Paume** is a major exhibition space dedicated to photography and video art. It's not quite as well lit as you might expect from the first impression of the soaring, light-filled foyer, but it's a top venue for catching major retrospectives of photographers.

Musée Jacquemart-André

Shops

Le 66

MAP P.36, POCKET MAP C6

66 av des Champs-Elysées Ⓜ George V. Ⓦ le66.fr.

This stylishly designed glass-walled concept store stocks a great selection of high-end, often lesser-known, streetwear labels such as Commune de Paris and Maison Père for both men and women, as well as accessories, international art books and magazines.

Artcurial

MAP P.36, POCKET MAP D6

61 av Montaigne Ⓜ Franklin-D.-Roosevelt. Ⓦ librairie.artcurial.com.

Arguably the best art bookshop in Paris, set in an elegant townhouse. It sells French and foreign editions, houses a gallery which puts on interesting exhibitions, and there's also a stylish Italian vegetarian restaurant.

Chanel

MAP P.36, POCKET MAP C6

51 av Montaigne Ⓜ Franklin-D.-Roosevelt. Ⓦ chanel.com.

Born in 1883, Gabrielle "Coco" Chanel engendered a way of life that epitomized elegance, class and refined taste. Her most famous signatures are the legendary No. 5 perfume, the black evening dress and the once-omnipresent tweed suit.

Louis Vuitton

MAP P.36, POCKET MAP C5

101 av des Champs-Elysées Ⓜ George V. Ⓦ louisvuitton.com.

You might have to fend off the crowds but the enormous flagship store offers you the best of LV – a "bag bar", jewellery emporium and men's and women's ready-to-wear collections.

Séphora

MAP P.36, POCKET MAP C6

70 av des Champs-Elysées Ⓜ Franklin-D.-Roosevelt. ⓉⓌ sephora.fr.

A huge perfume and cosmetics emporium, stocking every conceivable brand, including *Séphora*'s own line of fun, reasonably priced cosmetics. There are lots of testers, and you can get free makeovers plus pampering and beauty consultations from the solicitous sales staff. It's also open until close to midnight, handy if you're out on the town without your lipstick.

Cafés

Café Jacquemart-André

MAP P.36, POCKET MAP D5

158 bd Haussmann Ⓜ Miromesnil/St-Philippe-du-Roule. Ⓦ musee-jacquemart-andre.com.

This, the city's most sumptuously appointed *salon de thé*, is set within the splendid Musée Jacquemart-André. The high ceilings are decorated with detailed frescoes by Tiepolo and the walls hung with antique tapestries. In summer you can sit out on the lovely terrace, set in the mansion's interior courtyard. On the menu are light lunches and exquisite cakes and pastries. No reservations.

Ladurée

MAP P.36, POCKET MAP C6

75 av des Champs-Elysées Ⓜ George V. Ⓦ laduree.fr.

This Champs-Elysées branch of the *Ladurée* tea rooms, with its luxurious gold and green decor, is perfect if you're in need of a shopping break. It's justly famed for its melt-in-the-mouth *macarons* with their gooey fillings, and the light-as-air meringues and millefeuilles are just as good.

Restaurants

L'Ardoise

MAP P.36. POCKET MAP A14

28 rue du Mont Thabor Ⓜ Tuileries. Ⓦ lardoise-paris.com.

Ladurée

A modern *bistrot* with a friendly atmosphere (the chef frequently pops out of the kitchen to greet diners) and an imaginative take on the classics: think langoustine ravioli, scallops in their shells with herb butter, and banana and caramel crème brûlée. With a three-course set menu for under €40, this is a good-value, reliable choice. €€

Le Drugstore

MAP P.36. POCKET MAP C5
133 av des Champs Elysées Ⓜ George V. Ⓦ publicisdrugstore.com.
With prime views of the Arc de Triomphe, food overseen by top chef Eric Fréchon and cool decor by Tom Dixon, this moderately priced brasserie is one of the better offerings on the Champs. The food ranges from the trusty *jambon beurre* (ham baguette), caesar salad and dainty finger food to more substantial dishes, including sumptuous Wagyu beef. €€

Edith Néo Bistro

MAP P.36, POCKET MAP B6
9 rue Jean Giraudoux, Ⓦ padam-hotel.com.
In 2023, the PADAM hotel opened its doors in the heart of Paris' golden triangle. The hotel has a sleek art deco feel and a neo-bistro style restaurant called Edith offering breakfast, lunch and dinner. €€

Loulou

MAP P.36, POCKET MAP B14
Musée des Arts Décoratifs, 107 rue de Rivoli Ⓜ Tuileries/Concorde. Ⓦ loulou-paris.com.
The Musée des Arts Décoratifs' restaurant enjoys a splendid setting, overlooking the Tuileries gardens and the Louvre; in warmer weather you can sit out on the lovely *terrasse* and soak up the views. The interior is attractive too, with its stylish black-and-white "tulip" chairs, marble floor and wicker panelling. On the menu you'll find a mix of French and Italian food, such as pasta and pistachio sauce, truffle pizza and peppered steak. €€

Pierre Gagnaire

MAP P.36, POCKET MAP C5
Hôtel Balzac, 6 rue Balzac Ⓜ George-V. Ⓦ pierregagnaire-lerestaurant.com.
Eating at the highly acclaimed, three-Michelin-starred Pierre Gagnaire is a gastronomic adventure. The seven-course

menu dégustation of modern French food might feature such dishes as oyster with cuttlefish, sailor clams and mussels in Kientzheim butter with crunchy fennel and black garlic; the desserts are amazing. €€€

Le Relais de l'Entrecote

MAP P.36, POCKET MAP C6

15 rue Marbeuf Ⓜ Franklin-D.-Roosevelt. Ⓦ relaisentrecote.fr.

Don't worry if a menu isn't forthcoming here – there isn't one. The only dish is *steak frites*, widely considered among the best in Paris and served with a delicious sauce, the ingredients of which are a closely kept secret. No reservations are taken so you may have to queue, or arrive early. €€

Bars

Le George V Bar

MAP P.36, POCKET MAP C6

Four Seasons Hotel George V, 31 av George V Ⓜ George V. Ⓦ fourseasons.com/paris.

The luxury George hotel's bar is a plush affair, with velvet Louis XVI style chairs, wood panelling and a glittering chandelier, a sumptuous place for heady cocktails and intimate rendezvous.

The Place To...

MAP P.36, POCKET MAP C3

47 av de Wagram Ⓜ Ternes. Ⓦ theplaceto. paris.

If you're looking for a wide choice of affordable food, from burgers to mushroom risotto, plus a varied drinks menu, all set amid a warm, friendly atmosphere and vintage decor, then this popular bar-restaurant is definitely the place to be.

Club

Jazz Club Etoile

MAP P.36, POCKET MAP A4

81 blvd Gouvion Saint-Cyr Ⓦ jazzclub-paris.com.

Located in the lobby of the *Méridien Etoile* hotel, this renowned club has played host to such jazz legends as Lionel Hampton and Cab Calloway and continues to attract top names in French and international jazz, as well as soul and blues.

THE CHAMPS-ELYSÉES AND TUILERIES

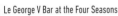

Le George V Bar at the Four Seasons

The Eiffel Tower area

The swathe of the 7e arrondissement from the Eiffel Tower east to St-Germain has little in common with the rest of the Left Bank. Boutique bars and bohemians are few, while mansions and public monuments dominate. Dwarfed by the tower, which casts its timeless spell, the district is also defined by the great military edifices of the Ecole Militaire and Hôtel des Invalides. On a more human scale are the exotic museum of non-Western art, the Musée du Quai Branly, and the intimate Musée Rodin. Across the river, the swish strip of the 16e arrondissement that runs alongside the Seine echoes the staid monumental tone, though a handful of museums – in particular the Palais de Tokyo, the Musée Guimet and the Cité de l'Architecture – offer some of the city's most exciting exhibitions.

Eiffel Tower

MAP P.44, POCKET MAP B8
Ⓜ RER Champ de Mars–Tour Eiffel.
Ⓦ toureiffel.paris. Charge – different prices depending on the level and whether you use the lift or not.

It's hard to believe that the **Eiffel Tower**, the quintessential symbol both of Paris and the brilliance of industrial engineering, was designed to be a temporary structure for the 1889 Exposition Universelle. When completed, the 300m tower was the tallest building in the world. Outraged critics protested against this "grimy factory chimney", though Eiffel himself thought it was beautiful in its sheer structural efficiency: "To a certain extent," he wrote, "the tower was formed by the wind itself".

Try and book online well in advance, or turn up before opening time, otherwise you'll face long queues to get in (especially for the lift); even if you've booked online, you'll still have to wait to go through bag checks. It's absolutely worth it,

however, not just for the view, but for the exhilaration of being inside the structure, a thrill intensified by the renovation of the first level in 2014 in which part of the floor was replaced with glass. The views of the city are usually clearer from the second level, but there's something irresistible about taking the lift all the way up. After dark the tower is lit by a double searchlight, and for the first five minutes of every hour thousands of effervescent lights fizz about the structure.

Palais de Chaillot

MAP P.44, POCKET MAP A7
Ⓜ Trocadéro.

From behind its elaborate park and fountains, the sweeping arcs of the **Palais de Chaillot** seem designed to embrace the view of the Eiffel Tower, which stands on the far side of the river. The totalitarian Modernist-Classical architecture dates the palace to 1937, when it was built as the showpiece of the Exposition Universelle, one of Paris's regular trade and culture jamborees. The central terrace between the palace's two wings provides a perfect platform for photo opportunities, curio sellers and skateboarders.

Cité de l'Architecture et du Patrimoine

MAP P.44, POCKET MAP A7–B7
Palais de Chaillot, 1 place du Trocadéro
Ⓜ Trocadéro. Ⓦ citedelarchitecture.fr.
Charge.

The **Cité de l'Architecture et du Patrimoine**, in the east wing of the Palais de Chaillot, is a splendid museum of architecture. On the loftily vaulted ground floor, the Galerie des Moulages displays giant plaster casts taken from great French buildings at the end of the nineteenth century. You'd never guess these moulds weren't the real thing, and they vividly display the development of national (mainly church) architecture from the Middle Ages to the nineteenth century. The top floor offers a sleek rundown of the modern and contemporary, including a reconstruction of an apartment from Le Corbusier's Cité Radieuse,

in Marseille. The Galerie des Peintures Murales, with its radiant, full-scale copies of great French frescoes, occupies the top floors.

Musée National de la Marine

MAP P.44, POCKET MAP A7
Palais de Chaillot, place du Trocadéro
Ⓜ Trocadéro. Ⓦ aamm.fr. Charge; check online for times and admission.
This museum boasts an excellent collection spanning several centuries of French maritime and naval history.

Cineaqua

MAP P.44, POCKET MAP B7
Jardins du Trocadéro Ⓜ Trocadéro.
Ⓦ aquariumdeparis.com. Charge.
This high-concept, subterranean aquarium-multimedia complex, consisting of the rather unlikely combination of animation workshops, state-of-the-art tanks, a film museum and classic movie screenings, somehow works and should appeal to any cartoon-loving kid.

Musée de l'Homme

MAP P.44, POCKET MAP B7

Cité de l'Architecture et du Patrimoine

Palais du Chaillot, place du Trocadéro
Ⓜ Trocadéro. Ⓦ museedelhomme.fr.
Charge.

The city's anthropological museum, revamped in 2015 to much acclaim, asks fundamental questions about humankind's origins (and future) through an incredible collection of prehistoric artefacts, including a Cro-Magnon skull and mammoth-tusk sculptures, as well as eighteenth-century anatomical waxworks and high-tech digital touchscreens.

Musée Guimet

MAP P.44, POCKET MAP B7

6 place d'Iéna Ⓜ Iéna. Ⓦ guimet.fr. Charge.
The **Musée National des Arts Asiatiques-Guimet** boasts a stunning display of Asian, and especially Buddhist, art. Four floors groan under the weight of imaginatively displayed statues of Buddhas and gods, and a covered courtyard provides an airy space in which to show off the museum's world-renowned collection of Khmer sculpture. The Buddhist statues of the Gandhara civilization, on the first floor, betray a fascinating debt to Greek sculpture, while the fierce demons from Nepal, the many-armed gold gods of South India and the pot-bellied Chinese Buddhas are stunningly exotic. One of the most moving exhibits is one of the simplest: a two-thousand-year-old blown-glass fish from Afghanistan.

Founder Emile Guimet's original collection, brought back from Asia in 1876, is exhibited in the temple-like Galeries du Panthéon Bouddhique, at 19 avenue d'Iéna (same hours and ticket as museum).

Palais Galliera

MAP P.44, POCKET MAP B7

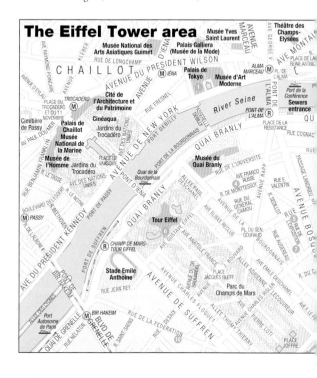

The Eiffel Tower area

10 av Pierre 1er de Serbie Ⓜ **Iéna/Alma-Marceau.** Ⓦ **palaisgalliera.paris.fr. Charge.**
Behind the Palais de Tokyo, the grandiose **Palais Galliera** – another Neoclassical hulk – is home to the Musée de la Mode, which houses a magnificent collection of clothes and accessories from the eighteenth century to the present day.

Musée Yves Saint Laurent

MAP P.44, POCKET MAP C7
5 Av. Marceau Ⓜ Iéna/Alma-Marceau.
Ⓦ museeyslparis.com.
The Musée Yves Saint Laurent exhibits the couturier's body of work on the legendary premises of his former haute couture house where 200 tailors and seamstresses once worked. A great film about the designer's life plays on a loop in the theatre.

Palais de Tokyo

MAP P.44, POCKET MAP B7

Palais Galliera

13 av du Président Wilson Ⓜ **Iéna/Alma-Marceau.** Ⓦ **palaisdetokyo.com. Charge.**
Spread over four floors, the **Palais de Tokyo** is one of the largest contemporary art spaces in Europe. Its industrial-looking concrete walls and exposed piping creates a

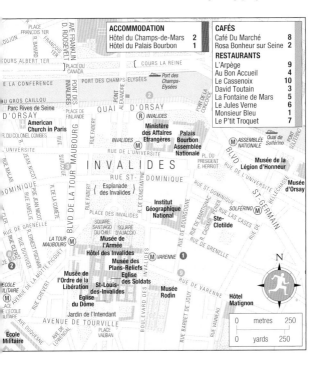

ACCOMMODATION

Hôtel du Champs-de-Mars	2
Hôtel du Palais Bourbon	1

CAFÉS

Café Du Marché	8
Rosa Bonheur sur Seine	2

RESTAURANTS

L'Arpège	9
Au Bon Accueil	4
Le Cassenoix	10
David Toutain	3
La Fontaine de Mars	5
Le Jules Verne	6
Monsieur Bleu	1
Le P'tit Troquet	7

Musée du Quai Branly

sense of 'work in progress', while a changing flow of exhibitions and events – anything from a show by Paris-born Louise Bourgeois to a temporary "occupation" by squatter-artists – keeps the atmosphere lively, with an exciting, countercultural buzz.

Musée d'Art Moderne de Paris (MAM)

MAP P.44, POCKET MAP B7
11 av du Président Wilson Ⓜ léna/Alma-Marceau. Ⓦ mam.paris.fr. Charge.

While it's no competition for the Pompidou, the cool white Musée d'Art Moderne de la Ville de Paris is a more contemplative space, offering a fitting Modernist setting for the city's own collection of modern art. Paris-based artists such as Braque, Chagall, Delaunay, Derain, Léger and Picasso are well represented in its strong early twentieth-century collection, and many works have Parisian themes. The enormous centrepieces are two versions of Matisse's *La Danse* and Dufy's giant mural, *La Fée Électricité*, commissioned by the electricity board, which fills an entire curved room with 250

lyrical panels recounting the story of electricity from Aristotle to the 1930s. Temporary exhibitions fill the ground-floor space.

Place de l'Alma

MAP P.44, POCKET MAP C7
Ⓜ Alma-Marceau.

From most angles, **place de l'Alma** looks like just another busy Parisian junction, with cars rattling over the cobbles and a métro entrance on the pavement. Over in one corner, however, stands a replica of the flame from the Statue of Liberty, which was given to France in 1987 as a symbol of Franco-American relations.

This golden torch has been adopted by mourners from all over the world as a memorial to Princess Diana, who was killed in the underpass beneath in 1997.

The Sewers Museum (Musée des Egouts)

MAP P.44, POCKET MAP C7
Place de la Résistance Ⓜ Alma-Marceau/ RER Pont de l'Alma. Ⓦ musee-egouts. paris.fr. Charge.

The Musée des Egouts, or **Sewers Museum**, is one of Paris's more unusual attractions – a small, visitable section of the sewers, or *les égouts.* Underground, it's dark, damp and noisy from the gushing water; the main exhibition runs along a gantry walk poised above a main sewer. The photographs, lamps, specialized sewermen's tools and other antique flotsam and jetsam form a surprisingly interesting history of the city's water supply and waste management. The air down here is as smelly and unappealing as you might expect, so those of a nervous disposition might want to give it a miss.

Rue Cler and around

MAP P.44, POCKET MAP C8
Ⓜ La Tour-Maubourg.

A little further upstream, the **American Church** on quai d'Orsay, together with the American College nearby at 31 av Bosquet, is a focal point in the well-organized life of Paris's large American community, its notice board usually plastered with job and accommodation offers and requests. Immediately to the south, and in stark contrast to the austerity of much of the rest of the quarter, lies a villagey wedge of early nineteenth-century streets between avenue Bosquet and the Invalides. Chief among them is **rue Cler**, whose food shops act as a kind of permanent market. The cross-streets, rue de Grenelle and rue St-Dominique, are full of neighbourhood shops, posh *bistrots* and little hotels.

Parc du Champs de Mars

MAP P.44, POCKET MAP B8–C9

Ⓜ Ecole Militaire.

Parading back from the Eiffel Tower are the long, rectangular and tourist-thronged gardens of the **Champs de Mars**, leading to the eighteenth-century **École Militaire**, originally founded in 1751 by Louis XV for the training of aristocratic army officers and attended by Napoleon, among other fledgling leaders.

Musée du Quai Branly

MAP P.44, POCKET MAP B7–8

37 Quai Branly Ⓜ Iéna/RER Pont de l'Alma. Ⓦ quaibranly.fr. Charge.

A short distance upstream of the Eiffel Tower, on quai Branly, stands the intriguing **Musée du Quai Branly**, designed by the French state's favourite architect, Jean Nouvel. The museum – which gathers together hundreds of thousands of non-European objects bought or purloined by France over the centuries – was the brainchild of President Chirac, whose passion for what he would no doubt call *arts primitifs* helped secure funding. Nouvel's elaborate design, which aims to blur the divide between structure and environment, unfurls in a long glazed curve, pocked with coloured boxes, through the middle of an enormous garden. Inside, areas devoted to Asia, Africa, the Americas and the Pacific ("Oceania") snake through dimly lit rooms lined by curving "mud" walls in brown leather. The 3,500 folk artefacts on display at any one time – Hopi kachina dolls, ancient Hawaiian feather helmets – are as fascinating as they are beautiful; the tone of the place, however, is muddled. While the objects are predominantly displayed – and easily experienced – as works of art, there's an uneasy sense that they are being presented above all in terms of their exotic "otherness". This is not helped when the museum loses the courage of its convictions, shifting into outdated anthropological mode, using written (and often poorly translated) panels to give lofty cultural context.

Hôtel des Invalides

MAP P.44, POCKET MAP D8

Ⓜ Varenne/La Tour-Maubourg. Ⓦ musee-armee.fr.

There's no missing the overpowering facade of the **Hôtel des Invalides**, topped by its resplendently gilded dome. Despite its palatial, crushingly grand appearance, it was built as a home for wounded soldiers in the reign of Louis XIV – whose foreign wars gave the building a constant supply of residents, and whose equestrian statue lords over a massive central arch. It today houses two churches – one for the soldiers, the other intended as a mausoleum for the king but now containing the mortal remains of Napoleon – and the Musée de l'Armée, an enormous national war museum (see page 48). The most interesting sections of the museum are detailed below, but the remainder, dedicated to the history of the French army from Louis XIV up to the 1870s, is really for fanatics only.

Musée de l'Armée

MAP P.44, POCKET MAP D8

Hôtel des Invalides Ⓜ La Tour-Maubourg/
Varenne. Ⓦ musee-armee.fr. Charge, also
valid for Napoleon's tomb.

By far the most affecting galleries
of the vast **Musée de l'Armée** cover
the two world wars, beginning
with Prussia's annexation of Alsace-
Lorraine in 1871 and ending with
the defeat of the Third Reich.
The battles, the resistance and the
slow liberation are documented
through imaginatively displayed
war memorabilia combined with
stirring contemporary newsreels,
most of which have an English-
language option. The simplest
artefacts – a rag doll found on
a battlefield, plaster casts of
mutilated faces, an overcoat caked
in mud from the trenches – tell
a stirring human story, while
un-narrated footage, from the
Somme, Dunkirk and a bomb
attack on a small French town,
flicker across bare walls in grim
silence. The collection of medieval
and Renaissance armour in the
west wing of the royal courtyard
is also worth admiring. Highlights
include highly decorative
seventeenth-century Italian suits,
and two dimly lit chambers of
beautifully worked Chinese and
Japanese weaponry.

Musée des Plans-Reliefs

MAP P.44, POCKET MAP D8

Ⓦ museedesplansreliefs.culture.fr. Same
hours and ticket as the Musée de l'Armée.

Up under the roof of the east
wing, the **Musée des Plans-
Reliefs** displays an extraordinary
collection of super-scale models
of French ports and fortified
cities. Essentially giant three-
dimensional maps, they were
created in the seventeenth and
eighteenth centuries to plan
defences or plot potential artillery
positions. The eerie green glow
of their landscapes only just
illuminates the long, tunnel-like
attic; the effect is rather chilling.

Eglise des Soldats

MAP P.44, POCKET MAP D8

Entrance from main courtyard of Les
Invalides. Free.

The lofty "Soldiers' Church" is
the spiritual home of the French
army, its proud simplicity standing
in stark contrast to the elaborate
Eglise du Dôme, which lies on
the other side of a dividing glass
wall – an innovation that allowed
worshippers to share the same high
altar without the risk of coming
into social contact. The walls are
hung with almost one hundred
enemy standards captured on the
battlefield, part of a collection of
some three thousand that once
adorned Notre-Dame.

Eglise du Dôme

MAP P.44, POCKET MAP D8

Entrance from south side of Les Invalides.
Same hours and ticket as the Musée de
l'Armée (see page 48).

Some find the lavish **Eglise
du Dôme**, or "royal church",
gloriously sumptuous – others
find it overbearing. A perfect
example of the architectural
pomposity of Louis XIV's day,
with grandiose frescoes and
an abundance of Corinthian
columns and pilasters, it is now a
monument to Napoleon.

Napoleon's tomb

MAP P.44, POCKET MAP D8

Eglise du Dôme. Ⓦ napoleon.org Same
hours and ticket as the Musée de l'Armée
(see page 48).

On December 14, 1840, Napoleon
was finally laid to rest in the crypt
of the Eglise du Dôme. Brought
home from St Helena twenty
years after his death, his remains
were carried through the streets
from the newly completed Arc
de Triomphe to the Invalides.
As many as half a million people
came out to watch the emperor's
last journey, and Victor Hugo
commented that "It felt as if the
whole of Paris had been poured to
one side of the city, like liquid in

a vase which has been tilted". He now lies in a giant sarcophagus of smooth red porphyry, encircled with Napoleonic quotations of staggering but largely truthful conceit, and overshadowing the nearby tombs of two of his brothers as well as his son, the King of Rome, whose body was brought here on Hitler's orders in 1940. Another chapel upstairs holds Marshal Foch, the Supreme Commander of Allied forces in World War I.

Musée Rodin

MAP P.44, POCKET MAP D8

79 rue de Varenne Ⓜ Varenne. Ⓦ musee-rodin.fr. Charge for museum and garden, and separately.

The setting of the **Musée Rodin** is superbly elegant, a beautiful eighteenth-century mansion which the sculptor leased from the state in return for the gift of all his work upon his death. Bronze versions of major projects like *The Burghers of Calais*, *The Thinker*, *The Gate of Hell* and *Ugolino* are exhibited in the large gardens – the last-named of these works forms the centrepiece of the ornamental pond, and there's also a pleasant outdoor café.

Inside, the passionate intensity of the sculptures contrasts with the graceful wooden panelling and chandeliers. The museum is usually very crowded with visitors eager to see much-loved works like *The Hand of God* and the touchingly erotic *The Kiss*, which was originally designed to portray Paolo and Francesca da Rimini, from Dante's *Divine Comedy*, in the moment before they were discovered and murdered by Francesca's husband. Rodin once self-deprecatingly referred to it as "a large sculpted knick-knack following the usual formula"; art critics today like to think of it as the last masterwork of figurative sculpture before the whole art form was reinvented – largely by Rodin himself. Paris's

Kiss is one of only four marble versions of the work, but hundreds of smaller bronzes were turned out as money-spinners.

It's well worth lingering over the museum's vibrant, impressionistic clay works, small studies that Rodin took from life. In fact, most of the works here are in clay or plaster, as these are considered to be Rodin's finest achievements – after completing his apprenticeship, he rarely picked up a chisel, in line with the common nineteenth-century practice of delegating the task of working up stone and bronze versions to assistants. Instead, he would return to his plaster casts again and again, modifying and refining them and sometimes deliberately leaving them "unfinished".

Don't miss the room devoted to Camille Claudel, Rodin's pupil, model and lover. Among her works is the painfully allegorical *The Age of Maturity*, symbolizing her ultimate rejection by Rodin, and a bust of the artist himself. Claudel's perception of her teacher was so akin to Rodin's own that he considered it his self-portrait.

Hôtel des Invalides

Cafés

Cafe Du Marche

MAP P.44, POCKET MAP C8
38 rue Cler Ⓜ La-Tour-Maubourg.
Big, busy café-brasserie in the rue
Cler market serving reasonably
priced meals, with hearty salads
and market-fresh *plats du jour*.
Outdoor seating, with a covered
terrace in winter.

Rosa Bonheur sur Seine

MAP P.44, POCKET MAP D7
Near Pont Alexandre III Ⓜ Invalides.
Ⓦ rosabonheur.fr.
On a floating barge moored
alongside the Parc Rives de
Seine, this café-bar, offshoot of
the popular *Rosa Bonheur* in the
Parc des Buttes-Chaumont, is the
perfect place for a relaxing coffee
or cocktail, or a pizza from their
riverside food truck.

Restaurants

L'Arpege

MAP P.44, POCKET MAP E8
84 rue de Varenne Ⓜ Varenne. Ⓦ alain-
passard.com.
Elite chef Alain Passard puts the
spotlight on vegetables at this
Michelin-starred restaurant –
grilled turnips with chestnuts, or
beetroot baked in salt crust are
astonishingly good – but you'll also
find plenty of other exhilarating
dishes. Reserve well in advance and
dress up. €€€

Au Bon Accueil

MAP P.44, POCKET MAP C8
14 rue de Monttessuy Ⓜ Duroc/Vaneau.
Ⓦ aubonaccueilparis.com.
Practically in the shadow of the
Eiffel Tower, this relaxed but
upbeat wine-*bistrot* offers fresh,
well-considered dishes, such as a
salad of prawns and lemon verbena,
and veal liver with Jerusalem
artichoke purée. There are a few
outside tables. €€

Le Cassenoix

MAP P.44, POCKET MAP A9
56 rue de la Fédération Ⓜ Dupleix. Ⓦ le-
cassenoix.fr.
Cosy and friendly neighbourhood
bistrot, conveniently near the Eiffel
Tower, serving sizeable portions
of traditional and modern French
food, such as *gamabas a la plancha*
with basil risotto or quali with foie
gras, with a good selection of wines
by the glass. €

David Toutain

MAP P.44, POCKET MAP D7
29 rue Surcouf Ⓜ Invalides/La Tour
Maubourg. Ⓦ davidtoutain.com.
An intimate, contemporary
restaurant, with lots of natural
wood and light, serving original,
creative cuisine made with
seasonal ingredients, especially
farm-fresh veg and delicate fish.
Typical dishes include beetroot
rolls, scallops in Jerusalem
artichoke bouillon, and smoked
eel with black sesame sauce.
Booking essential. €€

La Fontaine de Mars

MAP P.44, POCKET MAP C8
129 rue Saint-Dominique Ⓜ La Tour-
Maubourg. Ⓦ fontaine-de-mars.com.
Pink checked tablecloths,
leather banquettes, tiled floor,
outside tables, attentive service;
this is quintessential France
– the Obama family certainly
enjoyed it. The food is meaty,
southwestern French fare: think
snails, *magret de canard* and
boudin sausages. €€

Le Jules Verne

MAP P.44, POCKET MAP B8
Eiffel Tower Ⓜ Bir-Hakeim. Ⓦ restaurants-
toureiffel.com.
It's not only the food, overseen
by star chefs Frédéric Anton and
Thierry Marx, that's elevated here,
but the restaurant too: it's 125m
up the Eiffel Tower. Best at dinner,
but the weekday lunch is more
affordable. Reserve well in advance
and dress smartly. €€€

Monsieur Bleu

MAP P.44, POCKET MAP B7
Palais de Tokyo, 20 Ave de New York
Ⓜ léna/Alma-Marceau. Ⓦ monsieurbleu-
restaurant.com.

The more stylish of the two
restaurants inside this cutting-
edge gallery, *Monsieur Bleu* is an
elegant, high-ceilinged Art Deco
dining room with an outdoor
terrace, perfect in summer for
stunning views of the Eiffel
Tower. The food – a mix of
traditional French and fusion
cuisine – is well prepared and
tasty, and not too high-priced
considering the location. The
gallery's other restaurant, *Les
Grands Verres*, is a more casual,
self-consciously hip hangout,
serving modern French cuisine; it
also has a cool cocktail bar. €€€

Le P'tit Troquet

MAP P.44, POCKET MAP C8
28 rue de l'Exposition Ⓜ Ecole Militaire.
Ⓦ lepetittroquet.fr.

This tiny, discreet family
restaurant has a nostalgic feel
with its marble tables, tiled floor
and ornate zinc bar. Its cuisine,
popular with the diplomats of the
quartier, as well as tourists, focuses
on traditional meaty classics,
such as lamb shank and *boeuf
bourguignon*, served with flair. It
also makes an effort to provide
some gluten-free options. €

THE EIFFEL TOWER AREA

Monsieur Bleu

The Grands Boulevards and passages

Built on the old city ramparts, the Grands Boulevards are the eight broad streets that extend in a long arc from the Église de la Madeleine eastwards. In the nineteenth century the boulevards, with their fashionable cafés, street theatre and puppet shows, were where "Paris vivant" was to be found. A legacy from this heyday, brasseries, cafés, theatres and cinemas (notably the splendid Art Deco cinemas Le Grand Rex and Max Linder Panorama; see page 173) still abound. To the south of the Grands Boulevards lies the city's main commercial and financial district, while just to the north, beyond the glittering Opéra Garnier, are the large department stores Galeries Lafayette and Printemps. Rather more well-heeled shopping is concentrated on the rue St-Honoré in the west and the streets around aristocratic place Vendôme, lined with top couturiers, jewellers and art dealers. Scattered around the whole area are the delightful passages – nineteenth-century arcades that hark back to shopping from a different era.

Musée Grévin

MAP P.54, POCKET MAP G5
10 bd Montmartre ⓂGrands-Boulevards.
Ⓦ grevin-paris.com. Charge.

A remnant from the fun-loving times on the Grands Boulevards are the waxworks in the **Musée Grévin**, comprising mainly French personalities and the usual bunch of Hollywood actors. The best thing about the museum is the original rooms: the magical Palais des Mirages (Hall of Mirrors), built for the Exposition Universelle in 1900; the theatre with its sculptures by Bourdelle; and the 1882 Baroque-style Hall of Columns.

Opéra Garnier

MAP P.54, POCKET MAP F5
ⓂOpéra. Ⓦoperadeparis.fr. Charge; see page 61 for booking information for performances.

The ornate **Opéra Garnier**, built by Charles Garnier for Napoléon III, exemplifies the Second Empire in its show of wealth and hint of vulgarity. The theatre's facade is a concoction of white, pink and green marble, colonnades, rearing horses and gleaming gold busts. No less opulent is the interior with its spacious gilded-marble and mirrored lobbies. The auditorium is all red velvet and gold leaf, hung with a six-tonne chandelier; the colourful ceiling was painted by Chagall in 1964 and depicts scenes from well-known operas and ballets jumbled up with Parisian landmarks. You can visit the interior and auditorium outside of rehearsals; entry is on the corner of rues Scribe and Auber.

Place Vendôme

MAP P.54, POCKET MAP A13
Ⓜ Opéra.

Built by Versailles architect Hardouin-Mansart, **place Vendôme** is one of the city's most impressive set pieces. It's a pleasingly symmetrical, eight-sided square, enclosed by a harmonious ensemble of elegant mansions, graced with Corinthian pilasters and steeply pitched roofs. Once the grand residences of tax collectors and financiers, they now house such luxury establishments as the *Ritz* hotel, Cartier, Bulgari and other top-flight jewellers, lending the square a decidedly exclusive air. No. 12, now occupied by Chaumet jewellers, is where Chopin died, in 1849.

Somewhat out of proportion with the rest of the square, the centrepiece is a towering triumphal column, surmounted by a statue of Napoleon dressed as Caesar. It was raised in 1806 to celebrate the Battle of Austerlitz and features bronze reliefs of scenes of the battle spiralling their way up.

Eglise de la Madeleine

MAP P.54, POCKET MAP E6
Ⓜ Madeleine. Ⓦ lamadeleineparis.fr.com.

Originally intended as a monument to Napoleon's army, the imperious-looking **Eglise de la Madeleine** is modelled on the Parthenon, surrounded by Corinthian columns and fronted by a huge pediment depicting The Last Judgement. Inside, the wide single nave is decorated with Ionic columns and surmounted by three huge domes – the only source of natural light. A theatrical stone sculpture of the Magdalene being swept up to heaven by two angels draws your eye to the high altar, and above is a half-dome with a fresco commemorating the concordat signed between the Church and Napoleon, healing the rift after the Revolution.

Place de la Madeleine

MAP P.54, POCKET MAP E6
Ⓜ Madeleine. Flower market.

Place de la Madeleine is home to some of Paris's top gourmet food stores, one of the best known being Fauchon (see page 57). On the east side is one of the city's oldest flower markets, dating to 1832.

Rue St-Honoré

MAP P.54, POCKET MAP A13–D15
Rue St-Honoré – especially its western end and the Faubourg St-Honoré – hosts top fashion designers and art galleries. All the classic couturiers such as Hermès, Yves Saint Laurent and Christian Dior are here.

Palais Royal

MAP P.54, POCKET MAP B14–C14
Ⓜ Palais Royal-Musée du Louvre. Free.

The **Palais Royal** was built for Cardinal Richelieu in 1624, though little now remains of the original palace. The current building, mostly dating from the eighteenth century, houses various governmental bodies and the Comédie Française, long-standing venue for the classics of French theatre. To the rear lie sedate

Jardin du Palais-Royal

gardens with fountains and avenues of clipped limes, bounded by stately eighteenth-century mansions built over arcades housing quirky antique and designer shops. You'd hardly guess that for a time these peaceful arcades and gardens were a site of gambling dens, brothels and funfair attractions until the prohibition on public gambling in 1838 put an end to the fun. Folly, some might say, has returned – in the form of contemporary artist Daniel Buren's black-and-white-striped pillars. They're rather like sticks of Brighton rock of varying heights, dotted about the main courtyard in front of the palace.

Galerie Véro-Dodat

MAP P.54, POCKET MAP C14
Between rue Croix-des-Petits-Champs and rue Jean-Jacques Rousseau Ⓜ Palais Royal-Musée du Louvre.
With its tiled floors, ceiling decorations and mahogany shop

fronts divided by faux marble columns, **Galerie Véro-Dodat** is one of the most attractive and homogeneous *passages*. Fashionable new shops rub shoulders with older businesses, such as R.F. Charle at no. 17, specializing in the repair and sale of vintage stringed instruments.

Galerie Vivienne

MAP P.54, POCKET MAP C13–14
Links rue Vivienne with rue des Petits-Champs Ⓜ Bourse.
Sporting a flamboyant décor of Grecian and marine motifs, charming **Galerie Vivienne** harbours fashion and design shops, as well as the delightful antiquarian bookshop, *Librairie Jousseaume*, once frequented by Balzac, Dumas and Hugo.

Passage Choiseul

MAP P.54, POCKET MAP B13
Links rue des Petits Champs and rue St Augustin Ⓜ Pyramides.

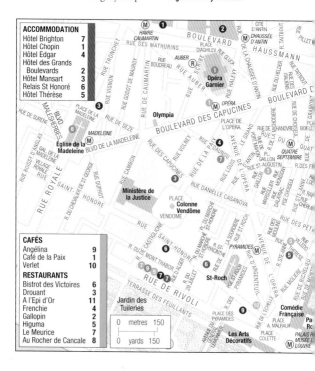

ACCOMMODATION

Hôtel Brighton	7
Hôtel Chopin	1
Hôtel Edgar	4
Hôtel des Grands Boulevards	2
Hôtel Mansart	3
Relais St Honoré	6
Hôtel Thérèse	5

CAFÉS

Angélina	9
Café de la Paix	1
Verlet	10

RESTAURANTS

Bistrot des Victoires	6
Drouant	3
A l'Epi d'Or	11
Frenchie	4
Gallopin	2
Higuma	5
Le Meurice	
Au Rocher de Cancale	8

The passages

Conceived by town planners in the early nineteenth century to protect pedestrians from mud and horse-drawn vehicles, the *passages*, elegant glass-roofed shopping arcades, were for decades left to crumble and decay. Many have been renovated and restored to something approaching their former glory, and chic boutiques have moved in alongside the old-fashioned traders and secondhand dealers. Most are closed at night and on Sundays.

Evocatively described by Louis-Ferdinand Céline in his autobiographical *Death on Credit*, the **passage Choiseul** shelters takeaway food stores, discount clothes and shoe shops, art galleries and well-known supplier of art materials, Lavrut (no. 52).

Passage des Panoramas

MAP P.54, POCKET MAP G6
Off rue Vivienne Ⓜ Grands-Boulevards.
This characterful grid of arcades is known for its fine restaurants,

stamp and coin dealers and vintage postcards. The restaurant at no. 57 is worth a look for its carved wood ornamentation dating from the 1900s, as is *Caffè Stern* at no. 47, which used to house an old print shop and still has its original 1834 decor.

Passages Jouffroy and Verdeau

MAP P.54, POCKET MAP G5
Off bd Montmartre Ⓜ Grands-Boulevards.
Across boulevard Montmartre, **passage Jouffroy** is full of the

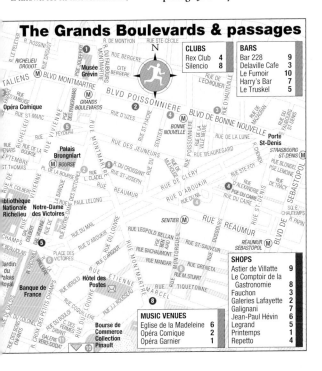

The Grands Boulevards & passages

CLUBS	
Rex Club	4
Silencio	8

BARS	
Bar 228	9
Delaville Cafe	3
Le Fumoir	10
Harry's Bar	7
Le Truskel	5

SHOPS	
Astier de Villatte	9
Le Comptoir de la Gastronomie	8
Fauchon	3
Galeries Lafayette	2
Galignani	7
Jean-Paul Hévin	6
Legrand	5
Printemps	1
Repetto	4

MUSIC VENUES	
Eglise de la Madeleine	6
Opéra Comique	2
Opéra Garnier	1

Passage du Grand-Cerf

kind of stores that make shopping an adventure rather than a chore. *Galerie Fayet* sells antique and modern walking canes, opposite a shop stocking every conceivable fitting and furnishing for a doll's house; near the romantic *Hôtel Chopin* (see page 158), Librairie du Passage displays fine art books along the passageway, and Ciné-Doc appeals to cinephiles with its collection of old film posters. Crossing rue de la Grange-Batelière, you enter the equally enchanting **passage Verdeau**, perhaps the lightest of the arcades, with its high glass ceiling sheltering antiquarian books and old prints.

Passage du Grand-Cerf

MAP P.54, POCKET MAP D14–E14
Between rue St-Denis and rue Dessoubs Ⓜ Etienne-Marcel.

The lofty, three-storey **passage du Grand-Cerf** arcade is stylistically the best of all. The wrought-iron work, glass roof and plain-wood shop fronts have all been cleaned, attracting stylish contemporary design, jewellery and fairtrade boutiques. There's always something quirky and original on display in the window of Le Labo (no. 4), specializing in lamps and other lighting fixtures made from recycled objects, while As'Art, opposite, is a treasure-trove of home furnishings and objects from Africa.

Bibliotheque Nationale Richelieu

MAP P.54, POCKET MAP C13
58 rue de Richelieu Ⓜ Bourse. Ⓦ bnf.fr. Charge.

The French National Library, a huge, forbidding building that dates to the 1660s, has recently undergone renovation. Parts of the library remain open for exhibitions, but check the website for updates. The Cabinet des Monnaies, Médailles et Antiques, a display of coins and ancient treasures, is currently closed and will be moved to grander rooms as part of the renovations. There's no restriction on entering the library, nor on peering into the atmospheric reading rooms, though many of the books have now been transferred to the new François Mitterrand site in the 13e (see page 118).

Shops

As well as the shops below, be sure to check out the *passages*, fertile hunting ground for curios and one-off buys.

Astier de Villatte

MAP P.54, POCKET MAP B14
173 rue St-Honoré ⓂPalais Royal.
Ⓦastierdevillatte.com.

An atmospheric old shop full of oak cabinets displaying stylish ceramic dinnerware. The pieces manage to seem elegant and rustic at the same time, with their milky white glaze and slightly unfinished look.

Le Comptoir de la Gastronomie

MAP P.54, POCKET MAP D14
34 rue Montmartre Ⓜ Etienne Marcel.
Ⓦcomptoirdelagastronomie.com.

The walls of this lovely old-fashioned shop are stacked high with foie gras, *saucisses*, hams, terrines, oils and wine. You can also buy takeaway baguettes or dine on delicious cassoulet, onion soup and roast duck in the attached restaurant.

Fauchon

MAP P.54, POCKET MAP E6
24–30 place de la Madeleine Ⓜ Madeleine.
Ⓦstores.fauchon.com.

A cornucopia of extravagant and beautiful groceries, charcuterie and wines. Just the place for presents of tea, jam, truffles, chocolates, exotic vinegars and mustards.

Galeries Lafayette

MAP P.54, POCKET MAP F5
40 bd Haussmann Ⓜ Chaussée d'Antin.
Ⓦhaussmann.galerieslafayette.com.

This venerable upmarket department store occupies three separate buildings. The main store is mainly devoted to women's fashion and accessories, there's a huge parfumerie, and a floor devoted to shoes – all under a superb 1900 dome. Mens' fashion and accessories take up the four floors of the adjoining building, while just down the road at no. 35 is Lafayette Maison/Gourmet: a luxury foodhall topped with four floors of quality kitchenware, linen and furniture.

Galignani

MAP P.54, POCKET MAP A14
224 rue de Rivoli Ⓜ Concorde.
Ⓦgalignani.fr.

Reputedly the first English bookshop opened on the Continent, dating back to the early 1800s. The stock is top-notch and includes fiction, fine art and children's books.

Jean-Paul Hévin

MAP P.54, POCKET MAP A14
231 rue St-Honoré ⓂTuileries.
Ⓦjeanpaulhevin.com.

Jean-Paul Hévin is one of Paris's best chocolatiers. His sleek shop displays an array of elegantly presented tablets of chocolate, bearing little descriptions of their aroma and characteristics as though they were choice

Galeries Lafayette

wines; try for example the São Tomé, with its "grande intensité aromatique".

Legrand

MAP P.54, POCKET MAP C14
1 rue de la Banque ⓜ Bourse. ⓦ caves-legrand.com.

This beautiful old wine shop is the place to stock up on your favourite vintages and discover some little-known ones too. There's also a bar (noon–7pm) for drinks, *saucisson* and pâté.

Printemps

MAP P.54, POCKET MAP F5
64 bd Haussmann ⓜ Havre-Caumartin. ⓦ printemps.com.

This venerable old department store stocks a wide range of luxury brands, with three floors devoted to womenswear, plus a whole floor given over to shoes and one to accessories. The seventh floor is now a wonderful sustainable shopping space with upcycling, vintage and secondhand popups as well as a large preloved designer space where you can buy and sell.

Repetto

MAP P.54, POCKET MAP B13
22 rue de la Paix ⓜ Opéra. ⓦ repetto.com.

This long-established supplier of ballet shoes has branched out to produce attractive ballerina pumps in assorted colours, much coveted by the fashion crowd.

Cafés

Angelina

MAP P.54, POCKET MAP A14
226 rue de Rivoli ⓜ Tuileries. ⓦ angelina-paris.fr.

One of the city's best-known *salons de thé*, dating back to 1903 and sporting an ornate decor. The hot chocolate is legendary, and the pastries equally exquisite. It's also good for breakfast or a light lunch.

Café de la Paix

MAP P.54, POCKET MAP F6
Cnr of place de l'Opéra and bd de Capucines ⓜ Opéra. ⓦ cafédelapaix.fr.

This grand café counts Emile Zola, Tchaikovsky and Oscar Wilde among its illustrious past *habitués*. Sit in the sumptuous interior or watch the world go by from the *terrasse*.

Verlet

MAP P.54, POCKET MAP B14
256 rue St-Honoré ⓜ Palais Royal-Musée du Louvre. ⓦ verlet.fr.

A heady aroma of freshly ground coffee greets you as you enter this old-world coffee merchant and café. Choose from around thirty varieties, such as Mokka Harar d'Ethiopie. There's also a selection of teas and cakes.

Restaurants

Bistrot des Victoires

MAP P.54, POCKET MAP C14
6 rue de la Vrillère ⓜ Bourse. ☎ 01 42 61 43 78.

Located just behind the chic place des Victoires, but very reasonably priced for the area, this charming, old-fashioned *bistrot*, with zinc bar, mustard-coloured walls and globe lamps, serves good old standbys such as *confit de canard* and *poulet rôti*, as well as huge salads and hearty *tartines* – recommended is the *savoyarde* with bacon, potatoes and gruyère. Good-value Sunday brunch, too. €

Drouant

MAP P.54, POCKET MAP B13
16–18 rue Gaillon ⓜ Opéra. ⓦ drouant.com.

Legendary restaurant *Drouant*, the setting for the annual Goncourt and Renaudot literary prizes, is run by famed chef Antoine Westermann, who puts a contemporary spin on bourgeois cuisine. The starters and desserts show off the chef's creative flair –

Le Meurice

you can choose four of each served in small portions if you wish. €€

A l'Epi d'Or

MAP P.54, POCKET MAP C14
25 rue Jean-Jacques Rousseau ⓂLouvre-Rivoli. ⓌWfrancoisepiege.com.
Christian Louboutin is a fan of this perfect locals' *bistrot* that dishes up comforting, homely standards such as steaks and *tarte tatin*, as well as its signature dish, *agneau à la cuillère* (slow-cooked lamb). €

Frenchie

MAP P.54, POCKET MAP D13
5 rue du Nil Ⓜ Sentier. Ⓦfrenchie-ruedenil.com.
It's famously hard to reserve a table, but definitely worth the effort: Frenchie, run by Greg Marchand, is an innovative neo-*bistrot*, reinventing French classics and using only the freshest ingredients. The five-course tasting menu (with countless little extras and *amuse-bouches*) might include dishes such as roast lamb with chickpeas, zaatar and harissa, or beef with ceps and samphire. If you can't get a reservation, try

and bag a table (no bookings) at the *Frenchie bar à vins* opposite, where you can sample interesting wines and snack on sharing platters. €€

Gallopin

MAP P.54, POCKET MAP C13
40 rue Notre-Dame-des-Victoires
Ⓜ Bourse. Ⓦgallopin.com.
An utterly endearing old brasserie with all its original brass and mahogany fittings, and a beautiful painted glass roof in the back room. The classic French dishes, especially the foie gras *maison*, are well above par. €€

Higuma

MAP P.54, POCKET MAP B14
32bis rue Ste Anne Ⓜ Pyramides.
Ⓦhiguma.fr.
The pick of the numerous Japanese canteens in this area, *Higuma* serves up cheap, filling staples like ramen, pork katsu curry and yaki udon. Sit at the counter and watch the chefs at work, or go for a table in one of the two dining rooms. It's popular and you may have to queue at lunchtime. €

Le Meurice

MAP P.54, POCKET MAP A14
Hôtel Le Meurice, 228 rue de Rivoli
Ⓜ Tuileries. Ⓦ dorchestercollection.com.
This sumptuous historic restaurant, decorated in Louis XVI style with a few flashes of modern flair from Philippe Starck, is one of the most beautiful dining rooms in Paris. With its two Michelin stars and Alain Ducasse at the helm, it also does top-notch cuisine based on the best and freshest ingredients. There's a lunch set menu or go for the *menu dégustation*. €€€

Au Rocher de Cancale

MAP P.54, POCKET MAP D14
78 rue Montorgueil Ⓜ Etienne-Marcel.
Ⓣ 01 42 21 31 03.
This historic café-restaurant, dating back to 1848, stands out on the foodie rue Montorgueil for the quality and price of its fresh seafood and good wine list. You can also order well-executed burgers and salads, as well as more traditional French food. Desserts are equally good – the Carambar crème brûlée is exceptional. €

Bars

Bar 228

MAP P.54, POCKET MAP A14
Hôtel Le Meurice 228 rue de Rivoli
Ⓜ Tuileries. Ⓦ dorchestercollection.com.
Secreted away inside the luxury *Hôtel Meurice*, *Bar 228* with its glorious belle époque frescoes, mahogany wood panelling and leather armchairs is the place to treat yourself to pre-dinner cocktails; there's often live jazz too.

Delaville Cafe

MAP P.54, POCKET MAP H6
34 bd de la Bonne Nouvelle Ⓜ Bonne-Nouvelle. Ⓦ delavilleparis.com.
This ex-bordello, with grand staircase, gilded mosaics and marble columns, draws crowds of pre-clubbers who throw back a mojito or two before going on to one of the area's nightclubs. DJs reign till the early hours on Thurs, Fri and Sat from 10pm.

Le Fumoir

MAP P.54, POCKET MAP C15
6 rue de l'Amiral de Coligny Ⓜ Louvre-Rivoli. Ⓦ lefumoir.com.
Animated chatter rises above a mellow jazz soundtrack and the sound of cocktail shakers in this coolly designed and relaxing bar-restaurant, situated just by the Louvre. You can browse the international press and there's also a restaurant and library at the back.

Harry's Bar

MAP P.54, POCKET MAP B13
5 rue Daunou Ⓜ Opéra. Ⓣ 01 42 61 71 14.
Legendary *Harry's Bar*, where George Gershwin is said to have composed An American in Paris, is a classic. It's popular with American expats and locals alike, who come for its old-fashioned ambience and cocktails, especially the Bloody Mary, which the bar claims to have invented.

Le Truskel

MAP P.54, POCKET MAP C13
12 rue Feydeau Ⓜ Bourse. Ⓦ truskel.com.
This pub-club often screens live sports in the early evening, followed by live gigs, and then DJs and dancing later on. Drinks are inexpensive and you're pretty much guaranteed a fun night out.

Clubs

Rex Club

MAP P.54, POCKET MAP H6
5 bd Poissonnière Ⓜ Bonne-Nouvelle.
Ⓦ rexclub.com.
The clubbers' club: serious about its music, which is strictly electronic, notably techno, played through a top-of-the-line sound system. Attracts big-name DJs.

Silencio

MAP P.54, POCKET MAP D13

142 rue Montmartre Ⓜ Bourse. Ⓦ silencio-club.com.

A very cool club, attracting an arty media crowd, hidden away down three flights of stairs underneath the *Social Club*; it's owned by film director David Lynch, who designed the sleek 1950s decor, inspired by the club in *Mulholland Drive*. Up until 11pm it's members only; after that doors open to the public, though you still have to look the part to get in.

Music venues

Eglise de la Madeleine

MAP P.54, POCKET MAP E6

Place de la Madeleine Ⓜ Madeleine. Ⓦ lamadeleinedeparis.fr.

A grand, regular venue for organ recitals, to which admission is usually free, and choral concerts. The church has a long and venerable musical tradition.

Gabriel Fauré, who was organist here for a time, wrote his famous Requiem for the church, premiered here in 1888.

Opéra Comique

MAP P.54, POCKET MAP G5

Place Boieldieu Ⓜ Richelieu-Drouot. Ⓦ opera-comique.com.

The *Opéra Comique* offers a richly varied repertoire, often lesser-known nineteenth-century operas, as well as obscure works by well-known composers.

Opéra Garnier

MAP P.54, POCKET MAP F5

8 rue Scribe Ⓜ Opéra. Ⓦ operadeparis.fr.

The *Opéra Garnier* is generally used for ballets and smaller-scale opera productions than those put on at the Opéra Bastille. For programme and booking details, consult their website or phone the box office. Tickets can cost as little as €10 if you don't mind having no view; otherwise, they range from €25 to over €200.

The Opéra Garnier

Beaubourg and Les Halles

One of the city's most recognizable and popular landmarks, the Pompidou Centre, or Beaubourg as the building is known locally, draws large numbers of visitors to its excellent modern art museum and high-profile exhibitions. Its groundbreaking architecture provoked a storm of controversy on its opening in 1977, but since then it has won over critics and public alike. By contrast, nearby Les Halles, a huge shopping mall and transport hub built at around the same time as the Pompidou Centre to replace the old food market that once stood there, has struggled to endear itself to the city's inhabitants. However, a major revamp, designed to open up the space and make it more appealing, has gone some way to rescuing its tarnished image. It's also worth seeking out some of Les Halles' surviving old *bistrots* and food stalls, which preserve traces of the old market atmosphere.

Centre Pompidou

MAP P.64, POCKET MAP E15
Ⓜ Rambuteau/Hôtel-de-Ville.
Ⓦ centrepompidou.fr.

Centre Pompidou

At the heart of one of Paris's oldest districts stands the resolutely modern **Centre Pompidou**. Wanting to move away from the traditional idea of galleries as closed treasure-chests and create something more open and accessible, the architects Renzo Piano and Richard Rogers stripped the "skin" off the building and made the "bones" visible. The infrastructure was put on the outside: escalator tubes and utility pipes, brightly colour-coded according to their function, climb around the exterior in a crazy snakes-and-ladders fashion. The centre's main draw is its modern art museum and exhibitions, but there are also cinemas, a performance space and the Galerie de Photographies (free), which organizes exhibitions drawn from the centre's extensive archive of photographs. One of the added treats of the museum is that you get to ascend the transparent escalator on the outside of the building, affording superb views.

Atelier Brancusi

Musée National d'Art Moderne

MAP P.64, POCKET MAP E15
Pompidou Centre Ⓜ Rambuteau/Hôtel-de-Ville. Charge.

The **Musée National d'Art Moderne** collection, spread over floors four and five of the Pompidou Centre, is one of the finest of its kind in the world. Only a small fraction of the more than 100,000 works can be displayed at any one time, though with the 2010 opening of its sister gallery, the Pompidou Metz, and a pop-up gallery in Malaga, Spain, many more can now be enjoyed by the public.

The galleries are regularly rehung, but broadly speaking floor five covers the years 1905 to 1965 and level four the 1970s to the present day. Fauvism, Cubism, Dada, abstract art, Surrealism and Abstract Expressionism are all well represented. There's a particularly rich collection of Matisses, ranging from early Fauvist works to his late masterpieces – a standout is his *Tristesse du Roi*, a moving meditation on old age and memory. Other highlights include a number of Picasso's and Braque's early Cubist paintings and a substantial collection of Kandinskys. A whole room is devoted to the characteristically colourful paintings of Robert and Sonia Delaunay, while the mood darkens in later rooms with unsettling works by Surrealists Magritte, Dalí and Ernst. Contemporary artists regularly featured include Sophie Calle, Christian Boltanski, video artist Pierre Huyghe, and Daniel Buren, whose works are easy to spot with their trademark stripes, exactly 8.7cm in width.

Atelier Brancusi

MAP P.64, POCKET MAP E15
Pompidou Centre Ⓜ Rambuteau/Hôtel-de-Ville. Free.

The **Atelier Brancusi** is the reconstructed home and studio of sculptor Constantin Brancusi. He bequeathed the contents of his atelier to the state on condition that the rooms be arranged exactly as he left them, and they provide a fascinating insight into how the artist lived and worked. Studios one and two are crowded with Brancusi's trademark abstract bird and column shapes in highly polished brass and marble, while studios three and four comprise the artist's private quarters.

BEAUBOURG AND LES HALLES

Quartier Beaubourg

MAP P.64, POCKET MAP E15

Ⓜ Rambuteau/Hôtel-de-Ville.

The lively **quartier Beaubourg** around the Pompidou Centre also offers much in the way of visual art. The colourful, swirling sculptures and fountains, in the pool in front of the Eglise St-Merri on the south side of the Pompidou Centre, were created by Jean Tinguely and Niki de Saint Phalle. North of the Pompidou Centre, numerous commercial galleries take up the contemporary art theme on rue Quincampoix, a narrow, pedestrianized street lined with fine old houses.

Les Halles

MAP P.64, POCKET MAP D15

Ⓜ Les-Halles/RER Châtelet-Les-Halles.

Described by Zola as "le ventre (the stomach) de Paris", **Les Halles** was Paris's main food market for over eight hundred years until,

despite widespread opposition, it was moved out to the suburbs in 1969. It was replaced by a large, ugly underground shopping and leisure complex, the **Forum des Halles**, as well as a major métro/RER interchange (métro Châtelet-les Halles), the largest in Europe. Widely acknowledged as an architectural disaster, it underwent a major facelift, completed in 2018. The most striking feature of the revamp is **La Canopée**, a vast, undulating, metal-and-glass roof, inspired by a rainforest canopy, which lets much-needed light flood into the lower floors. At ground level, the whole area has been made more inviting with re-landscaped gardens, wide promenades, *pétanque* courts and playgrounds.

The Forum des Halles shops, spread over four levels, are mostly devoted to high-street fashion and homeware, though there's also a large Fnac bookshop. Cultural offerings

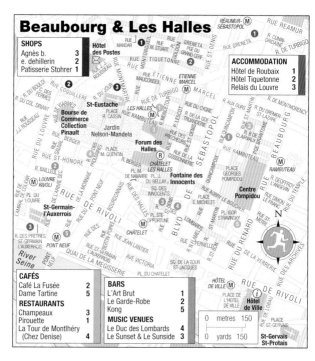

Beaubourg & Les Halles

SHOPS
Agnès b. — 3
e. dehillerin — 2
Patisserie Stohrer — 1

ACCOMMODATION
Hôtel de Roubaix — 1
Hôtel Tiquetonne — 2
Relais du Louvre — 3

CAFÉS
Café La Fusée — 2
Dame Tartine — 5

RESTAURANTS
Champeaux — 3
Pirouette — 1
La Tour de Montlhéry (Chez Denise) — 4

BARS
L'Art Brut — 1
Le Garde-Robe — 2
Kong — 3

MUSIC VENUES
Le Duc des Lombards — 4
Le Sunset & Le Sunside — 3

Bourse de Commerce

include two cinemas, a music and drama school, and a centre for hip-hop – La Place (Ⓦlaplace.paris), the first anywhere of its kind.

Little remains of the old working-class quarter, but you can still catch a flavour of the old market atmosphere in some of the surrounding bars and *bistrots* and on pedestrianized **rue Montorgueil** to the north, where traditional grocers, butchers and fishmongers still ply their trade.

Bourse de Commerce (Collection Pinault)

MAP P.64, POCKET MAP C14
2 rue de Viarmes Ⓜ Les-Halles/
RER Châtelet-Les-Halles.
Ⓦ collectionpinaultparis.com.
Facing the Canopée at the other end of the Les Halles gardens stands the striking **Bourse de Commerce**, the city's former corn market, an eighteenth-century circular building under a glass cupola, which reopened as a major new museum of contemporary art in 2021. The artworks, including pieces by Damien Hirst and Mark Rothko, will come from the huge collection built up by the luxury goods billionaire François Pinault, who already has an art museum in Venice and has long been seeking a Paris outlet for his collection.

St-Eustache

MAP P.64, POCKET MAP D14
Ⓜ Les-Halles/RER Châtelet-Les-Halles.
The beautiful church of **St-Eustache** was built between 1532 and 1637. It's Gothic in structure, with soaring naves and graceful flying buttresses, and Renaissance in decoration – all Corinthian columns, pilasters and arcades. Molière was baptized here, and Rameau and Marivaux are buried here.

Fontaine des Innocents

MAP P.64, POCKET MAP D15
Ⓜ Les-Halles/RER Châtelet-Les-Halles.
The **Fontaine des Innocents**, a perfectly proportioned Renaissance fountain decorated with reliefs of water nymphs, is Paris's oldest surviving fountain – dating from 1549. On warm days shoppers sit around its edge, drawn to the cool of its cascading waters. It is named after the cemetery that used to occupy this site, the Cimetière des Innocents.

Kong

cookware, laid out like a traditional ironmonger's, with narrow aisles and no fancy displays, stocks a superb selection of copper and pewter pans, knives and other utensils at reasonable prices.

Patisserie Stohrer

MAP P.64, POCKET MAP D14
51 rue Montorgueil ⓂSentier.
Discover what *pain aux raisins* should really taste like at this wonderful patisserie, in business since 1730 and preserving its lovely old decor.

Cafés

Cafe La Fusée

MAP P.64, POCKET MAP E15
168 rue Saint-Martin ⓂRambuteau. ☎01 42 76 93 99.
A vibrant, authentic café-bar, with cosy nooks inside and seats on the terrace under a cheery red-and-white-striped awning. Come for a filling breakfast, a simple lunch of croque monsieur, say, or an evening drink and snack, all at reasonable prices for the area.

Dame Tartine

MAP P.64, POCKET MAP E15
2 rue Brisemiche ⓂRambuteau/Hôtel-de-Ville.
Overlooking the Stravinsky fountain, with outdoor seating under shady plane trees, this popular café is a handy pit stop, offering cheap and tasty, open toasted sandwiches and soups, and a set menu for children.

Shops

Agnès b.

MAP P.64, POCKET MAP D14
2–4 & 6 rue du Jour ⓂLes-Halles/RER Châtelet-Les-Halles.
Agnès b. pays scant regard to fashion trends, creating chic, timeless, understated clothes for men, women and children. Her best-known staples are the snap cardigan and well-made T-shirts that don't lose their shape.

e. dehillerin

MAP P.64, POCKET MAP C14
18–20 rue Coquillière ⓂLes-Halles/RER Châtelet-Les-Halles. Ⓦedehillerin.fr.
Dating back to 1820, this supplier of professional-quality

Restaurants

Champeaux

MAP P.64, POCKET MAP D15
Forum des Halles ⓂEtienne-Marcel/Châtelet. Ⓦrestaurant-champeaux.com.
Installed under the new Les Halles Canopée, this contemporary

brasserie run by Alain Ducasse cuts a dash with its long cocktail bar, marble-topped tables, black leather banquettes and huge glass windows. In a novel touch, large departure boards of the kind you see at train stations flick up the menu at regular intervals and add to the general air of hum and bustle. Try one of the signature soufflés (think cheese, lobster, or pistachio and salted caramel) or well-prepared classics such as filet de boeuf, duck, or pan-fried foie gras. €€

Pirouette

MAP P.64, POCKET MAP D14
5 rue Mondétour Ⓜ Etienne-Marcel.
Ⓦ restaurantpirouette.com.
This sleek restaurant has gained a name for serving beautifully presented, innovative French food in a relaxed, contemporary atmosphere, with fresh, bright flavours, lots of light choices and delicious veggie dishes. There's also a really good wine list, with many wines available by the glass. €€

La Tour de Montlhéry (Chez Denise)

MAP P.64, POCKET MAP D15
5 rue des Prouvaires Ⓜ Louvre-Rivoli/
Châtelet. ☏ 01 42 36 21 82.
An old-style late-night Les Halles *bistrot*, packed with diners at long tables tucking into substantial meaty French dishes, such as *daube* of beef with perfectly cooked chips. €€

Bars

L'Art Brut

MAP P.64, POCKET MAP E15
78 rue Quincampoix Ⓜ Les Halles/
Rambuteau. Ⓦ barbrutbistrot.fr.
A small, friendly bar with a bohemian vibe, partly lent by the changing display of paintings and photos by young artists on the walls. A lively crowd is drawn here in the evenings by its relatively cheap drinks and generous cheese and charcuterie platters.

Le Garde-Robe

MAP P.64, POCKET MAP C15
41 rue de l'Arbre Sec Ⓜ Louvre-Rivoli. ☏ 01 49 26 90 60.
An animated, cosy bar à vins that – with its bare-board floors, retro wallpaper and globe lights – manages to feel effortlessly stylish. The wines are superb, with mostly biodynamic and natural choices. A couple of simple and unusual lunchtime menus focus on organic ingredients, with tasty veggie choices; in the evenings the likes of cheese and charcuterie plates, croques and foie gras take over.

Kong

MAP P.64, POCKET MAP C15
5th floor, 1 rue du Pont-Neuf Ⓜ Pont Neuf.
Ⓦ kong.fr.
A lift whisks you up to this cool, Philippe Starck-designed bar-restaurant atop the flagship Kenzo building. Happy hour daily, club nights Thurs, Fri & Sat.

Music venues

Le Duc des Lombards

MAP P.64, POCKET MAP D15
42 rue des Lombards Ⓜ Châtelet.
Ⓦ ducdeslombards.com.
Stylish jazz club with nightly performances featuring gypsy jazz, blues, ballads and fusion.

Le Sunset & Le Sunside

MAP P.64, POCKET MAP D15
60 rue des Lombards Ⓜ Châtelet.
Ⓦ sunset-sunside.com.
Two clubs in one: *Le Sunside* on the ground floor features mostly traditional jazz, while the downstairs *Sunset* is a venue for electric and fusion jazz. Charge to enter, but free entry to some jam sessions.

The Marais

Full of splendid old mansions, narrow lanes and buzzing bars and restaurants, the Marais is one of the most seductive areas of central Paris, known for its sophistication and artsy leanings, and for being the neighbourhood of choice for LGBTQ+ Parisians. The quarter boasts a concentration of fascinating museums, including the Carnavalet history museum and the Musée Picasso, as well as some fine commercial art galleries housed in handsome Renaissance buildings.

Musée d'Art et d'Histoire du Judaïsme

MAP P.70, POCKET MAP E15–F15
71 rue du Temple ⓜ Rambuteau.
ⓦ mahj.org. Charge.

Housed in the attractively restored Hôtel de Saint-Aignan, the **Musée d'Art et d'Histoire du Judaïsme** traces Jewish culture and history, mainly in France. The result is a comprehensive collection, as educational as it is beautiful.

Highlights include a Gothic-style Hanukkah lamp, one of the very few French-Jewish artefacts to survive from the period before the expulsion of the Jews from France in 1394; an Italian gilded circumcision chair from the seventeenth century; and a completely intact, late nineteenth-century Austrian Sukkah, a temporary dwelling for the celebration of the harvest.

The museum also holds the Dreyfus archives, with one room devoted to the notorious Dreyfus Affair. The wrongful conviction of Captain Alfred Dreyfus caused deep divisions in French society, stoking up anticlerical, socialist sympathies on the one hand and conservative, anti-Semitic feelings on the other.

The last few rooms contain a significant collection of paintings and sculpture by Jewish artists – Marc Chagall, Samuel Hirszenberg, Chaïm Soutine and Jacques Lipchitz – who came to live in Paris at the beginning of the twentieth century. The Holocaust is only briefly touched on, since it's dealt with in depth by the Mémorial de la Shoah (see page 74).

Hôtel Soubise – Musée des Archives Nationales

MAP P.70, POCKET MAP F15
60 rue des Francs-Bourgeois
ⓜ Rambuteau/St-Paul.
ⓦ archivesnationales.culture.gouv.fr.
Charge.

The entire block enclosed by rue des Quatre Fils, rue des Archives, rue Vieille-du-Temple and rue des Francs-Bourgeois, was once filled by a magnificent, early eighteenth-century palace complex. Only half remains, but it is utterly splendid, especially the colonnaded courtyard of the **Hôtel Soubise**, with its Rococo interiors and vestigial fourteenth-century towers on rue des Quatre Fils. The hôtel houses the city archives, and a number of key documents, such as the Edict of Nantes and Marie-Antoinette's last letter, are on display in its **Musée des Archives Nationales**. The opulent ground-floor Chambre du Prince is the scene of chamber music recitals, held here most Saturday evenings.

Musée Picasso

MAP P.70, POCKET MAP G15

5 rue de Thorigny Ⓜ Chemin Vert/St-Paul.
Ⓦ museepicassoparis.fr. Charge. To avoid long queues, reserve tickets online in advance.

Behind the elegant classical facade of the seventeenth-century Hôtel Salé lies the **Musée Picasso**, home to the largest collection of Picassos anywhere, representing almost all the major periods of the artist's life from 1905 onwards.

Many of the works were owned by Picasso, and on his death in 1973 were seized by the state in lieu of taxes owed. The result is an unedited body of work, which, although perhaps not among the most recognizable of Picasso's masterpieces, provides an insight into the person behind the myth. Some of the most engaging works on display are his more personal ones, for example the contrasting portraits of his lovers Dora Maar and Marie-Thérèse.

The museum also holds a substantial number of Picasso's ceramics and sculptures, some of which he created from recycled household objects. 2023 was the 50th anniversary of Picasso's death and inspired a handful of cultural events in the museum and at landmarks across the capital.

Musée Cognacq-Jay

MAP P.70, POCKET MAP G16

8 rue Elzévir Ⓜ St-Paul.
Ⓦ museecognacqjay.paris.fr. Free.

The compact **Musée Cognacq-Jay** occupies the fine Hôtel Donon. The Cognacq-Jay family built up the Samaritaine department store and were noted philanthropists and lovers of European art. Their collection of eighteenth-century pieces on show includes a handful of works by Canaletto, Fragonard, Rubens and Rembrandt, as well as an exquisite still life by Chardin, displayed in beautifully carved wood-panelled rooms filled with Sèvres porcelain and Louis XV furniture.

Musée Carnavalet

MAP P.70, POCKET MAP G16

16 rue des Francs-Bourgeois Ⓜ St-Paul.
Ⓦ carnavalet.paris.fr. Free.

The **Musée Carnavalet** is a fascinating museum, which charts the history of Paris from

Hôtel de Soubise

The Marais

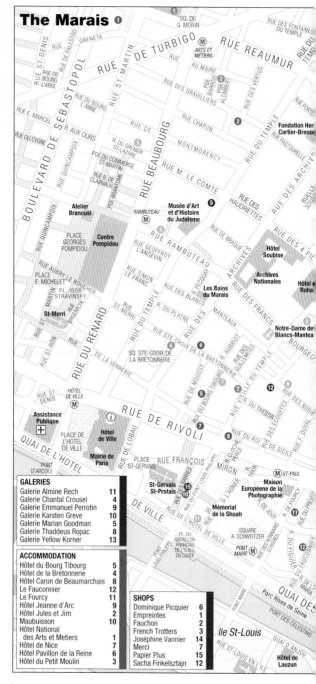

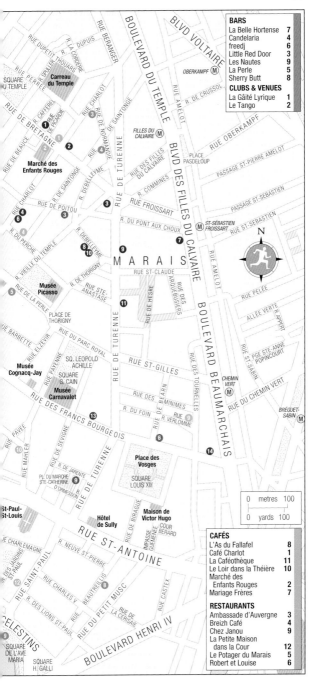

BARS

La Belle Hortense	7
Candelaria	4
freedj	6
Little Red Door	3
Les Nautes	9
La Perle	5
Sherry Butt	8

CLUBS & VENUES

La Gâîté Lyrique	1
Le Tango	2

CAFÉS

L'As du Fallafel	8
Café Charlot	1
La Caféothèque	11
Le Loir dans la Théière	10
Marché des Enfants Rouges	2
Mariage Frères	7

RESTAURANTS

Ambassade d'Auvergne	3
Breizh Café	4
Chez Janou	9
La Petite Maison dans la Cour	12
Le Potager du Marais	5
Robert et Louise	6

Hammams

Hammams, or Turkish baths, are one of the unexpected delights of Paris. Much more luxurious than the standard Swedish sauna, these are places to linger and chat, and you can usually pay extra for a massage and a gommage – a rubdown with a rubber glove – followed by mint tea to recover. One of the most attractive is to be found at Les Bains du Marais (31–33 rue des Blancs-Manteaux; Ⓜ Rambuteau/ St-Paul; Ⓦ bainsdumarais.com), as much a posh health club as a hammam, with a chichi clientele and glorious interior. Sauna and steam room by the hour; massage/gommage charged separately. There are exclusive sessions for women and men as well as mixed sessions, for which you have to bring a swimsuit.

its origins up to the *belle époque* through a huge and extraordinary collection of paintings, sculptures, decorative arts and archaeological finds, occupying over 140 rooms. The museum's setting in two beautiful Renaissance mansions, Hôtel Carnavalet and Hôtel Le Peletier, surrounded by attractive formal gardens, is reason enough to visit.

Inside is a succession of recreated salons and boudoirs full of richly sculpted wood panelling and tapestries from the time of Louis XII to Louis XVI. A number of rooms are devoted to the belle époque, evoked through paintings of the period and some wonderful Art Nouveau interiors, among which is the sumptuous peacock-green interior designed by Alphonse Mucha for Fouquet's jewellery shop in the rue Royal. Also well preserved is José-Maria Sert's Art Deco ballroom, with its extravagant gold-leaf decor and grand-scale paintings, including one of the Queen of Sheba with a train of elephants. The rooms dedicated to the French Revolution are compelling, with exhibits ranging from models of the guillotine to decimal clocks. There are also temporary exhibitions; in 2023, on Philippe Stark for example.

The Jewish quarter: rue des Rosiers

MAP P.70, POCKET MAP F16
Ⓜ St-Paul.

The narrow, pedestrianized rue des Rosiers has been the city's **Jewish quarter** ever since the twelfth century. Despite the incursion of trendy boutiques, it just about manages to retain a Jewish flavour, with the odd delicatessen, kosher food shop and Hebrew bookstore, as well as a number of falafel takeaways – testimony to the influence of the North African Sephardim, who, since the end of World War II, have sought refuge here from the uncertainties of life in the former French colonies.

Place des Vosges

MAP P.70, POCKET MAP G16
Ⓜ St-Paul.

A grand square of handsome pink brick and stone mansions built over arcades, the **place des Vosges** is a masterpiece of aristocratic elegance and the first example of planned development in the history of Paris. It was built by Henri IV and inaugurated in 1612 for the wedding of Louis XIII and Anne of Austria; a replica of Louis' statue stands hidden by chestnut trees in the middle of the grass-and-gravel gardens at the square's centre.

Today, well-heeled Parisians pause in the arcades to browse art, antique and clothing shops, and lunch alfresco in the restaurants while buskers play classical music. Unusually for Paris, you're allowed to sprawl on the grass in the garden.

Maison de Victor Hugo

MAP P.70, POCKET MAP G17
Place des Vosges Ⓜ St-Paul.
Ⓦ maisonsvictorhugo.paris.fr. Free.
Among the many celebrities who made their homes in place des Vosges was Victor Hugo; his house at no. 6, where he wrote much of *Les Misérables*, is now a museum. Hugo's life is evoked through a sparse collection of memorabilia, portraits and photographs. What the museum conveys, though, is an idea of his prodigious creativity: as well as being a prolific writer, he enjoyed drawing and designed his own furniture. Some of his sketches and Gothic-style furniture are on display, and a Chinese-style dining room that he designed for his house in Guernsey is re-created in its entirety.

Les Bains du Marais

Hôtel de Sully

MAP P.70, POCKET MAP G17
62 rue St-Antoine Ⓜ St-Paul. Ⓦ hotel-de-sully.fr.
The exquisite Renaissance **Hôtel de Sully** (not open to the public) is the headquarters of the Centre des Monuments Nationaux, which looks after more than a hundred national monuments and publishes numerous guides and books, many of which are on sale in the excellent ground-floor bookshop. The mansion's attractive garden is a peaceful place for a rest stop and a handy shortcut from the place des Vosges to rue St-Antoine.

The Quartier St-Paul-St-Gervais

MAP P.70, POCKET MAP E16–F17
Ⓜ St-Paul.
The southern section of the Marais, below rues de Rivoli and St-Antoine, is quieter than the northern part and has some picturesque corners. One of these is cobbled rue des Barres, perfumed with the scent of roses from nearby gardens and the occasional waft of incense from

Mémorial de la Shoah

the church of St-Gervais-St-Protais, a late Gothic construction that looks somewhat battered on the outside owing to a direct hit from a shell fired from a Big Bertha howitzer in 1918. Its interior contains some lovely stained glass, carved misericords and a seventeenth-century organ – Paris's oldest. Worth exploring further east is Village St-Paul, a network of courtyards and streets housing antique, one-off interior-design and art shops.

Mémorial de la Shoah

MAP P.70, POCKET MAP F17

17 rue Geoffroy l'Asnier ⓂSt-Paul/Pont-Marie. Ⓦmemorialdelashoah.org. Free. Since 1956 this has been the site of the Mémorial du Martyr Juif Inconnu (Memorial to an Unknown Jewish Martyr), a sombre crypt containing a large black marble Star of David. In 2005 President Chirac opened a new museum here and unveiled a Wall of Names: four giant slabs of marble engraved with the names of the 76,000 Jews sent to death camps from 1942 to 1944.

The excellent museum gives an absorbing account of the history of Jews in France, and especially Paris, during the German occupation. There are last letters from deportees to their families, videotaped testimonies from survivors, numerous ID cards and photos. The museum ends with the Mémorial des Enfants, an overwhelming collection of photos of 2,500 French children, each with the dates of their birth and their deportation.

Maison Europeenne de la Photographie

MAP P.70, POCKET MAP F16

5–7 rue de Fourcy ⓂSt-Paul. Ⓦmep-fr.org. Charge.
A gorgeous Marais mansion, the early eighteenth-century Hôtel Hénault de Cantobre, has been turned into a vast and serene space dedicated to the art of contemporary photography. Temporary shows are combined with a revolving exhibition of the Maison's permanent collection; young photographers and news photographers get a look-in, as well as artists using photography

in multimedia creations or installation art.

Hôtel de Ville

MAP P.70, POCKET MAP E16
Ⓜ Rambuteau/Hôtel-de-Ville.

The **Hôtel de Ville**, the seat of the city's mayor, is a gargantuan mansion in florid neo-Renaissance style, modelled on the previous building which burned down during the Commune in 1871. It stages regular free, highly popular exhibitions on Parisian themes (entrance 5 rue Lobau). The road along the river from here to the Port de l'Arsenal has been made into an attractive pedestrianized riverside walk, an extension of the Parc Rives de Seine on the Left Bank (see page 101).

The Haut Marais

MAP P.70, POCKET MAP F14/15–G14/15

The northern part of the Marais, the "**haut Marais**", is currently the favoured strolling ground of bobo (bourgeois-bohemian)

Parisians, drawn by the art galleries, design and fashion shops, cocktail bars and the **Carreau du Temple** arts centre (Ⓦcarreaudutemple.eu). The main thoroughfare is rue de Bretagne, with its cafés and traditional shops. The adjacent **Marché des Enfants-Rouges**, one of the smallest and oldest food markets in Paris, makes a good lunchtime stop (see page 77).

Fondation Henri Cartier-Bresson

MAP P.70, POCKET MAP F14
79 rue des Archives Ⓜ Arts et Métiers.
Ⓦ henricartierbresson.org. Charge.

The **Fondation Henri Cartier-Bresson** moved out of its old premises in Montparnasse in 2018 and enjoys more than double the space in its new Marais home. The foundation houses the archive of the great Parisian photojournalist and showcases the work of his contemporaries and of younger photographers.

Hôtel de Ville

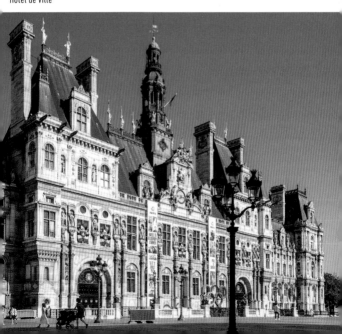

Shops

Dominique Picquier

MAP P.70, POCKET MAP F15

10 rue Charlot Ⓜ Filles du Calvaire.
Ⓦ dominiquepicquier.com.

"A tribute from the town to the country" is how this textile designer describes her beautiful hand-printed fabrics of swirling orchids, delicate mimosas and daisies. She also does a stylish range of accessories, such as tote bags, purses and travel bags.

Empreintes

MAP P.70, POCKET MAP G14

5 rue de Picardie Ⓜ Saint-Sébastien-Froissart. Ⓦ empreintes-paris.com.

The first of its kind in France, this arts and crafts concept store occupies an attractive, light-filled space, spread over four floors, and presents a wide-ranging collection of ceramics, jewellery, ornaments, tableware and much else, all hand-crafted in French workshops. Some works are expensive one-offs, others part of a more affordable limited edition. It's a nice place to linger even if you don't buy, especially as there's a café and a bookshop too.

Fauchon

MAP P.70, POCKET MAP G14

14 rue de Bretagne, Ⓦ fauchon.com.

In 2023, Fauchon opened a new boutique dedicated to teas and infusions in the Marais, focussing on its unique concept of made-to-measure infusions.

French Trotters

MAP P.70, POCKET MAP G15

128 rue Vieille du Temple Ⓜ Saint Sébastien-Froissart. Ⓦ frenchtrotters.fr.

A well-curated collection of lesser-known fashion labels, as well as the store's own-brand casual-chic clothing for men and women. There's also a good range of homeware and accessories.

Joséphine Vannier

MAP P.70, POCKET MAP H16

4 rue du Pas de la Mule Ⓜ Bastille.
Ⓦ chocolats-vannier.com.

This inventive chocolatier sells chocolate-shaped accordions, violins, books, Eiffel Towers and Arcs de Triomphe – exquisite creations, almost too perfect to eat.

Merci

MAP P.70, POCKET MAP G15

111 blvd Beaumarchais Ⓜ St-Sébastien-Froissart. Ⓦ merci-merci.com.

Set in a huge old wallpaper factory, this hip and original concept store sells an attractive range of women's clothing alongside homeware and jewellery; the clothes are not especially cheap, but all profits go to charity. There are three good eating options too, including the cosy Used Books Café, lined with secondhand books.

Papier Plus

MAP P.70, POCKET MAP F16

9 rue du Pont-Louis-Philippe Ⓜ Hôtel-de-Ville. Ⓦ papierplus.com.

Fine-quality colourful stationery, including notebooks, photo albums and artists' portfolios.

Sacha Finkelsztajn

MAP P.70, POCKET MAP F16

27 rue des Rosiers Ⓜ Hôtel-de-Ville.
Ⓦ laboutiquejaune.fr.

A marvellous Jewish deli for takeaway snacks and goodies: challah bread, apple strudel, boreks, *gefilte* fish, aubergine purée, tarama, *blinis* and *borscht*. There's a handful of tables for eating in.

Cafés

L'As du Fallafel

MAP P.70, POCKET MAP F16

34 rue des Rosiers Ⓜ St-Paul. ☏ 01 48 87 63 60.

The sign above the doorway of this falafel shop in the Jewish quarter reads "*Toujours imité, jamais égalé*" ("Always copied, but never equalled"), a boast that few would challenge, given the queues. Takeaway falafels, or pay a bit more and sit in the buzzing little dining room.

Café Charlot

MAP P.70, POCKET MAP G14
38 rue de Bretagne Ⓜ Filles du Calvaire.
Ⓦ cafecharlot-paris.com.
You'll need to fight for a seat on the terrace of this white-tiled retro-chic café, which bursts at the seams on weekends with local hipsters and in-the-know tourists. The food – a mix of French and American standards – is not that special, but it's a great place for a drink and a spot of people-watching.

La Caféothèque

MAP P.70, POCKET MAP F16
52 rue de l'Hôtel-de-Ville Ⓜ Pont Marie.
Ⓦ lacafeotheque.com.
This arty, aromatic coffee house, with its nest of cosy rooms, provides the perfect setting to relax on plump hessian-covered seating over a brew and make use of the free wi-fi. Coffee is taken seriously here, with daily specials and a three-cup *dégustation* option in addition to espressos, flat whites and the like.

Le Loir dans la Théière

MAP P.70, POCKET MAP F16
3 rue des Rosiers Ⓜ St-Paul.
Ⓦ leloirdanslatheiere.com.
A characterful *salon de thé* decorated with antique toys and Alice in Wonderland murals. It's a popular spot for meeting friends and lounging about on comfy sofas, while feasting on delicious home-made cakes and pastries (the lemon meringue pie is to die for) or excellent vegetarian quiches.

Marché des Enfants Rouges

MAP P.70, POCKET MAP G14
39 rue de Bretagne Ⓜ Filles-du-Calvaire.
In addition to fresh fruit, veg and cheese, this popular food market

Marché des Enfants Rouges

is the place to come for street food – rôtisserie, Japanese, couscous, crêpes, Lebanese, Italian, Creole – which you can eat at communal picnic tables.

Mariage Frères

MAP P.70, POCKET MAP F16
30 rue du Bourg-Tibourg Ⓜ Hôtel-de-Ville.
Ⓦ mariagefreres.com.
A classy, colonial-style *salon de thé* in the *Mariages Frères* tea emporium, with a choice of over five hundred brews.

Restaurants

Ambassade d'Auvergne

MAP P.70, POCKET MAP E14
22 rue du Grenier St-Lazare Ⓜ Rambuteau.
Ⓦ ambassade-auvergne.fr.
Suited, moustachioed waiters serve scrumptious, filling Auvergnat cuisine that would have made Vercingetorix proud. There's a set menu, but you may well be tempted by some of the house specialities such as the roast Marvejols lamb. Among the after-dinner treats are a cheese plate and divine chocolate mousse. €€

Breizh Café

Breizh Café

MAP P.70, POCKET MAP G15
109 rue Vieille du Temple Ⓜ St-Paul.
Ⓦ breizhcafe.com.

A Breton café, serving the best crêpes in the Marais (and arguably the city), with traditional fillings like ham and cheese, as well as more exotic options such as smoked herring, which you can wash down with one of around sixty different ciders. Leave room for dessert, as Valrhona chocolate is used in the sweet crêpes. It's very popular, so book ahead. €

Chez Janou

MAP P.70. POCKET MAP G16
2 rue Roger Verlomme Ⓜ Chemin Vert.
Ⓦ chezjanou.com.

A fiercely popular Provençal restaurant serving generous portions of traditional southern food and over eighty different types of *pastis*, so you can whet your appetite like a true local. Tables are cramped, so unless you can snaffle one on the sunny terrace you'll be sitting cosily, elbow to elbow, with your neighbours. €

La Petite Maison dans la Cour

MAP P.70, POCKET MAP F17
9 rue St Paul Ⓜ St-Paul.
Ⓦ lapetitemaisondanslacour.fr.

Hidden away in a courtyard (part of the Village St Paul; see page 74) off the main road, this attractive restaurant-*salon de thé*, with its pretty *terrasse*, is a tranquil spot for lunch or an afternoon cup of one of the best hot chocolates in town, made with Madagascar chocolate and organic milk. The menu is short but everything is locally sourced and homemade, including savouries such as split-pea and bacon broth, quiches, and herbed chicken with black rice. €

Le Potager du Marais

MAP P.70, POCKET MAP E15
22 rue Rambuteau Ⓜ Rambuteau. ☎ 01 57 40 98 57.

Come early or book in advance for a place at this organic vegan restaurant, with only 25 covers at a long communal table. Dishes include seitan stew with red wine and mushrooms, and buckwheat pancakes. €

Robert et Louise

MAP P.70. POCKET MAP F15
64 rue Vieille du Temple Ⓜ Hôtel-de-Ville.
Ⓦ robertetlouise.com.

The welcome at this rustic *bistrot*, with its exposed beams and wooden tables, is as warm and hearty as the meaty dishes on offer. Start with foie gras or a blood sausage, then choose between steak, lamb chops, duck confit or *andouillette* (tripe sausage). €

Bars

La Belle Hortense

MAP P.70, POCKET MAP F16
31 rue Vieille du Temple Ⓜ St-Paul.
Ⓦ cafeine.com.

You can sip a glass of wine while reading or chatting in this friendly little wine/champagne-bar-bookshop with book-lined walls and a zinc bar. There's a snug room with sofas at the back, but you'll be lucky to get a seat there later on.

Candelaria

MAP P.70, POCKET MAP G14
52 rue de Saintonge Ⓜ Filles du Calvaire.
Ⓦ candelaria-paris.com.

A speakeasy-style cocktail bar, set at the back of a taco bar; push open what looks like a broom-cupboard door and you'll find yourself in a small, stone-walled, dimly lit bar. You might be lucky to snag one of the low tables, otherwise you'll have to squeeze in around the bar where you can watch the expert staff mix up some exotic concoctions such as La Guêpe Verte, made of pepper-infused tequila, lime, agave syrup and coriander.

freedj

MAP P.70, POCKET MAP E16
35 rue Ste-Croix de la Bretonnerie
Ⓜ Hôtel-de-Ville. Ⓦ freedj.fr.

This stylish gay bar draws the young and *très looké* – beautiful types. It's friendly, though, and features some big sounds (house, disco-funk) in the basement club.

Little Red Door

MAP P.70, POCKET MAP G14
60 rue Charlot Ⓜ Filles du Calvaire/Temple.
Ⓦ lrdparis.com.

A discreet cocktail bar with snug candle-lit interior. Settle into a velvet sofa and have fun choosing one of the original, award-winning cocktails. It soon gets very crowded, so either arrive early or be prepared to negotiate with the doorman.

Les Nautes

MAP P.70, POCKET MAP F17
1 quai des Célestins Ⓜ Pont Marie/Sully
Morland. Ⓦ lesnautes-paris.com.

Occupying an idyllic spot on the riverbank opposite the Ile Saint-Louis, the extensive *terrasse* of *Les Nautes* is the perfect place for chilling out on over a beer on a warm evening. It's also a good place for live music, such as rock, reggae and jazz, and it hosts regular DJ nights.

La Perle

MAP P.70, POCKET MAP F15
78 rue Vieille du Temple Ⓜ St-Paul.
Ⓦ cafelaperle.com.

An 'emperor's new clothes' kind of place that maintains a *très cool* reputation. Always packed with an arty indie crowd drinking cheap beer, despite being somewhat scruffy and playing generic dance music.

Sherry Butt

MAP P.70. POCKET MAP G17
20 rue Beautreillis Ⓜ St-Paul/Bastille.
Ⓦ sherrybuttparis.com.

This cool, New York-style cocktail bar serves creative drinks such as the popular La Belle en Bulle (pisco, pear syrup, lemon juice and champagne). The leather sofas and low lighting create a laidback, intimate atmosphere.

Clubs and venues

La Gaîté Lyrique

MAP P.70, POCKET MAP E13
3 bis rue Papin Ⓜ Réaumur-Sébastopol/
Arts-et-Métiers. Ⓦ gaiete-lyrique.net.

La Gaîté Lyrique

A centre for digital arts and contemporary music, housed in a nineteenth-century theatre. After years of closure, it was given a radical makeover – the architects restored the facade and splendid marble foyer and entrance hall, while opening up the interior to accommodate various performance spaces, including a state-of-the-art concert hall. The busy programme of events includes exhibitions, dance, theatre and art installations.

Le Tango
MAP P.70, POCKET MAP F14
13 rue au Maire Ⓜ Arts-et-Métiers. Ⓦ tangoparis.com.
Unpretentious gay and lesbian club with a Sunday-afternoon tea dance, with proper slow dances as well as tangos. Friday and Saturday nights start with anything from camp 1980s disco classics to world music, turning into a full-on club around midnight.

Galleries

Galerie Almine Rech
MAP P.70, POCKET MAP G15
64 rue de Turenne Ⓜ St-Sébastien-Froissart. Ⓦ alminerech.com.
Installed in an elegant gallery, Rech represents around fifty artists, including Ugo Rondinone and Jeff Koons.

Galerie Chantal Crousel
MAP P.70, POCKET MAP F15
10 rue Charlot Ⓜ Filles du Calvaire. Ⓦ crousel.com.
This gallery, which has been around since 1980, represents mostly foreign and some French artists – such as Gabriel Orozco and Mona Hatoum – who work in a variety of media. It also promotes the work of emerging video artists.

Galerie Emmanuel Perrotin
MAP P.70, POCKET MAP G15
76 rue de Turenne Ⓜ St-Sébastien-Froissart. Ⓦ perrotin.com.
One of the most influential galleries on the French contemporary art scene, Perrotin has exhibited French artists such as Sophie Calle, as well as international names including the likes of Takashi Murakami and Maurizio Cattelan.

Galerie Karsten Greve

MAP P.70, POCKET MAP G15

5 rue Debelleyme Ⓜ St-Sébastien-
Froissart Ⓦ galerie-karsten-greve.com.
Paris branch of the German gallery,
showing the work of notable
twentieth-century artists such as Louise
Bourgeois and Willem de Kooning.

Galerie Marian Goodman

MAP P.70, POCKET MAP F15

79 rue du Temple Ⓜ Rambuteau.
Ⓦ mariangoodman.com.
This offshoot of the famed New
York gallery has exhibited Jean-
Marc Bustamante, Steve McQueen
and Rineke Dijkstra, among many
other big names.

Galerie Thaddeus Ropac

MAP P.70, POCKET MAP G15

7 rue Debelleyme Ⓜ Filles-du-Calvaire.
Ⓦ ropac.net.
Recent exhibitions at this
well-established gallery include
Robert Rauschenberg and
Robert Mapplethorpe. Also
well worth a visit is Ropac's
enormous outpost in Pantin,
near La Villette, which
specialises in showing large-scale
installations.

Galerie Yellow Korner

MAP P.70, POCKET MAP G16

8 rue des Francs Bourgeois Ⓜ St-Paul.
Ⓦ yellowkorner.com.
This contemporary photography
gallery, which has outposts
throughout Europe, showcases
both established and up-and-
coming talent.

Galerie Karsten Greve

Bastille and Bercy

A symbol of revolution since the toppling of the Bastille prison in 1789, the Bastille quarter used to belong in spirit and style to the working-class districts of eastern Paris. After the construction of the opera house in the 1980s, however, it became a magnet for artists, fashion folk and young people, who over the years brought with them stylish shops and an energetic nightlife. However, some of the working-class flavour lingers on in the furniture workshops off rue du Faubourg-St-Antoine, testimony to a long tradition of cabinet making and woodworking in the district. To the south lies Bercy, once the largest wine market in the world, its warehouses now converted into restaurants and shops.

Place de la Bastille

MAP P.84, POCKET MAP H17
Ⓜ Bastille.

The huge **place de la Bastille** is where Parisians congregate to celebrate Bastille Day on July 14, though hardly anything survives of the prison – the few remains have been transferred to square Henri-Galli at the end of boulevard Henri-IV. At the centre of the *place* is a column (Colonne de Juillet) surmounted by a gilded Spirit of Liberty, erected to commemorate the July Revolution of 1830 that replaced the autocratic Charles X with the "Citizen King" Louis-Philippe. The square is usually clogged with traffic, though a refurbishment, currently underway, should make it a greener and more pedestrian-friendly space.

Place d'Aligre market

MAP P.84, POCKET MAP L9
Ⓜ Ledru-Rollin.

The **place d'Aligre market**, between avenue Daumesnil and rue du Faubourg St-Antoine, is a lively, raucous affair, particularly at weekends. The square itself is given over to clothes and bric-a-brac stalls, selling anything from old gramophone players to odd bits of crockery. It's along the adjoining rue d'Aligre where the market really comes to life though, with the vendors, many of Algerian origin, doing a frenetic trade in fruit and veg.

Promenade Plantée

MAP P.84, POCKET MAP L10
Ⓜ Bastille.

The **Promenade Plantée** is a stretch of disused railway line, much of it along a viaduct, ingeniously converted into an elevated walkway and planted with trees and flowers. Starting near the beginning of avenue Daumesnil, just south of the Bastille opera house, it is reached via a flight of stone steps – or lifts – with a number of similar access points all the way along. It takes you to the Parc de Reuilly, then descends to ground level and continues nearly as far as the *périphérique*, from where you can follow signs to the Bois de Vincennes. The whole walk is around 4.5km long.

Viaduc des Arts

MAP P.84, POCKET MAP L9–10
Ⓜ Bastille. Ⓦ leviaducdesarts.com.

The arches of the Promenade Plantée's viaduct have been converted into attractive spaces for artisans' studios and craft shops, collectively known as the **Viaduc des Arts**, and include furniture and tapestry restorers, interior designers, cabinetmakers, violin- and flute-makers, embroiderers and fashion and jewellery designers.

Parc Floral

POCKET MAP M11

Bois de Vincennes Ⓜ Chateau de Vincennes, then bus #112, or a fifteen-minute walk. Free except high summer weekends.

The **Parc Floral** is one of the city's best gardens. Flowers are always in bloom in the Jardin des Quatre Saisons, and there are some enchanting walks amid pines and rhododendrons. Children will enjoy the adventure playground and minigolf of Parisian monuments, and in spring and summer there are exhibitions and concerts.

Parc Zoologique de Paris

POCKET MAP M11

Bois de Vincennes Ⓜ Porte Dorée. Ⓦ parczoologiquedeparis.fr. Charge.

Paris's **zoo** uses fake rocks and boulders to re-create as natural a habitat as possible for the 1,000-odd animals, including giraffes, lions and endangered species. Animals are grouped by region, such as Madagascar, Patagonia and Guyana.

Château de Vincennes

POCKET MAP M10

Ⓜ Château-de-Vincennes. Ⓦ chateau-de-vincennes.fr. Charge.

On the northern edge of the *bois* is the **Château de Vincennes** – erstwhile royal medieval residence, then state prison, porcelain factory, weapons dump and military training school. It presents a rather austere aspect on first sight, but is worth visiting for its beautiful Flamboyant-Gothic **Chapelle Royale**, completed in the mid-sixteenth century and decorated with superb Renaissance stained-glass windows. Nearby, in the renovated fourteenth-century *donjon* (keep), you can see some fine vaulted ceilings and Charles V's bedchamber, as well as graffiti left by prisoners.

An inhabitant of the Parc Zoologique de Paris

Bastille and Bercy

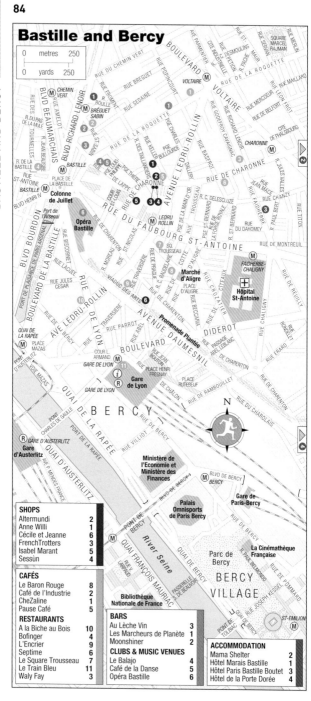

Bercy Village

MAP P.84, POCKET MAP M12

Ⓜ Cour St-Emilion.

Bercy Village is a complex of rather handsome old wine warehouses stylishly converted into shops, which, unusually for Paris, are open on a Sunday. There are also plenty of restaurants and wine bars – popular spots before or after a film at the giant Bercy multiplex cinema at the eastern end of Cour Saint Emilion.

Parc de Bercy

MAP P.84, POCKET MAP M12

Ⓜ Bercy/Cour St-Emilion.

The contemporary-style **Parc de Bercy** incorporates elements of the old warehouse site, such as disused railway tracks and cobbled lanes. The western section of the park is a fairly unexciting expanse of grass, but the area to the east has arbours, rose gardens, lily ponds and an orangerie.

La Cinémathèque Francaise

MAP P.84, POCKET MAP M11–12

51 rue de Bercy Ⓜ Bercy.

Ⓦ cinematheque.fr.

The **Cinémathèque**, a striking glass, zinc and stone building designed by Guggenheim architect Frank Gehry and resembling a falling pack of cards, houses a huge archive of films dating back to the earliest days of cinema. Regular retrospectives of French and foreign films are screened in its four cinemas, and it also has an engaging **museum** (Charge), with early cinematic equipment, silent film clips and costumes – such as the dress worn by Vivienne Leigh in *Gone With The Wind*.

La Cinémathèque Française

Shops

Altermundi

MAP P.84, POCKET MAP L9

39 rue de Charonne Ⓜ Ledru-Rollin.
Ⓦ altermundi.com.

This eco-friendly shop, one of a growing number in the capital, stocking colourful sustainable homeware and men's', women's' and children's fashion, including cute baby clothes.

Anne Willi

MAP P.84, POCKET MAP L9

13 rue Keller Ⓜ Ledru-Rollin/Voltaire.
Ⓦ annewilli.com.

Completely original pieces of clothing in gorgeous, luxurious fabrics, from layered, casual-chic sets to one-piece geometric studies of the body.

Cécile et Jeanne

MAP P.84, POCKET MAP L10

49 av Daumesnil Ⓜ Gare-de-Lyon.

Reasonably priced and innovative jewellery from local artisans in one of the Viaduc des Arts showrooms.

FrenchTrotters

MAP P.84, POCKET MAP L9

30 rue de Charonne Ⓜ Ledru-Rollin.
Ⓦ frenchtrotters.fr.

Trendy concept store, stocking homeware, bath products and above all men's and women's clothing, including covetable own-brand Breton shirts, as well as unusual international and French labels, such as Commune de Paris and Filippa K.

Isabel Marant

MAP P.84, POCKET MAP L9

16 rue de Charonne Ⓜ Ledru-Rollin.
Ⓦ isabelmarant.com.

Marant has established an international reputation for her feminine and flattering clothes in quality fabrics such as silk and cashmere. Prices are above average, but not exorbitant.

Sessun

MAP P.84, POCKET MAP L9

34 rue de Charonne Ⓜ Ledru-Rollin.
Ⓦ sessun.com.

This bright and spacious boutique on the trendy rue de Charonne sells all the womenswear you could want, from pretty prints and basic Ts to elegant winter coats and cosy knits. Good value given the quality.

Cafés

Le Baron Rouge

MAP P.84, POCKET MAP L9

1 rue Théophile-Roussel Ⓜ Ledru-Rollin.
Ⓦ lebaronrouge.net.

This *bar à vins* is as close as you'll get to the spit-on-the-floor, saloon stereotype of the old movies. Stallholders and shoppers from the place d'Aligre market gather for a light lunch or an *apéritif* during the day, especially on Sundays, with a younger crowd appearing later on. Join the locals on the pavement lunching on *saucisson*, mussels or Cap Ferrat oysters washed down with a glass of Muscadet.

Café de l'Industrie

MAP P.84, POCKET MAP H16

16 rue St-Sabin Ⓜ Bastille.
Ⓦ cafédelindustrieparis.fr.

One of the best Bastille cafés (actually two cafés, across the road from each other), packed out every evening. Rugs on the floor around solid old wooden tables, mounted rhinoceros heads, old black-and-white photos on the walls and an unpretentious crowd.

CheZaline

MAP P.84, POCKET MAP L8

85 rue de la Roquette Ⓜ Voltaire. ☎ 01 43 71 90 75.

This great-value gourmet deli puts a creative spin on picnic food – eat in if you're lucky to bag one of the few tables, or take out baguettes (ham, artichoke and pesto; roasted

Anne Willi

cod with tapenade), deli salads and daily changing specials.

Pause Café

MAP P.84, POCKET MAP L9
41 rue de Charonne, cnr rue Keller
Ⓜ Ledru-Rollin. ☏ 01 48 06 80 33.
Or maybe "Pose Café" – given its popularity with the *quartier*'s young and fashionable (sunglasses are worn at all times) who bag the pavement tables at lunch and *apéritif* time. Service is predictably insouciant.

Restaurants

A la Biche au Bois

MAP P.84, POCKET MAP H18
45 av Ledru-Rollin Ⓜ Gare de Lyon. ☏ 01 43 43 34 38.
The queues leading out through the conservatory at the front are a strong indicator of the popularity of this restaurant, which mixes charming service with keenly priced, well-produced food. The house specialities include a rich *coq au vin* and game dishes in season. Four-course lunch and dinner set menu

(with magnificent cheese platter included). €

Bofinger

MAP P.84, POCKET MAP H17
7 rue de la Bastille Ⓜ Bastille.
Ⓦ bofingerparis.com.
This big and bustling fin-de-siècle Alsatian brasserie, with its splendid, perfectly preserved coloured-glass dome, is a favourite of operagoers and tourists. Specialities are seafood and steaming dishes of sauerkraut; don't miss the delicious profiteroles for dessert. €

L'Encrier

MAP P.84, POCKET MAP L10
55 rue Traversière Ⓜ Ledru-Rollin.
Ⓦ lencrierbydo.fr.
The interior of exposed brick walls and wood beams complements the good-value, homely fare served up by pleasant staff in this cooperative-run restaurant near the Viaduc des Arts. The food has a southwestern influence and might include goose breast in honey or pear with Roquefort. €

Septime

MAP P.84, POCKET MAP M9

80 rue de Charonne Ⓜ Charonne.
Ⓦ septime-charonne.fr.
This highly acclaimed neo-*bistrot* turns out inventive, delicate food matched with a fine list of natural wines. Dishes might include asparagus with oranges and ricotta, or steamed cod with pickled turnips and yuzu sauce. The four-course lunch menu is particularly good value; dinner is a seven-course tasting menu affair. Book three weeks in advance. If you can't get a table, you could try its affiliated seafood tapas bar two doors up, *Clamato*, which takes walk-ins only. €€

Le Square Trousseau

MAP P.84, POCKET MAP L9
1 rue Antoine Vollon Ⓜ Ledru-Rollin.
Ⓦ squaretrousseau.com.
At once elegant – cream leather banquettes, marble columns, decorative ceiling – and cheerful, this *brasserie*, opposite a park and playground near the Marché Aligré, is as convenient for hungry families (chalk is supplied for decorating the paper tablecloths) as it is for a relaxed lunch. The menu features French dishes both traditional and modern, from chestnut and cep soup or frogs' legs to cheeseburgers and lobster with *frites*. €€

Le Train Bleu

Le Train Bleu

MAP P.84, POCKET MAP L10
Gare de Lyon ⓜ Gare de Lyon. ⓦ le-train-bleu.com.

Le Train Bleu's stunning decor is straight out of a bygone era – everything drips with gilt, and chandeliers hang from frescoed ceilings. The French cuisine is good, if a tad overpriced. €€

Waly Fay

MAP P.84, POCKET MAP M8
6 rue Godefroy-Cavaignac ⓜ Charonne/Faidherbe-Chaligny. ⓦ walyfay.fr.

West African restaurant with a cosy, stylish atmosphere. Smart young Parisians come here to dine on richly spiced stews and other West African delicacies at a moderate cost. €€

Bars

Au Lèche Vin

MAP P.84, POCKET MAP H16
13 rue Daval ⓜ Bastille.

Appealing, rough-around-the edges little bar, dotted with kitsch religious decor. The statue of Mary in the window sets the tongue-in-cheek tone; the pictures in the toilet, on the other hand, are far from pious. It gets packed very quickly at night with a young, cosmopolitan crowd, knocking back cheap beer and house wine.

Les Marcheurs de Planète

MAP P.84, POCKET MAP L8
73 rue de la Roquette ⓜ Voltaire. ⓦ jusdebox.fr.

Good old-fashioned Parisian atmosphere with an effortlessly cool, vaguely retro vibe, with chess tables, posters and a wild-haired owner. More than 150 wines are on offer, plus excellent cheeses and charcuterie dishes, as well as traditional French dishes such as *pot au feu* and steak.

Moonshiner

MAP P.84, POCKET MAP K8
5 rue Sedaine ⓜ Bréguet-Sabin. ☎ 09 50 73 12 99.

Deliciously hidden away behind the cold room in an otherwise unremarkable pizzeria, this speakeasy-style bar is a good spot to snuggle down on a leather sofa with a well-mixed gin, vodka or (especially) whisky cocktail. Try if you dare the "Back to Basil" gin fizz, featuring the somewhat unusual libation ingredients of olive oil and basil.

Clubs and music venues

Le Balajo

MAP P.84, POCKET MAP H17
9 Rue de Lappe ⓦ balajo.fr/.

A real mix of musical styles is hosted at this institution of a Pris nightclub that's been around since the 1930s. Depending on the day of the week, you'll find hip hop, RnB and salsa on offer; on a Monday afternoon, there's even a tea dance.

Café de la Danse

MAP P.84, POCKET MAP H17
5 passage Louis-Philippe ⓜ Bastille. ⓦ cafedeladanse.com. Open nights of concerts only.

Rock, pop, world and folk music played in an intimate and attractive space.

Opéra Bastille

MAP P.84, POCKET MAP H17
120 rue de Lyon ⓜ Bastille. ⓦ operadeparis.fr.

Opened in 1989 to a rather mixed reception, the amorphous glass-and-steel opera house building still inspires a fair amount of controversy, but no matter – its performances are nearly always a sell-out. Tickets start from €15, but most are in the €65–100 range.

The Quartier Latin

The Quartier Latin has been associated with students ever since the Sorbonne was established in the thirteenth century. The name derives from the Latin spoken at the medieval university, which perched on the slopes of the Montagne Ste-Geneviève. Many colleges remain in the area to this day, along with some fascinating vestiges of the medieval city, such as the Gothic church of St-Séverin and the Renaissance Hôtel de Cluny, site of the national museum of the Middle Ages. Some of the quarter's student chic may have worn thin in recent years – notably around the now-too-famous place St-Michel – and high rents have pushed scholars and artists out of their garrets; but the cafés, restaurants and arty cinemas are still packed with students, making this one of the most relaxed areas of Paris for going out.

The riverbank

MAP P.92, POCKET MAP D17–E18
Ⓜ St-Michel.

The **riverbank** *quais* east of place St-Michel are ideal for wandering and enjoying a good browse among the old books, postcards and prints sold from the **bouquinistes**, whose green kiosks line the parapets. There are wonderful views across the river to Notre-Dame from square Viviani, a welcome patch of grass around the corner from the celebrated English-language bookshop **Shakespeare and Company** (see page 96). The mutilated church behind the square is **St-Julien-le-Pauvre** (Ⓜ-Michel/ Maubert-Mutualité). The same age as Notre-Dame, it used to be the venue for university assemblies until rumbustious students tore it apart in 1524. For the most dramatic view of Notre-Dame, walk along the riverbank as far as the tip of the Ile St-Louis and the Pont de Sully.

The Huchette quarter

MAP P.92, POCKET MAP D17
Ⓜ St-Michel.

The touristy bustle is at its worst around **rue de la Huchette**, just east of the place St-Michel, but look beyond the cheap bars and overpriced Greek kebab-and-disco tavernas and you'll find some evocative remnants of medieval Paris. Connecting rue de la Huchette to the riverside is the narrow rue du Chat-qui-Pêche, a tiny slice of how Paris looked before Baron Haussmann flattened the old alleys to make room for his wide boulevards. One block south of rue de la Huchette, just west of rue St-Jacques, is the mainly fifteenth-century church of **St-Séverin**, whose entrance is on rue des Prêtres St-Séverin (Ⓜ St-Michel/ Cluny-La Sorbonne). It's one of the city's more intense churches, its windows filled with edgy stained glass by the modern French painter Jean Bazaine.

Musée National du Moyen Age

MAP P.92, POCKET MAP C18–D18
6 place Paul-Painlevé Ⓜ Cluny-La
Sorbonne. Ⓦ musee-moyenage.fr. Charge.
Medieval music concerts throughout the
week; see website for details; Charge.

The walls of the third-century
Roman baths are visible in the
garden of the **Hôtel de Cluny**,
a sixteenth-century mansion
built by the abbots of the
Cluny monastery as their Paris
pied-à-terre. It now houses the
rewarding **Musée National du
Moyen Age**, a treasure-trove of
medieval art. There's a feast of
medieval sculpture throughout,
along with wonderful stained
glass, books and curious objets
d'art, but the real beauties are
the **tapestries** that hang in most
rooms, including vivid depictions
of a grape harvest, a lover making
advances and a woman in a bath
that overflows into a duck pond.
The greatest of all is the stunning
La Dame à la Licorne ("The
Lady with the Unicorn") series,
displayed in its own chapel-
like chamber. Made in the late
fifteenth century, the set depicts
the five senses – along with
an ambiguous image that may
represent the virtue in controlling
them – in six luxuriantly detailed
allegoric scenes, each featuring
a richly dressed woman flanked
by a lion and a unicorn. On the
ground floor, the vaults of the
Roman baths are preserved intact.

The museum also has a busy
programme of medieval music
concerts; look out for the regular
"heure musicale".

The Sorbonne

MAP P.92, POCKET MAP C18–D18
Ⓜ Cluny-La Sorbonne/RER Luxembourg.

The traffic-free place de la
Sorbonne is a great place to sit
back and enjoy the Quartier Latin
atmosphere. Frowning over it are
the high walls of the **Sorbonne**,
which was once the most
important of the medieval colleges
huddled atop the Montagne Ste-
Geneviève. More recently it was a
flashpoint in the student riots of
1968. The frontage is dominated
by the Chapelle Ste-Ursule,
built in the 1640s by the great
Cardinal Richelieu, whose tomb
it contains.

Musée National du Moyen Âge

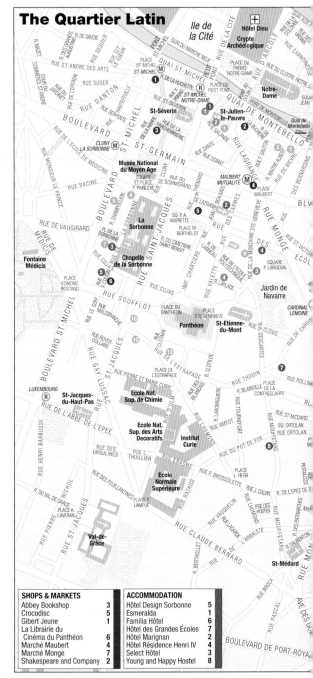

The Quartier Latin

SHOPS & MARKETS	
Abbey Bookshop	3
Crocodisc	5
Gibert Jeune	1
La Librairie du Cinéma du Panthéon	6
Marché Maubert	4
Marché Monge	7
Shakespeare and Company	2

ACCOMMODATION	
Hôtel Design Sorbonne	5
Esmeralda	1
Familia Hôtel	6
Hôtel des Grandes Écoles	7
Hôtel Marignan	2
Hôtel Résidence Henri IV	4
Select Hôtel	3
Young and Happy Hostel	8

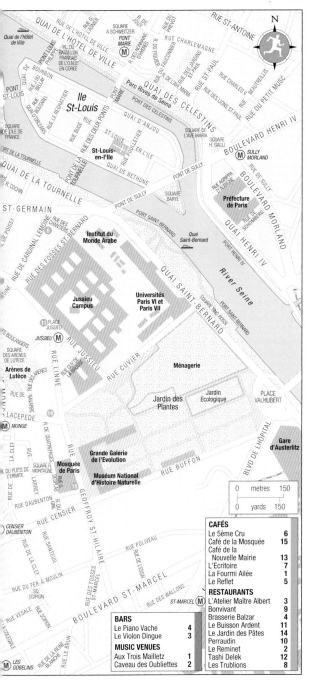

The Panthéon

The Panthéon

MAP P.92, POCKET MAP D19

Ⓜ Cardinal-Lemoine/RER Luxembourg.
Ⓦ paris-pantheon.fr. Charge for entry and ascent of dome.

Crowning the Montagne Ste-Geneviève, the largest and most visible of Paris's domes graces the bulky **Panthéon**, Louis XV's thank-you to Ste-Geneviève, patron saint of Paris, for curing him of illness. Completed only in 1789, after the Revolution it was transformed into a mausoleum, emblazoned with the words "Aux grands hommes la patrie reconnaissante" ("The nation honours its great men") beneath the pediment of the giant portico. The remains of giants of French culture, including Voltaire, Rousseau, Hugo and Zola, are entombed in the vast, barrel-vaulted crypt, along with Marie Curie, and Alexandre Dumas, who was "panthéonized" in 2002. The Classical nave displays a working model of **Foucault's Pendulum** swinging from the dome. French physicist Léon Foucault devised the experiment, conducted here in 1851, to demonstrate that while the pendulum appeared to rotate over a 24-hour period, it was in fact the Earth beneath it turning. From April to October you can climb up to the dome and enjoy wonderful panoramic views of the city.

St-Etienne-du-Mont

MAP P.92, POCKET MAP D19

Ⓜ Cardinal Lemoine.

The remains of Pascal and Racine, two seventeenth-century literary giants who didn't make it into the Panthéon, and a few relics of Ste-Geneviève, lie in the church of **St-Etienne-du-Mont**. The main attraction, however, is the fabulously airy interior, formed of a Flamboyant Gothic choir joined to a Renaissance nave, the two parts linked by a sinuous catwalk that runs around the interior, arching across the nave in the form of a carved rood screen – an extremely rare survival, as most French screens fell victim to Protestant iconoclasts, reformers or revolutionaries.

Institut du Monde Arabe

MAP P.92, POCKET MAP F18

1 rue des Fossés St-Bernard Ⓜ Jussieu/
Cardinal-Lemoine. Ⓦ imarabe.org. Charge
for museum entry.

A bold slice of glass and steel,
the stunning exterior of the
Institut du Monde Arabe
betrays architect Jean Nouvel's
obsession with light – its broad
southern facade, which mimics
a *moucharabiyah*, or traditional
Arab latticework, is made up
of thousands of tiny metallic
shutters. Originally designed to be
light-sensitive, they now open and
close just once an hour, and the
exhibition spaces are consequently
quite gloomy. Inside, a thoughtful
museum explores five themes
– Arabs, the sacred, cities,
beauty and daily life – through a
collection of exquisite ceramics,
metalwork and textiles.

The Paris mosque and hammam

MAP P.92, POCKET MAP J11

Entrance on rue Daubenton Ⓜ Jussieu.
Ⓦ mosqueedeparis.net. Charge.

Even in this quiet area, the **Paris
mosque**, built by Moroccan
craftsmen in the early 1920s,
feels like an oasis of serenity
behind its crenellated walls.
You can walk in the sunken
garden and patios with their
polychrome tiles and carved
ceilings, and relax at the laidback
café (see page 96), but non-
Muslims are asked not to enter
the prayer room.

Jardin des Plantes

MAP P.92, POCKET MAP F19–G19

Entrances at the corners of the park and
opposite rue Jussieu Ⓜ Jussieu/Censier
Daubenton., Ⓦ jardindesplantesdeparis.
fr. Free.

Behind the mosque, the **Jardin
des Plantes**, a medicinal herb
garden from 1626, now hosts
Paris's botanical gardens,
with avenues of trees, lawns,
hothouses, museums and an

old-fashioned **ménagerie**, also
France's oldest zoo.

Grande Galerie de l'Evolution

MAP P.92, POCKET MAP J11

Jardin des Plantes; entrance off rue Buffon
Ⓜ Censier-Daubenton/Gare d'Austerlitz.
Ⓦ jardindesplantesdeparis.fr. Charge.

Magnificent floral beds make a
fine approach to the collection
of buildings that forms the
**Muséum National d'Histoire
Naturelle** (Ⓦ mnhn.fr). Skip the
musty displays of paleontology,
anatomy, mineralogy and
paleobotany in favour of the
Grande Galerie de l'Evolution,
housed in a restored nineteenth-
century glass-domed building.
It doesn't actually tell the
story of evolution, but it does
feature a huge cast of life-sized
animals, some of them striding
dramatically across the space.
It's great fun for children, who
have a small interactive area
to themselves, the Galerie des
Enfants, on the first floor.

Café de la Mosquée, Paris mosque

Shops and markets

Abbey Bookshop

MAP P.92, POCKET MAP D17

29 rue de la Parcheminerie Ⓜ St-Michel. ☎ 01 46 33 16 24, ⓦ abbeybookshop.org.

An overstuffed warren with lots of used British and North American fiction and travel guides, plus knowledgeable, helpful staff – and free coffee.

Crocodisc

MAP P.92, POCKET MAP D18

40–42 rue des Ecoles Ⓜ Maubert-Mutualité. ⓦ crocodisc.com.

Everything from folk and Afro-Antillais to salsa and movie soundtracks, new and used, at good prices.

Gibert Jeune

MAP P.92, POCKET MAP D17

5 place St-Michel and around Ⓜ St-Michel. ⓦ gibert.com.

A Latin Quarter institution for student/academic books, with a number of stores on and around place St-Michel. There's a secondhand selection at no. 2 and foreign-language titles at no. 6.

La Librairie du Cinéma du Panthéon

MAP P.92, POCKET MAP C18

15 rue Victor Cousin Ⓜ Cluny-La Sorbonne. ⓦ cinelitterature.fr.

Superb store devoted to cinema, with books, not all in French, plus magazines and posters.

Marché Maubert

MAP P.92, POCKET MAP D18

Place Maubert Ⓜ Maubert-Mutualité.

One of the city's classic food markets, with a wonderful array of cheese, *saucisson* and fresh fruit and veg.

Marché Monge

MAP P.92, POCKET MAP H11

Place Monge Ⓜ Monge.

Just off "La Mouff" (the city's famed rue Mouffetard market, now mostly given over to classy food shops), this authentic market is set around the pretty Monge fountain and sells fabulous, pricey produce. Organic stalls on Sundays.

Shakespeare and Company

MAP P.92, POCKET MAP D17

37 rue de la Bûcherie Ⓜ Maubert-Mutualité. ⓦ shakespeareandcompany.com.

A Latin Quarter institution, this cosy, crowded literary haunt, run by Americans and staffed by earnest young Hemingway wannabes, sells Paris's best selection of English-language books. There are readings in the week; and a café worth checking out next door.

Cafés

Le 5ème Cru

MAP P.92, POCKET MAP E18

7 rue du Cardinal Lemoine Ⓜ Cardinal Lemoine. ⓦ 5ecru.com.

The shelves at this welcoming cave à manger are piled high with bottles from French artisan winemakers. Let the friendly staff advise you, then join the locals in the cosy dining area and order plates of excellent charcuterie, cheese and pâté.

Café de la Mosquée

MAP P.92, POCKET MAP J11

39 rue Geoffroy-St-Hilaire Ⓜ Monge. ☎ 01 43 31 14 32.

Drink mint tea and eat sweet cakes beside the courtyard fountain and fig trees of the Paris mosque. A haven of calm (except on weekend lunchtimes when it's a popular spot for festive families), the indoor salon has a beautiful Arabic interior where tasty tagines and couscous are served.

Café de la Nouvelle Mairie

MAP P.92, POCKET MAP D19

Shakespeare and Company

19 rue des Fossés-St-Jacques Cluny-La Sorbonne/RER Luxembourg. ☎ 01 44 07 04 41.
Sleek café/wine bar with some pavement seating and a relaxed feel generated by its older, university clientele. Serves good, modern food and plates of cheese or charcuterie.

L'Ecritoire

MAP P.92, POCKET MAP C18
3 place de la Sorbonne Ⓜ Cluny-La Sorbonne/RER Luxembourg. Ⓦ lecritoireparis.com.
This classic university café is right beside the Sorbonne, and has outside tables by the fountain.

La Fourmi Ailée

MAP P.92, POCKET MAP D17
8 rue du Fouarre Ⓜ Maubert-Mutualité. ☎ 01 43 29 40 99, Ⓦ la-fourmi-ailee. parisresto.com.
Simple, classically French food and speciality teas are served in this relaxed *salon de thé* with a pretty, tiled exterior. The high, cloud-painted ceiling, book-lined walls and background jazz add to the atmosphere.

Le Reflet

MAP P.92, POCKET MAP C18
6 rue Champollion Ⓜ Cluny-La Sorbonne. ☎ 01 43 29 97 27.
This artsy cinema café has a strong flavour of the *nouvelle vague*, with its scruffy black paint scheme, lights rigged up on a gantry and rickety tables packed with filmgoers and chess players. Perfect for a drink either side of a film at one of the art cinemas on rue Champollion, perhaps accompanied by a steak, quiche or salad from the short list of blackboard specials.

Restaurants

L'Atelier Maître Albert

MAP P.92, POCKET MAP E18
1 rue Maître Albert Ⓜ Maubert-Mutualité. Ⓦ ateliermaitrealbert.com.
One of chef-entrepreneur Guy Savoy's ventures, this contemporary rôtisserie specializes in top-notch spit-roast meats, though you can also find lighter dishes like cod casseroled with seasonal veg or a delicious starter of prawns stuffed with citrus butter. €€

Bonvivant

MAP P.92, POCKET MAP E18

7 rue des Ecoles Cardinal Lemoine.
Ⓦ bonvivant.paris.

This friendly wine bar with biodynamic wines serves sharing platters and pâtés, hummus or rillettes to nibble – and expands at the back into an elegant restaurant. Dishes range from gluten-free options, like Thai broth with steamed veg and soba, perhaps, to old French favourites. €

Brasserie Balzar

MAP P.92, POCKET MAP D18

49 rue des Ecoles Ⓜ Maubert-Mutualité.
Ⓦ brasseriebalzar.com.

Classic, high-ceilinged brasserie, long frequented by the literary intelligentsia of the Latin Quarter along with hordes of delighted tourists. Steak tartare, roast chicken or sauerkraut with sausage are perennial favourites. €€

Le Buisson Ardent

MAP P.92, POCKET MAP E19

25 rue Jussieu Ⓜ Jussieu.
Ⓦ lebuissonardent.fr.

Generous helpings of first-class cooking with vivacious touches: *velouté* of watermelon followed by lamb noisettes with a fennel and blue cheese fondant, for instance. The panelled dining room is grand, but the atmosphere is never less than convivial – and there's a cosy back room. €€

Brasserie Balzar

Le Jardin des Pâtes

MAP P.92, POCKET MAP E19

4 rue Lacépède Ⓜ Jussieu. ☎ 01 43 31 50 71.

Delicious home-made pasta that uses all manner of freshly ground, organic grains and is served with wonderful flourishes and garnishes. The room is stylish, fresh-feeling and airy – almost like a conservatory – and you'll pay a good price for a plate of pasta. €

Perraudin

MAP P.92, POCKET MAP D19

157 rue St-Jacques. Ⓜ RER Luxembourg. Ⓦ leperraudin.fr.

Quintessential Left Bank *bistrot* featuring solid cooking and an atmosphere thick with Parisian chatter floating above packed tables. €

Le Reminet

MAP P.92, POCKET MAP E17

3 rue des Grands-Degrés Ⓜ Maubert-Mutualité. ☎ 01 44 07 04 24.

This tiny *bistrot* is effortlessly stylish, with gilded mirrors and brass candlesticks at every table, and French windows opening out onto a leafy square. The classy food incorporates quality French ingredients and imaginative sauces. €€

Tashi Delek

MAP P.92, POCKET MAP D19

4 rue des Fossés-St-Jacques. Ⓜ RER Luxembourg. ☎ 01 43 26 55 55.

Sober-looking but cheery Tibetan restaurant serving tasty dishes from robust, warming noodle soups to the addictive, ravioli-like beef *momok* and a salty, soupy yak-butter tea. It's good value, with a *menu découverte* for two people. €

Les Trublions

MAP P.92, POCKET MAP D18

Rue de la Montagne Sainte-Geneviève. Ⓜ Maubert-Mutualité. Ⓦ lestrublions.fr.

This smart little bistrot is a friendly local favourite, delivering bright, creative food made with market-fresh ingredients in a soothingly contemporary dining room. The two- and three-course set lunch menus (are particularly good value. €

Bars

Le Piano Vache

MAP P.92, POCKET MAP D18

8 rue Laplace Ⓜ Cardinal-Lemoine. ☎ 01 46 33 75 03.

Left Bank favourite crammed with students, with cool music and a laidback atmosphere.

Le Violon Dingue

MAP P.92, POCKET MAP D18

46 rue de la Montagne-Ste-Geneviève Ⓜ Maubert-Mutualité. ☎ 01 43 25 79 93.

A long, dark student pub that's noisy and popular with young travellers. English-speaking bar staff and cheap drinks. The cellar bar stays open until 4.30am on busy nights.

Music venues

Aux Trois Mailletz

MAP P.92, POCKET MAP D17

56 rue Galande Ⓜ St-Michel. Ⓦ lestroismailletz.fr.

This corner café-resto transforms into a convivial piano bar in the evenings; later on a good jazz/cabaret bar sets up in the basement, often featuring fabulous world music artists.

Caveau des Oubliettes

MAP P.92, POCKET MAP D17

52 rue Galande Ⓜ St-Michel. Ⓦ caveau-des-oubliettes.com. Free.

Lively jazz jams – blues, Latin, African – bring vim and vibrancy to a gloomy, smoky dungeon setting. The Caveau des Oubliettes is housed in what was actually once a medieval prison.

St-Germain

St-Germain, the westernmost section of Paris's Left Bank, has long been famous as the haunt of bohemians and intellectuals. A few famous cafés preserve a strong flavour of the old times, but the dominant spirit these days is elegant, relaxed and seriously upmarket. At opposite ends of the quarter are two of the city's busiest and best-loved sights: to the east, bordering the Quartier Latin, spreads the huge green space of the Jardin du Luxembourg, while to the west stands the jaw-dropping Musée d'Orsay, a converted railway station with a world-beating collection of Impressionist paintings. Between the two you can visit the churches of St-Sulpice and St-Germain-des-Prés, or intriguing museums dedicated to the artists Delacroix and Maillol, but really, shopping is king. The streets around place St-Sulpice swarm with international fashion brands, while on the north side of boulevard St-Germain, antique shops and art dealers dominate.

Pont des Arts

MAP P.102, POCKET MAP C16
Ⓜ Pont Neuf.

The much-loved **Pont des Arts** offers a classic upstream view of

Pont des Arts

the Ile de la Cité, and provides a grand entrance to St-Germain under the watchful eye of the Institut de France, an august academic institution. It had become dangerously weighed down with thousands of "love locks" left by couples wanting to leave a symbol of their undying love, but these have now been removed and replaced with plates of glass.

Musée d'Orsay

MAP P.102, POCKET MAP A15
1 rue de la Légion d'Honneur Ⓜ Solférino/ RER Musée-d'Orsay. Ⓦ musee-orsay.fr. Charge.

Along the riverfront, on the western edge of St-Germain, the **Musée d'Orsay** dramatically fills a vast former railway station with paintings and sculptures dating between 1848 and 1914, including an unparalleled Impressionist and Post-Impressionist collection.

The museum's **ground floor**, spread out under a giant glass arch, is devoted to pre-1870 work, contrasting Ingres, Delacroix and other serious-minded painters and sculptors acceptable to the mid-nineteenth-century salons, with the relatively unusual works of Puvis de Chavannes, Gustave Moreau and the younger Degas. The influential Barbizon school and the Realists are also showcased, with works by Daumier, Corot and Millet preparing the ground for the early controversies of Monet's violently light-filled *Femmes au Jardin* (1867) and Manet's provocative *Olympia* (1863), which heralded the arrival of Impressionism. It's on **level five** that Impressionism proper is displayed. Hung against warmly lit, charcoal-grey walls, the vibrant colours and vigorous brushstrokes of even the almost-too-familiar Monets and Renoirs strike you afresh and seem almost to jump off the walls. The first painting to greet you, magnificent in its isolation, is Manet's scandalous *Déjeuner sur l'Herbe*, the work held to have announced the arrival of **Impressionism**. Thereafter follows masterpiece after masterpiece: Degas' *Dans un café (L'Absinthe)*, Renoir's *Bal du Moulin de la Galette*, Cézanne's *Joueurs de Cartes* and Monet's *Femme à l'Ombrelle* and *Coquelicots* ("Poppies"). You'll also find Degas' ballet dancer sculptures and small-scale landscapes, and outdoor scenes by Renoir, Sisley, Pissarro and Monet that owed much of their brilliance to the novel practice of setting up easels in the open. Berthe Morisot, the first woman to join the early Impressionists, is represented by her famous *Le Berceau*, among others.

On the **middle level** you'll find the various offspring of Impressionism. In works such as **Van Gogh**'s *La Nuit Etoilée*, with its fervid colours and disturbing rhythms, and **Gauguin**'s Tahitian paintings, there's an edgier, modern feel. More decorative effects are attempted by Pointillists such

Musée d'Orsay

as Seurat and Signac. On the **sculpture terraces**, Rodin's works are far and away the standouts. Try to find time, too, for the last few rooms, as well as levels two, three and four of the Pavillon Amont, which contain superb Art Nouveau furniture and objets d'art.

Parc Rives de Seine

MAP P.102, POCKET MAP C7, D7 & E7
Ⓜ Assemblée Nationale.

In 2013 the stretch of river between the Pont de l'Alma and Musée d'Orsay was turned into a pedestrianized promenade. It proved so successful that a similar stretch was opened up in 2017 on the Right Bank; it's possible to combine the two, now known together as the **Parc Rives de Seine**, in one 5.5km walk. The promenade is particularly lively on summer weekends when people come to picnic, play a game of chess over a cup of coffee, or simply relax in a deckchair and enjoy some of the finest views in the city. Occasional concerts and workshops are also held, and there are activities for children, including a climbing wall.

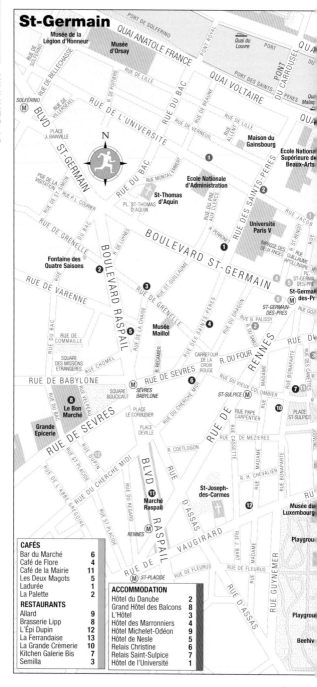

St-Germain

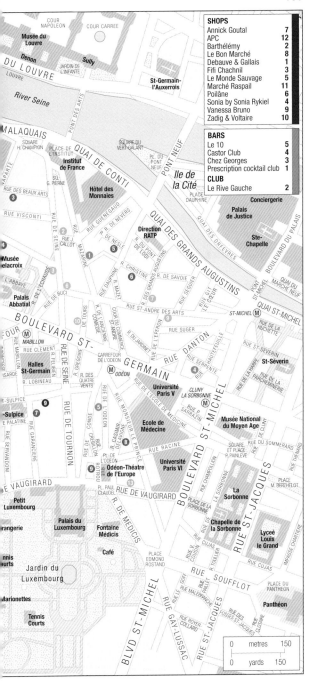

SHOPS

Annick Goutal	7
APC	12
Barthélémy	2
Le Bon Marché	8
Debauve & Gallais	1
Fifi Chachnil	3
Le Monde Sauvage	5
Marché Raspail	11
Poilâne	6
Sonia by Sonia Rykiel	4
Vanessa Bruno	9
Zadig & Voltaire	10

BARS

Le 10	5
Castor Club	4
Chez Georges	3
Prescription cocktail club	1

CLUB

Le Rive Gauche	2

Interior of Église St-Sulpice

Maison du Gainsbourg

MAP P.102, POCKET MAP A15
5 bis rue de Verneuil Ⓜ Rue du Bac/St-Germain-des-Prés. Ⓦ maisongainsbourg.fr
A new shrine to Serge opened in 2023 in Paris at the end of September. Visit his legendary interior and then, across the street at number 14, deep dive into his life and songwriting in a museum, book & gift shop and le Gainsbarre – café during the day and piano-bar at night.

Musée Delacroix

MAP P.102, POCKET MAP B17
6 rue de Furstemberg Ⓜ Mabillon/St-Germain-des-Prés. Ⓦ musee-delacroix.fr. Charge.
The **Musée Delacroix** is tucked away halfway down rue de Furstemberg, opposite a tiny square and backing onto a secret garden. Although the artist's major work is exhibited permanently at the Louvre (see page 30) and the Musée d'Orsay (see page 104), this museum, housed in the studio where the artist lived and worked from 1857 until his death in 1863, displays a refreshingly intimate collection including a scattering of personal belongings and minor exhibitions of his work.

Place St-Germain-des-Prés

MAP P.102, POCKET MAP B17
Ⓜ St-Germain-des-Prés.
Place St-Germain-des-Prés is the hub of the *quartier*, with the *Deux Magots* café (see page 107) on the corner of the square, *Flore* (see page 107) adjacent and *Lipp* (see page 108) across the boulevard St-Germain. All are renowned for the number of philosophical-politico-literary backsides that have shone – and continue to shine – their seats, along with plenty of celebrity-hunters. Picasso's bust of a woman, dedicated to the poet Apollinaire, recalls the district's creative heyday.

St-Germain-des-Prés

MAP P.102, POCKET MAP B17
Place St-Germain-des-Prés Ⓜ St-Germain-des-Prés.
The ancient tower overlooking place **St-Germain-des-Prés** belongs to the church of St-Germain, all that remains of an enormous Benedictine monastery. Inside, the transformation from Romanesque to early Gothic is just about visible under the heavy green and gold nineteenth-century paintwork. The last chapel on the south

side contains the tomb of the philosopher René Descartes.

St-Sulpice

MAP P.102, POCKET MAP B18
Place St-Sulpice Ⓜ St-Sulpice.

The enormous, early eighteenth-century church of **St-Sulpice** is an austerely Classical building with Doric and Ionic colonnades and Corinthian pilasters in the towers. There are three Delacroix murals in the first chapel on the right, but most visitors come to see the gnomon, a kind of solar clock whose origins and purpose were so compellingly garbled in *The Da Vinci Code*.

Jardin du Luxembourg

MAP P.102, POCKET MAP B18/19–C18/19
Ⓜ Odéon/RER Luxembourg.

Fronting onto rue de Vaugirard, the **Jardin du Luxembourg** is the chief green space of the Left Bank, its atmosphere a beguiling mixture of the formal and the relaxed. At the centre, the round pond and immaculate floral parterres are overlooked by the haughty Palais du Luxembourg, seat of the French Senate. Students sprawl on the garden's famous metal chairs, children sail toy yachts, watch the puppets at the *guignol*, or run about in the playgrounds, and old men play boules or chess. The southwest corner is dotted with the works of famous sculptors.

Musée du Luxembourg

MAP P.102, POCKET MAP B18
19 rue de Vaugirard Ⓜ Odéon/RER Luxembourg. Ⓦ museeduluxembourg.fr. Hours and prices vary.

The **Musée du Luxembourg**, at the top end of rue de Vaugirard, hosts temporary art exhibitions that rank among the most ambitious in Paris – recent shows have included Alphonse Mucha and Pissarro.

Musée Maillol

MAP P.102, POCKET MAP A17
61 rue de Grenelle Ⓜ Rue du Bac. Ⓦ museemaillol.com.

The **Musée Maillol** shares its space with the post-Impressionist Aristide Maillol's sculpted female nudes and temporary exhibitions on modern and contemporary art. Note that the museum is open only during exhibitions – check the website for dates.

Jardin du Luxembourg

Shops

Annick Goutal

MAP P.102, POCKET MAP B17
12 place St-Sulpice Ⓜ St-Sulpice.
Ⓦ goutalparis.com.

This family-run business, started by Goutal in the 1980s, is still going strong, producing exquisite perfumes, all made from natural essences and presented in old-fashioned ribbed-glass bottles.

APC

MAP P.102, POCKET MAP B18
38 rue Madame Ⓜ St-Sulpice. Ⓦ apc.fr.

This chain is perfect for young, urban basics. Simple cuts and fabrics create a minimal, Parisian look.

Barthélémy

MAP P.102, POCKET MAP E8
51 rue de Grenelle Ⓜ Rue du Bac. Ⓣ 01 42 22 82 24.

This aromatic nook sells carefully ripened seasonal cheeses to the rich and powerful, with attendants on hand to offer expert advice.

Le Bon Marché

MAP P.102, POCKET MAP E9
38 rue de Sèvres Ⓜ Sèvres-Babylone. Ⓣ 01 44 39 80 00, Ⓦ lebonmarche.com.

The world's oldest department store, founded in 1852, is a beautiful building and a classy place to shop – despite its name, this is a luxury emporium – with a legendary food hall.

Debauve & Gallais

MAP P.102, POCKET MAP A16
30 rue des Saints-Pères Ⓜ St-Germain-des-Prés/Sèvres-Babylone. Ⓦ debauve-et-gallais.fr.

A beautiful, ancient shop specializing in expensive, ambrosial chocolates.

Fifi Chachnil

MAP P.102, POCKET MAP A17
34 rue de Grenelle Ⓜ Rue du Bac. Ⓦ fifichachnil.com.

Soft lighting and sumptuous furnishings make this lingerie boutique feel more like a boudoir than a shop. Part-fantasy, part-Parisian chic, Chachnil's vintage-inspired, froufrou creations strike a careful balance between saucy and elegant.

Le Monde Sauvage

MAP P.102, POCKET MAP A17
31 bd Raspail Ⓜ Sèvres-Babylone. Ⓦ lemondesauvage.com/.

How about giving your home a bit of French chic? Homewares from cushions to bedspreads and throws.

Marché Raspail

MAP P.102, POCKET MAP A18
Bd Raspail, between rue du Cherche-Midi & rue de Rennes Ⓜ Rennes.

The Sunday organic market which takes over the broad central reservation of the boulevard is one of the classic experiences of bourgeois Paris. Come to people-watch as well as to browse, taste and shop.

Poilâne

MAP P.102, POCKET MAP A17
8 rue du Cherche-Midi Ⓜ Sèvres-Babylone. Ⓦ poilane.com.

This delicious-smelling bakery is the ultimate source of traditional sourdough *pain Poilâne*, and great for other baked treats.

Sonia by Sonia Rykiel

MAP P.102, POCKET MAP A17
6 rue de Grenelle Ⓜ St-Sulpice. Ⓦ soniarykiel.com.

Sonia Rykiel has been an area institution since opening a store on bd St-Germain in 1968; this is a younger, less expensive offshoot.

Vanessa Bruno

MAP P.102, POCKET MAP B17
25 rue St-Sulpice Ⓜ Odéon. Ⓦ vanessabruno.com.

Prices start in the hundreds for these effortlessly beautiful women's fashions with a hint of hippy chic.

Zadig & Voltaire

MAP P.102, POCKET MAP B18

1 & 3 rue du Vieux Colombier Ⓜ St-Sulpice. Ⓦ zadig-et-voltaire.com.

The clothes at this pricey Parisian chain have a wayward flair. There are two shops next door to each other selling clothes for women, men and children, the other only womenswear.

Cafés

Bar du Marché

MAP P.102, POCKET MAP B17

75 rue de Seine Ⓜ Mabillon. ☏ 01 43 26 55 15.

Buzzing café in the heart of the Buci market bustle, with *serveurs* kitted out in flat caps and market-trader dungarees.

Café de Flore

MAP P.102, POCKET MAP B17

172 bd St-Germain Ⓜ St-Germain-des-Prés. Ⓦ cafedeflore.fr.

The rival and neighbour of *Les Deux Magots*, with a trendier and more local clientele. Sartre, De Beauvoir, Camus et al used to hang out here – and there's still the odd reading or debate. Come for the famous morning hot chocolate. Prices are high.

Café de la Mairie

MAP P.102, POCKET MAP B17

8 place St-Sulpice Ⓜ St-Sulpice. ☏ 01 43 26 67 82.

A pleasant, ever-popular café on the sunny north side of the square, opposite the church.

Les Deux Magots

MAP P.102, POCKET MAP B17

170 bd St-Germain Ⓜ St-Germain-des-Prés., Ⓦ lesdeuxmagots.fr.

This historic Left Bank intellectual hangout has fallen victim to its own fame. Prices are ridiculous, but it's irresistible for people-watching. Come for breakfast (choose between the "Classique" or the "Hemingway").

Ladurée

MAP P.102, POCKET MAP B16

21 rue Bonaparte Ⓜ St-Germain-des-Prés. Ⓦ laduree.com.

Elegant outpost of *Ladurée*'s mini empire, with a conservatory at the back and a decadent Second Empire lounge upstairs. The famous *macarons* are out of this world, but they also do a good, if pricey, brunch.

La Palette

MAP P.102, POCKET MAP B16

43 rue de Seine Ⓜ Odéon. Ⓦ cafelapaletteparis.com.

This venerable art-student hangout is now frequented more by art dealers, though it's still very relaxed, and the decor of paint-spattered palettes is superb. There's a roomy *terrasse* outside.

Restaurants

Allard

MAP P.102, POCKET MAP C17

41 rue St-André-des-Arts Ⓜ Odéon. Ⓦ restaurant-allard.fr.

Proudly unreconstructed restaurant serving meaty, rich standards. If it

Café de la Mairie

wasn't for the almost exclusively international clientele, you could be dining in another century. €€

Brasserie Lipp

MAP P.102, POCKET MAP B17
151 bd St-Germain Ⓜ St-Germain-des-Prés.
Ⓦ brasserielipp.fr.

One of the most celebrated of the classic Paris brasseries, the haunt of the successful and famous; *Lipp* has a wonderful 1900s wood-and-glass interior. Decently priced *plats*, including the famous *choucroute* (sauerkraut), but exploring the *carte* gets expensive. €€

L'Épi Dupin

MAP P.102, POCKET MAP E9
11 rue Dupin Ⓜ Sèvres-Babylone. ☎ 01 42 22 64 56, Ⓦ restaurantdupin.com.

This contemporary *bistrot* serves up imaginative seasonal food. There are two sittings – go for the second if you want to take your time. €€

La Ferrandaise

MAP P.102, POCKET MAP C18
8 rue de Vaugirard Ⓜ St-Germain-des-Prés.
Ⓦ laferrandaise.com.

Arty photos of cows line the walls, and beef dominates the

L'Épi Dupin

menu – though you'll also find dishes such as minced cod with ratatouille. €€

La Grande Crèmerie

MAP P.102, POCKET MAP C17
8 rue Grégoire de Tours Ⓜ Odéon.
Ⓦ lagrandecremerie.paris.fr.

They keep it simple but impeccable at this contemporary-rustic wine bar, serving the very best produce – white Italian ham with truffles, black pudding with toast – alongside natural and organic wines. The amazing food, friendly staff and warm space make this a godsend on this touristy stretch. €

Kitchen Galerie Bis

MAP P.102, POCKET MAP C17
25 rue des Grands-Augustins Ⓜ St-Michel.
Ⓦ zekitchengalerie.fr.

This sleek, modern restaurant offers innovative cooking, fusing Mediterranean cuisine with Asian flavours; a main course might be grilled mackerel with an apricot and cumin dressing. Go for the *menu découverte* and you'll be getting the chef's choices; it's a steal, particularly compared to prices in the area. €€

Semilla

MAP P.102, POCKET MAP B17
54 rue de Seine Ⓜ Mabillon.
Ⓦ semillaparis.com.

This stand-out modern *bistrot* serves up fantastically good food – an enticing mixture of fusion cuisine and updated French classics. Bookings taken up to 8.30pm or wait at the bar for a table. €€

Bars

Le 10

MAP P.102, POCKET MAP C18
10 rue de l'Odéon Ⓜ Odéon. Ⓦ lebar10.com.

Classic Art Deco-era posters line the walls of this small, dark, studenty bar. The vaulted cellar bar gets noisy in the small hours.

Castor Club

Castor Club

MAP P.102, POCKET MAP C17

14 rue Hautefeuille Ⓜ Odéon. ☏ 09 50 64 99 38.

An excellent and relatively laidback cocktail bar with speakeasy decor, serving good craft cocktails. Try the Chirac 95, made with Calvados, complemented by a cool playlist of American country, rockabilly, soul and jazz.

Chez Georges

MAP P.102, POCKET MAP B17

11 rue des Canettes Ⓜ Mabillon. ☏ 01 43 26 79 15.

This dilapidated wine bar, with its venerable zinc counter, is one of the few authentic addresses in an area ever-more dominated by theme pubs. The young, studenty crowd gets good-naturedly rowdy later on in the cellar bar.

Prescription cocktail club

MAP P.102, POCKET MAP C17

23 rue Mazarine Ⓜ Odéon.
Ⓦ prescriptioncocktailclub.com.

This trendy, exclusive cocktail bar hides a glamorously plush interior behind its artfully blank facade. It's chic and restrained earlier in the evening, turning into a madhouse later on.

Club

Le Rive Gauche

MAP P.102, POCKET MAP A17

1 rue du Sabot Ⓜ St-Germain-des-Prés.
Ⓦ rive-gauche.paris.

A stylish set flocks to this plush little place for its club nights – funk, electro, groove, disco and pop. It's been around since the 1970s and still has some of its gold-mirror mosaic decor. Contact them via the website for the admittance password and free entry.

Montparnasse and southern Paris

Montparnasse divides the well-heeled opinion formers of St-Germain and the 7e from the relatively anonymous populations to the south. Long a kind of borderland of theatres, cinemas and cafés, Montparnasse still trades on its association with the wild characters of the interwar years. The artistic and literary glitterati have mostly ended up in Montparnasse cemetery, but cafés favoured by the likes of Picasso are still going strong on boulevard du Montparnasse, and there are plentiful artistic attractions: from the intimate museums dedicated to sculptors Zadkine and Bourdelle, to the contemporary exhibits at the Fondation Cartier and Fondation Cartier-Bresson. Further south, the riverside offers some intriguing attractions: to the east, the cutting-edge Paris Rive Gauche, and to the west, the futuristic Parc André-Citroën.

Tour Montparnasse

MAP P.112, POCKET MAP E11
33 av du Maine Ⓜ Montparnasse-
Bienvenüe. Ⓦ tourmontparnasse56.com.
Charge.

View of Tour Montparnasse

At the station end of boulevard du Montparnasse, the 200-metre-high **Tour Montparnasse** skyscraper is one of the city's principal and most despised landmarks. That said, the 360º

Musée Bourdelle

view from the top is better than the one from the Eiffel Tower, in that it includes the Eiffel Tower – and excludes the Tour Montparnasse. It also costs less to ascend, and queues are far shorter. The 56th-storey café-gallery offers a tremendous view westward; sunset is the best time to visit.

Jardin Atlantique

MAP P.112, POCKET MAP E11
Access by lifts on rue Cdt. R. Mouchotte and bd Vaugirard, or by the stairs alongside platform #1 in Montparnasse station Ⓜ Montparnasse-Bienvenüe.
Montparnasse station was once the great arrival and departure point for travellers heading across the Atlantic, a connection commemorated in the unexpected **Jardin Atlantique**, suspended above the train tracks behind the station. Hemmed in by cliff-like high-rise apartment blocks, the park is a fine example of Parisian flair, with fields of Atlantic-coast grasses, wave-like undulations in the lawns (to cover the irregularly placed concrete struts underneath) and well-hidden ventilation holes that reveal sudden glimpses of TGV roofs and rail sleepers below.

Musée Bourdelle

MAP P.112, POCKET MAP E10
16–18 rue A. Bourdelle Ⓜ Montparnasse-Bienvenüe/Falguière. Ⓦ bourdelle.paris.fr. Free, charge during temporary exhibitions.
One block northwest of the tower, the **Musée Bourdelle** has been built around the atmospheric atelier of the early twentieth-century sculptor. Rodin's pupil and Giacometti's teacher, Antoine Bourdelle, created bronze and stone works that move from a naturalistic style – as in the series of Beethoven busts – towards a more geometric Modernism, seen in his better-known, monumental sculptures, some of which sit in the garden.

Musée Zadkine

MAP P.112, POCKET MAP F10–11
100bis rue d'Assas Ⓜ Vavin/RER Port-Royal. Ⓦ zadkine.paris.fr. Free; charge during exhibitions.
The cottage-like home and garden studios of Russian-born Cubist sculptor Ossip Zadkine, where he lived from 1928 to

1967, are occupied by the tiny **Musée Zadkine**. A mixture of elongated figures and blockier works are displayed in the intimate rooms, while Cubist bronzes are scattered about the minuscule garden, sheltering under trees or emerging from clumps of bamboo.

Fondation Cartier pour l'Art Contemporain

MAP P.112, POCKET MAP F11–12
261 bd Raspail. Ⓜ Raspail.
Ⓦ fondationcartier.com. Charge.

Rue Schoelcher and boulevard Raspail, on the east side of Montparnasse cemetery, have some interesting examples of twentieth-century architecture, from Art Nouveau to the translucent glass-and-steel facade of the **Fondation Cartier pour l'Art Contemporain**. Designed in 1994 by Jean Nouvel, the venue presents contemporary installations, videos, graffiti and multimedia – often by foreign artists little known in France – in high-quality temporary exhibitions that use the light-filled spaces to maximum advantage.

The Catacombs

MAP P.112, POCKET MAP F12
Place Denfert-Rochereau Ⓜ Denfert-Rochereau. Ⓦ catacombs.paris.fr. Charge.

For a surreal, somewhat chilling experience, head down into the **catacombs** below place Denfert-Rochereau, formerly place d'Enfer (Hell Square). Abandoned quarries stacked with millions of bones, cleared from overstocked charnel houses and cemeteries between 1785 and 1871, the catacombs are said to hold the remains of around six million Parisians, more than double the population of the city, not counting the suburbs. Lining the gloomy passageways, long thigh bones are stacked end-on,

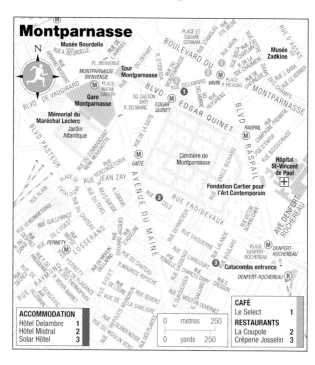

The Catacombs

forming a wall to keep in the smaller bones and shards, which can be seen in dusty heaps behind. These femoral walls are further inset with gaping, hollow-eyed skulls, forming elaborate geometric patterns, while plaques carrying macabre quotations loom out of the gloom. It's a fascinating place, but note that there are a good couple of kilometres to walk, and it can quickly become claustrophobic. Book tickets online in advance to avoid long queues to get in.

Montparnasse cemetery

MAP P.112, POCKET MAP E11–F12
Bd Edgar Quinet Ⓜ Raspail/Gaîté/Edgar Quinet. Free.

Second in size and celebrity to Père Lachaise, **Montparnasse cemetery** is an intriguing city of the dead, its ranks of miniature temples paying homage to illustrious names from Baudelaire to Beckett; pick up a free map at the entrance gate. The unembellished joint grave of Jean-Paul Sartre and Simone de Beauvoir lies right of the main entrance, while down avenue de l'Ouest, which follows the western wall,

you'll find the tombs of Baudelaire, the painter Soutine, Dadaist Tristan Tzara and Ossip Zadkine. Across rue Emile-Richard, in the eastern section, lie car-maker André Citroën, Guy de Maupassant, César Franck, and the notable victim of French anti-Semitism at the end of the nineteenth century, Captain Dreyfus.

Parc André-Citroën

MAP P.116
Quai André-Citroën Ⓜ Balard.

The riverfront south of the Eiffel Tower is a dull swathe, bristling with office blocks and miniature skyscrapers; it's brightened up at the southwestern extreme of the city limits by the **Parc André-Citroën**, the site of the old Citroën motor works. This is not a park for traditionalists: there is a central grassy area, but elsewhere concrete terraces and walled gardens with abstract themes define the Modernist space. Its best features are the huge glasshouses full of exotic-smelling shrubs, the capricious set of automated fountains – on hot days you'll see excitable teens dashing to and fro

Montparnasse Cemetery

through its sudden spurts – and the tethered balloon (charge), which rises and sinks regularly on calm days (consult ⓦballondeparis.com to check conditions).

Allée des Cygnes

MAP P.116, POCKET MAP A8–9
Ⓜ **Bir-Hakeim**.

One of Paris's most charming walks leads down from the

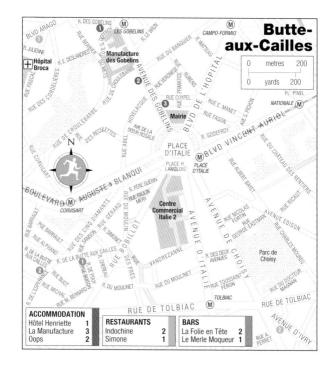

middle of the Pont de Bir-Hakeim along the tree-lined **Allée des Cygnes**, a narrow, mid-stream island built up on raised concrete embankments. Once you've taken in the views of the Eiffel Tower and both banks of the river, admired the passing coal barges and visited the curious small-scale version of the Statue of Liberty at the southern tip of the island, you might just share Samuel Beckett's opinion of the place – it was one of his favourite spots in Paris.

Manufacture des Gobelins

MAP P.112, POCKET MAP H12
42 ave des Gobelins Ⓜ Les Gobelins.
Ⓦ mobiliernational.culture.gouv.fr. Gallery (open during exhibitions only) Charge. Workshops Guided tours (1hr 30min; French only); charge; book online.

Manufacture des Gobelins

The highest-quality tapestries have been created in the **Gobelins** workshops for some four hundred years. The gallery stages temporary exhibitions of historic and contemporary tapestries, furnishings and textiles, while on the workshop tour you can watch the tapestries being made by painfully slow, traditional methods; each weaver completes between one and four square metres a year.

Butte-aux-Cailles

MAP P.114, POCKET MAP H12
Ⓜ Corvisart/Place d'Italie.
Between boulevard Auguste-Blanqui and rue Bobillot, the lively hilltop quarter of **Butte-aux-Cailles**, with its little streets and cul-de-sacs of prewar houses and studios, is typical

Butte-aux-Cailles

of pre-1960s Paris. The rue de la Butte-aux-Cailles itself is the animated heart of the area, lined with unpretentious, youthful and vaguely lefty bars and restaurants, most of which stay open late.

Paris Rive Gauche

MAP P.116, POCKET MAP K11–L12

Ⓜ Quai de la Gare/Bibliothèque François Mitterrand.

The easternmost edge of the 13e arrondissement, between

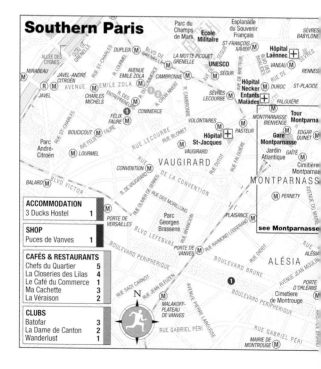

Southern Paris

ACCOMMODATION	
3 Ducks Hostel	1

SHOP	
Puces de Vanves	1

CAFÉS & RESTAURANTS	
Chefs du Quartier	5
La Closeries des Lilas	4
Le Café du Commerce	1
Ma Cachette	3
La Véraison	2

CLUBS	
Batofar	3
La Dame de Canton	2
Wanderlust	1

the river and the Austerlitz train tracks, has been transformed as part of the **Paris Rive Gauche** development. The **Passerelle Simone de Beauvoir**, a footbridge crossing the Seine in a double-ribbon structure, sets the tone, while tethered barges have made the area a nightlife attraction. The floating swimming pool, **Piscine Josephine Baker**, is a wonderful place to do a few laps, while south of rue Tolbiac, **Les Frigos** warehouse (Ⓦles-frigos.com), once used for cold-storage of produce destined for Les Halles, is now an anarchic studio space, with a bar-restaurant and occasional exhibitions.

Cité de la Mode et du Design

Cité de la Mode et du Design

MAP P.116, POCKET MAP K11
34 quai d'Austerlitz Ⓜ Austerlitz/Quai de la Gare. Ⓦcitemodedesign.fr.

The most recent Paris Rive Gauche development is the

Docks en Seine complex, which houses the **Cité de la Mode et du Design**, a fashion institute, whose intrusive design of twisting, lime-

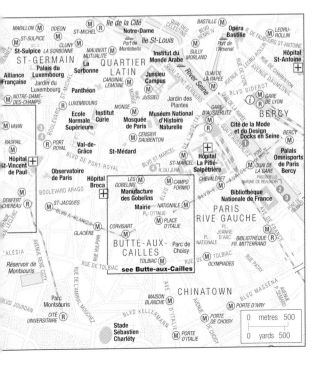

green tubes is supposed to recall the sinuous shape of the river. It hosts occasional exhibitions, a number of shops and a restaurant, as well as popular bars and clubs, including riverside *Wanderlust* (see page 121).

Chinatown

MAP P.116
Ⓜ Tolbiac.

Paris's best Southeast Asian cuisine is to be found in Chinatown, home to several East Asian communities. Avenues de Choisy and d'Ivry are full of Vietnamese, Chinese, Thai, Cambodian and Laotian restaurants and food shops, as is **Les Olympiades**, a tattily futuristic pedestrian area seemingly suspended between tower blocks and accessed by escalators from rue Nationale, rue de Tolbiac and avenue d'Ivry.

Bibliothèque Nationale de France

MAP P.116, POCKET MAP L12
Quai de la Gare Ⓜ Quai de la Gare/
Bibliothèque François Mitterrand, Ⓦ bnf.fr.
Charge for a reading room pass – over-16s only (bring ID).

Architect Dominique Perrault's **Bibliothèque Nationale de France** dominates this modernized section of the riverbank with four enormous L-shaped towers – intended to look like open books – framing a sunken pine copse. Glass walls alongside the trees allow dappled light to filter through to the underground library spaces. It's worth wandering around inside to experience the structure at first hand, and to see the pair of wonderful globes that belonged to Louis XIV. There are regular, high-quality exhibitions (admission varies).

The Bibliothèque Nationale de France

Shop

Puces de Vanves

MAP P.116, POCKET MAP E12
Av Georges-Lafenestre/av Marc-Sangnier
Ⓜ Porte-de-Vanves.

The city's best flea market for original finds, bric-a-brac and Parisian knick-knacks. It starts at daybreak and spreads along the pavements of avenues Marc-Sangnier and Georges-Lafenestre, petering out in place de la Porte-de-Vanves.

Cafés

Chefs du Quartier

MAP P.116, POCKET MAP J11
12 rue du Jura Les Gobelins.
Ⓦ chefsduquartier.fr.

This warm-hearted deli-café is a great spot for a cheap no-fuss lunch, either in the tiny dining room or to take away. The short menu focuses on a different cuisine daily, so you're as likely to be offered tabbouleh, veggie curry or quesadillas, all home-made. *Plat du jour* €7, Sat brunch €15.

Le Select

MAP P.112, POCKET MAP F11
99 bd du Montparnasse Ⓜ Vavin.
Ⓦ leselectmontparnasse.fr.

If you want to visit one of the great Montparnasse cafés, as frequented by Picasso, Matisse, Henry Miller and F. Scott Fitzgerald, make it this one. It's the least spoilt and most traditional of them all, and has the lowest prices – it's also conveniently located on the sunny side of the street. The food, however, can be disappointing.

Restaurants

La Closerie des Lilas

MAP P.116, POCKET MAP G11
171 Bd du Montparnasse Ⓜ Vavin/RER
Port-Royal. Ⓦ closeriedeslilas.fr/

La Coupole

If you're looking for haunts of Paris' star-studded past, start here. In a district famed for its brasseries, this one has hosted Cézanne, Picasso, Hemingway and Fitzgerald over the years. Expect leather banquettes and traditional fodder, on large menus offering everything from oyster platters to burger and chips. €€

Le Café du Commerce

MAP P.116, POCKET MAP B10
51 rue du Commerce Ⓜ Emile-Zola. ☎ 01
45 75 03 27, Ⓦ lecafeducommerce.com.
This huge, former workers' brasserie is a buzzing, dramatic place to eat, set on three lofty levels around a patio. Honest, high-quality meat is the speciality and the set lunch menu is a bargain. €

La Coupole

MAP P.112, POCKET MAP F11
102 bd du Montparnasse Ⓜ Vavin.
Ⓦ lacoupole-paris.com.
The largest and loveliest of the old Montparnasse brasseries. Now part of the *Flo* chain, it remains a genuine institution, its Art Deco interior buzzing with atmosphere. Tasty food choices range from

La Veraison

oysters to Welsh rarebit, with plenty of classics in between. €€

Crêperie Josselin

MAP P.112, POCKET MAP F11
67 rue du Montparnasse Ⓜ Edgar Quinet/ Montparnasse. ☎ 01 43 20 93 50.
Montparnasse is traditionally the Breton quarter of Paris (the station is on the direct line to northern France) and this crêperie couldn't be any more traditionally Breton, with its rustic decor and authentic buttery crêpes, washed down with jugs of cider. No reservations. €

Indochine

MAP P.114, POCKET MAP K12
86 av de Choisy Ⓜ Tolbiac. ☎ 01 44 24 28 08.
This is a better-than-average Vietnamese option in the heart of Paris's Chinatown, with tasty *banh xeo* pancakes, zingy fresh *pho* and *bun bo hue* soups, plus vermicelli, stir fries and grilled specialities. €

Ma Cachette

MAP P.116, POCKET MAP G11
8 rue des Chartreux Ⓜ Vavin/RER Port-Royal. ☎ 01 43 26 66 34.

Venture into the back streets of Montparnasse and you'll be rewarded with gems like this – a far cry from the heaving boulevard brasseries. Good ingredients simply served, like fresh fish fillets and veg, wok fried beef noodles, filet mignon de porc with tandoori sauce. You'll have to fight the locals for a table. €€

Simone

MAP P.114, POCKET MAP H12
33 blvd Arago Ⓜ Les Gobelins.
Ⓦ simonelerestolacave.com.
A minuscule homely neo-*bistrot*, with red walls, warm wood, shabby-chic *terrasse* chairs and open kitchen. Food is contemporary, featuring lots of fresh veg – pollack with asparagus, beetroot and fennel, for example.. Nearby, at 48 blvd Arago, is their offshoot wine bar, *Simone La Cave*, specializing in natural wines. €€

La Veraison

MAP P.116, POCKET MAP B10
64 rue de la Croix Nivert Ⓜ Commerce.
Ⓦ laveraison.com.
The open kitchen at this terrific, contemporary neighbourhood

bistrot turns out excellent modern French food – the likes of foie gras ravioli, beetroot gazpacho and duckling with sticky rice fritters – in a laidback space always brimming with happy locals. €€

Bars

La Folie en Tête

MAP P.114, POCKET MAP H12
33 rue Butte-aux-Cailles Ⓜ Place-d'Italie/ Corvisart. Ⓦ lafolieentete.wix.com/lesite.
The classic Butte-aux-Cailles bar: friendly and alternative, serving drinks and snacks in the day and playing a wide-ranging soundtrack, from world music to *chanson*, at night.

Le Merle Moqueur

MAP P.114, POCKET MAP H12
11 rue Butte-aux-Cailles Ⓜ Place-d'Italie/ Corvisart. Ⓣ 01 45 65 12 43.
This narrow, distressed-chic bar – which saw the Parisian debut of Manu Chao – serves up flavoured rums and 1980s French rock to a young, noisy crowd.

Clubs

Batofar

MAP P.116, POCKET MAP L12
Quai François Mauriac Ⓜ Quai-de-la-Gare. Ⓦ batofar.fr.
Moored in front of the Bibliothèque Nationale, this lighthouse boat is a quirky space for electro, hip-hop and experimental funk. Pay to enter.

La Dame de Canton

MAP P.116, POCKET MAP L12
Quai François Mauriac Ⓜ Quai-de-la-Gare. Ⓦ damedecanton.com.
Another kooky floating venue, *Batofar*'s neighbour is a beautiful Chinese junk that hosts relaxed but upbeat world music, *chanson* and DJ nights, along with edgy music hall and kids' shows.

Wanderlust

MAP P.116, POCKET MAP L11
36 Quai d'Austerlitz Ⓜ Gare d'Austerlitz. Ⓦ wanderlustparis.com.
This cool waterside club really comes into its own in summer when you can sip your cocktail on the vast rooftop terrace, looking out over the Seine, while a DJ plays an electro set.

Batofar

Montmartre and northern Paris

One of Paris's most romantic quarters, Montmartre is famed for its association with artists like Renoir, Degas, Picasso and Toulouse-Lautrec. It long existed as a hilltop village outside the city walls, and today the steep streets around the Butte Montmartre, Paris's highest point, preserve an attractively village-like atmosphere – although the crown of the hill, around place du Tertre, is overrun with tourists. The Butte is topped by the church of Sacré-Coeur and its landmark bulbous white domes. At the foot of the Butte is Pigalle, once best known for its sleazy strip clubs but now rapidly gentrifying and full of trendy bars and shops. Much of the 9e arrondissement is genteel, with elegant townhouses. Rather more rough-edged is the neighbouring 10e, though this too is changing, fast becoming one of the city's most vibrant areas, as young, hip Parisians move in. On the northern edge of the city, the mammoth St-Ouen market hawks everything from antiques to hand-me-downs.

Butte Montmartre

MAP P.124, POCKET MAP G3–H3
Ⓜ Anvers/Abbesses.

Despite being one of the city's chief tourist attractions, the slopes of the **Butte Montmartre** manage to retain the quiet, almost secretive, air of their rural origins, charming streets offering lovely views back over the city. The quickest way up is by the funicular, which is part of the city's métro system, but it's more fun to walk up through the winding streets from Abbesses métro.

Place des Abbesses

MAP P.124, POCKET MAP G3
Ⓜ Anvers/Abbesses.

Shady **place des Abbesses**, featuring one of Paris's few complete surviving Guimard Art Nouveau métro entrances, is the hub of a lively neighbourhood. The streets immediately around the square are relatively chichi for Montmartre, filled with buzzing wine bars, laidback restaurants and little boutiques – good to explore if you're after one-off outfits and accessories, and great to hang out in of an evening. From here you can head up rue de la Vieuville, from where the stairs in rue Drevet lead to the minuscule place du Calvaire, which has a lovely view back over the city.

Place Emile-Goudeau

MAP P.124, POCKET MAP G3
Ⓜ Abbesses/Anvers.

Halfway up steep, curving rue Ravignan is tiny **place Emile-Goudeau**, where Picasso, Braque and Juan Gris initiated the Cubist movement in an old piano factory known as the Bateau-Lavoir. The current building, a faithful reconstruction, is still occupied by studios. With its bench and little iron fountain, the *place* is a lovely spot to draw breath on your way up the Butte.

Place du Tertre

MAP P.124, POCKET MAP G3
Ⓜ Abbesses.

The bogus heart of Montmartre, the **place du Tertre** is best avoided: clotted with tour groups, overpriced restaurants, tacky souvenir stalls and jaded street artists. At the east end of the *place*, however, stands the serene church of **St-Pierre-de-Montmartre**, the oldest in Paris, along with St-Germain-des-Prés. Although much altered since it was built as a Benedictine convent in the twelfth century, the church retains its Romanesque and early Gothic character, with four ancient columns, probably leftovers from the Roman shrine that stood on the hill (which they knew as *mons mercurii* – Mercury's Hill).

Sacré-Coeur

MAP P.124, POCKET MAP G3
Ⓜ Anvers/Abbesses. sacre-coeur-monmartre.com Free. Charge to enter the Dome.

Crowning the Butte, **Sacré-Coeur** is a pastiche of Byzantine-style architecture, whose white tower and ice-cream-scoop dome has become an icon of the Paris skyline. Construction was started in the 1870s on the initiative of the Catholic Church to atone for the "crimes" of the revolutionary Commune, which first attempted to seize power from the heights of Montmartre. There's little to see in the soulless interior, but the view from the dome is fantastic – best enjoyed early in the morning or later in the afternoon if you don't want to look straight into the sun. **Square Willette**, at the foot of the monumental staircase, is named after the local artist who turned out on inauguration day to shout "Long live the devil!" Today the staircase acts as impromptu seating for visitors enjoying views, munching on picnics and tolerating the street entertainers; the crowds, and the guitar strumming, only increase as night falls.

Moulin de la Galette

MAP P.124, POCKET MAP G3
Rue Lepic Ⓜ Abbesses/Lamarck-Caulaincourt.

One atmospheric way to get to the top of the Butte is to head up rue Tholozé, turning right below the

Place des Abbesses

MONTMARTRE AND NORTHERN PARIS

Montmartre & northern Paris

SHOPS AND MARKETS

Arnaud Delmontel	5
Chezel	4
Ekyog	3
Gontran Cherrier	2
Puces de St-Ouen	1
Thanx God I'm a VIP	6

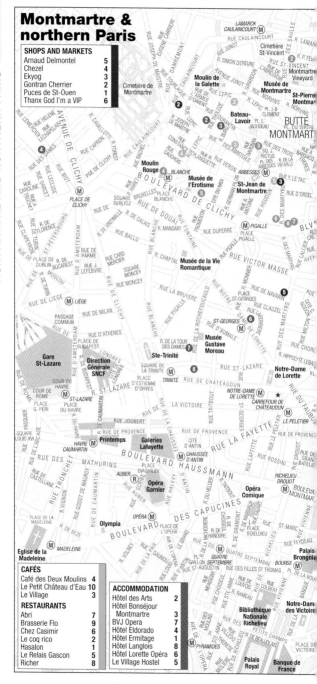

CAFÉS

Café des Deux Moulins	4
Le Petit Château d'Eau	10
Le Village	3

RESTAURANTS

Abri	7
Brasserie Flo	9
Chez Casimir	6
Le coq rico	2
Hasalon	1
Le Relais Gascon	5
Richer	8

ACCOMMODATION

Hôtel des Arts	2
Hôtel Bonséjour Montmartre	3
BVJ Opera	7
Hôtel Eldorado	4
Hôtel Ermitage	1
Hôtel Langlois	8
Hôtel Lorette Opéra	6
Le Village Hostel	5

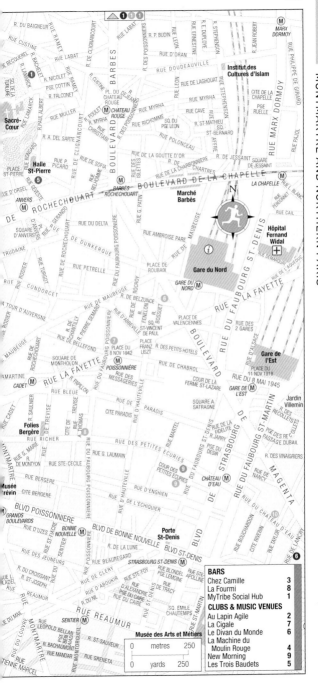

BARS

Chez Camille	3
La Fourmi	8
MyTribe Social Hub	1

CLUBS & MUSIC VENUES

Au Lapin Agile	2
La Cigale	7
Le Divan du Monde	6
La Machine du Moulin Rouge	4
New Morning	9
Les Trois Baudets	5

wooden **Moulin de la Galette** into rue des Norvins. The *moulin* is one of two survivors of Montmartre's forty-odd windmills (the other sits on an adjacent street corner, on top of a restaurant confusingly given the same name), and was once a *guingette*, holding fashionable dances – as immortalized by Renoir in his *Bal du Moulin de la Galette*, which hangs in the Musée d'Orsay.

Musée de Montmartre

MAP P.124, POCKET MAP G3
12 rue Cortot Ⓜ Lamarck-Caulaincourt.
Ⓦ museedemontmartre.fr. Charge.

The intriguing little **Musée de Montmartre**, set in two old houses (the Maison du Bel Air and the Hôtel Demarne) on a quiet street, recaptures something of the feel of the quarter's bohemian days, lining its period rooms with old posters, paintings and personal photos. The Maison du Bel Air was rented variously by Renoir, Dufy, Suzanne Valadon and her alcoholic son Utrillo. Valadon's studio was opened in 2014 for the first time to the public, and the three gardens have also been charmingly restored. You can walk round to the back of the

museum to see the neat terraces of the tiny **Montmartre vineyard** – which produces some 1,500 bottles a year. The streets leading off here are some of the quietest in Montmartre, and lovely for a romantic stroll.

Montmartre cemetery

MAP P.124, POCKET MAP F2–3
Entrance on av Rachel, underneath rue Caulaincourt Ⓜ Blanche/Place-de-Clichy.
Free.

West of the Butte, the **Montmartre cemetery** is an intimate, melancholy place: tucked down below street level in the hollow of an old quarry, its steep tomb-dotted hills create a sombre ravine of the dead. The graves of Nijinsky, Zola, Stendhal, Berlioz, Degas, Feydeau, Offenbach and Truffaut, among others, are marked on a free map available at the entrance.

Pigalle and SoPi

MAP P.124, POCKET MAP F3–H4
Ⓜ Pigalle.

The southern slopes of Montmartre are bordered by the boulevards de Clichy and Rochechouart. At the Barbès end of bd Rochechouart crowds teem around the cheap

Musée de Montmartre

The Moulin Rouge

Tati department stores and street vendors hawk textiles, watches and trinkets. The area where the two roads meet, around **place Pigalle**, has long been associated with sleaze, with sex shops, shows and streetwalkers vying for custom. The area is changing, however: the streets just south of place Pigalle have been rebranded **SoPi** ("South Pigalle") and are now some of the city's hippest. Most of the sleazy bars have closed and been replaced by trendy cocktail bars, bistros and organic grocers. Rues de Douai, Victor-Massé and Houdon sport a large number of electric guitar and hi-fi shops, while rue des Martyrs is one of Paris's most enjoyable gastro-streets, lined with fancy food and flower shops as it descends southwards from the Butte.

The Moulin Rouge

MAP P.124, POCKET MAP F3
82 bd de Clichy Ⓜ Blanche.
Ⓦ moulinrouge.fr. Charge.
Though its environs have lost the glamour they once had, you can't help but be drawn towards the tatty red windmill, its windows filled with photos of beaming showgirls. When Toulouse-Lautrec immortalized the **Moulin Rouge** in his paintings, it was one of many such bawdy, populist cabarets in the area; nowadays, it survives on its reputation, offering expensive Vegas-style dinner-and-show deals.

Musée de la Vie Romantique

MAP P.124, POCKET MAP F4
16 rue Chaptal Ⓜ St-Georges/Blanche/ Pigalle. Ⓦ vie-romantique.paris.fr. Free; admission varies for temporary exhibitions.
The **Musée de la Vie Romantique** evokes the era when this quarter was the home of Chopin, Delacroix, Dumas and other prominent figures in the Romantic movement. The bourgeois shuttered house, on a cobbled courtyard, once belonged to the painter Ary Scheffer; in addition to his sentimental portraits and the restored period interiors, you can see bits and pieces associated with his friend George Sand. The museum's *salon de thé*, located in the pretty garden, is a lovely place to unwind over a salad or quiche.

Musée Moreau

MAP P.124, POCKET MAP F4
14 rue de La Rochefoucauld Ⓜ Trinité.
Ⓦ musee-moreau.fr. Charge.

Musée Moreau

The little-visited **Gustave Moreau museum** was conceived by the artist himself, to be carved out of the house he shared with his parents for many years – you can visit their tiny apartments, crammed with furniture and trinkets. Connected by a beautiful spiral staircase, the two huge, studio-like spaces are no less cluttered: Moreau's decadent canvases hang cheek by jowl, every surface crawling with figures and decorative swirls, or alive with deep colours and provocative symbolism, as in the museum's *pièce de résistance*, *Jupiter and Sémélé*.

Place St-Georges

MAP P.124, POCKET MAP G4
Ⓜ St-Georges.

The handsome **place St-Georges** centres on a fountain topped by a bust of Paul Gavarni, a nineteenth-century cartoonist who made a speciality of lampooning the mistresses who were de rigueur for bourgeois males of the time. This was the mistresses' quarter – they were known as *lorettes*, after the nearby church of Notre-Dame-de-Lorette, built in the 1820s in the Neoclassical style. One the east side of place

St-Georges stands the extravagant Renaissance-style Hotel de la Paiva, built in the 1840s for Thérèse Lachmann, a famous Second Empire courtesan who married a marquis.

Faubourgs St-Denis and St-Martin

MAP P.124, POCKET MAP J5
Ⓜ Château d'Eau.

At the upper end of the 10e, the stations Gare du Nord and Gare de l'Est dominate, while to the south lies the fast-changing quarter of the **faubourgs St-Denis and St-Martin**, traditionally working class, but more and more popular with young Parisian bobos, priced out of the more affluent areas of the city. A growing number of cutting-edge *bistrots*, chic boutiques, delis and cocktail bars are colonizing the streets between Château d'Eau and Cadet métros.

Porte St-Denis and Porte St-Martin

MAP P.124, POCKET MAP K11
Ⓜ Strasbourg-St-Denis.

The **Porte St-Denis** and **Porte St-Martin** are two triumphal arches, marooned by traffic, at either end of the boulevard St-Denis. The Porte St-Denis was erected to celebrate Louis XIV's victories on the Rhine and bear the bas-reliefs *The Crossing of the Rhine* and *The Capture of Maastricht*. Some 200m east, the more graceful Porte St-Martin was built two years later in celebration of further victories.

Passage Brady

MAP P.124, POCKET MAP J6
Ⓜ Château d'Eau.

A number of hidden lanes and covered *passages* riddle this corner of the city; perhaps the best known is **passage Brady**, the hub of Paris's "Little India", lined with Indian barbers, grocers and restaurants. Further north, rue des Petites-Ecuries has a real buzz about it, with its boutiques, foodie shops and cutting-edge *bistrots*, as well as the renowned jazz and world music club, New Morning (see page 133).

Marché barbès

MAP P.124, POCKET MAP H3
Boulevard de la Chapelle Ⓜ Barbès-Rochechouart.

After World War I, when large numbers of North Africans were first imported to replenish the ranks of Frenchmen dying in the trenches, the swathe of Paris north of the Gare du Nord gradually became an immigrant ghetto. Today, while the *quartier* remains poor, it is a vibrant place; home to a host of mini communities, it's predominantly West African and Congolese but has pockets of South Asian, Haitian, Turkish and other ethnicities as well. Countless shops sell music and fabrics, but to get a feel for the place, head to the twice-weekly **Marché Barbès**, heaving with African groceries, exotic fish and halal meat.

Institut des Cultures d'Islam

MAP P.124, POCKET MAP J3
56 rue Stephenson Ⓜ La Chapelle/Marx Dormoy. Ⓦ institut-cultures-islam.org Free.

Opened in 2013, the **Institut des Cultures d'Islam** stages exhibitions of contemporary art from the Islamic world. These are usually fascinating and thought-provoking, with past exhibitions including Syrian artists responding to the current war and chaos in their country, and women artists depicting domestic life in the Middle East and Iran.

Passage Brady

Shops and markets

Arnaud Delmontel

MAP P.124, POCKET MAP G4
39 rue des Martyrs Ⓜ St-Georges.
Ⓦ arnaud-delmontel.com.
Exquisite Parisian patisserie with a funky twist, its *bavaroises, macarons* and tarts decorated in fresh candy colours. The award-winning bread is outstanding, too.

Chezel

MAP P.124, POCKET MAP G4
59 rue Condorcet Ⓜ Pigalle. ☏ 01 53 16 47 31.
One of the best of the three or four (the others come and go) little vintage fashion shops on this street. Prices from €30 to easily five times that for a classic – some serious designer wear finds its way here.

Ekyog

MAP P.124, POCKET MAP G3
89 R. des Martyrs Ⓜ Abbesses.
Ⓦ ekyog.com/en.
French sustainable women's clothing, designed in Paris, this brand has been around for nearly twenty years and continues to excel in timeless high-quality design.

Gontran Cherrier

MAP P.124, POCKET MAP F3
22 rue Caulaincourt Ⓜ Abbesses.
Ⓦ gontran-cherrier.com.
Gontran Cherrier bakes some of the most creative bread in Paris and disciples will trek across the city for his squid-ink buns filled with gravadlax, thin-crusted savoury tarts and signature sweet pastries.

Puces de St-Ouen

MAP P.124, POCKET MAP H1
Ⓜ Porte de Clignancourt.
Spreading beyond the *périphérique* at the northern edge of the city, between the Porte de St-Ouen and the Porte de Clignancourt, the *puces de St-Ouen* claims to be the largest flea market in the world, though nowadays it's predominantly a proper – and pricey – antiques market. Mainly selling furniture, with all sorts of fashionable junk like old café-bar

Puces de St-Ouen

counters, telephones, traffic lights, jukeboxes and the like, it offers many quirky treasures. Of the fourteen individual markets, you could concentrate on Marché **Dauphine**, good for movie posters, *chanson* and jazz records, comics and books, and Marché **Vernaison** for curios and bric-a-brac. Under the flyover of the *périphérique*, vendors hawk counterfeit clothing, sunglasses and pirated DVDs, while cup-and-ball scam merchants try their luck.

Thanx God I'm a VIP
MAP P.124, POCKET MAP F13
12 Rue de Lancry, ⓦ thanxgod.com.
A treasure trove of vintage fashion in the 10e with numerous outlets on the same street. There's a fantastic collection for both men and women, owing to owner Sylvie Chateigner's dedication and expertise for buying and selling. Clothes are colour coded on rails which could be good (or bad) for those naturally drawn to black, black, black.

Cafés

Café des Deux Moulins
MAP P.124, POCKET MAP F3
15 rue Lepic ⓜ Blanche.
Once a must-see for *Amélie* fans (she waited tables here in the film), this comfortably shabby retro diner/café is now a down-to-earth neighbourhood hangout once more – burly *ouvriers* in the morning, hipsters in the evening – and serves breakfasts, brunches and *plats* at good prices.

Le Petit Château d'Eau
MAP P.124, POCKET MAP J6
34 rue du Château d'Eau ⓜ Jacques-Bonsergent. ⓣ 01 42 08 72 81.
Lovely, peaceful old café-bar with zinc bar, gorgeous ceramic tiles on the walls, fresh flowers on the tables and a local crowd

enjoying coffee, wine and cheese/charcuterie platters or classic French *plats*.

Le Village
MAP P.124, POCKET MAP G3
36 rue des Abbesses ⓜ Abbesses.
A friendly café-bar with a teeny *terrasse* that extends across the pavement after dark. The interior is a retro delight – gleaming ceramic wall tiles, huge mirrors and a zinc bar. Equally good for a morning coffee, a light lunch of *croques* or salads, or an evening cognac, it's perfect for watching the world go by.

Restaurants

Abri
MAP P.124, POCKET MAP H4
92 rue du Faubourg-Poissonière ⓜ Poissonnière. ⓣ 01 83 97 00 00.
Behind the workaday exterior of this restaurant, chef Katsuaki Okiyama turns out some of the city's classiest cuisine – elegant French-Asian fusion dishes from the tiny open kitchen. Reserve weeks in advance for the no-choice tasting menus or come on Sat lunchtime for the gourmet toasted sandwiches (including dessert and a drink; arrive early). €€

Brasserie Flo
MAP P.124, POCKET MAP J5
7 cour des Petites-Ecuries ⓜ Château-d'Eau. ⓦ floderer-paris.com.
This dark and splendid old-time Alsatian brasserie is so beautiful that even the stroppy service and the crammed-in tourist/business clientele can't spoil the experience. Hearty brasserie food, with lots of fish and seafood, and butter in everything. €€

Chez Casimir
MAP P.124, POCKET MAP H4
6 rue de Belzunce ⓜ Gare-du-Nord.
ⓣ 01 48 78 28 80.

This no-frills corner *bistrot*, in a quiet spot a stone's throw from the Gare du Nord, is a gem: traditional but imaginative French cuisine with a fine brunch at weekends. €€

Le coq rico

MAP P.124, POCKET MAP G3
98 rue Lepic Ⓜ Abbesses/Blanche. Ⓦ lecoq-fils.com.

It's all about the birds at Antoine Westermann's chic, relatively formal Montmartre outfit, from the huge rôtisserie that turns out moist whole grilled chickens to the duck rillettes, roast pigeon and poultry soups. €€

Hasalon

MAP P.124, POCKET MAP G3
106 rue des Rosiers Ⓜ Porte de Clignancourt/Garibaldi. Ⓦ hasalonparis. com.

Following in the footsteps of New York and Tel Aviv, chef Eyal Shani has opened a Parisian address in Saint Ouen, featuring creative, avant-garde dishes with a Mediterranean focus. There are two services per evening and the atmosphere builds throughout the service, from peaceful beginnings to bustling energy. €€€

Le Relais Gascon

MAP P.124, POCKET MAP G3
6 rue des Abbesses & 13 rue de Joseph Maistre Ⓜ Abbesses. ☎ 01 42 58 58 22.

This noisy two-storey restaurant (upstairs is cosier) provides a welcome blast of Gascon heartiness. Enormous hot salads, good-value *plats* and set lunch menus. €

Richer

MAP P.124, POCKET MAP H5
2 rue Richer Ⓜ Poissonière/Bonne Nouvelle. Ⓦ lericher.com.

This light, modern dining room – a fresh update on the traditional all-day Parisian brasserie – offers coffee, wine and tapas all day long. It's the short seasonal menu that's really worth coming for, though, using fresh ingredients in innovative ways – perhaps steamed hake with beetroot puree, horseradish and Thai basil. No reservations. €

Bars

Chex Camille

MAP P.124, POCKET MAP G3
8 rue Ravignan Ⓜ Abbesses. ☎ 01 42 57 75 62.

With an effortlessly stylish decor – creamy walls, ceiling fans, a few old mirrors, mismatched seating – this tiny bar pulls a local crowd of all ages who could just as easily be enjoying a quiet chat as dancing to Elvis or raï.

La Fourmi

MAP P.124, POCKET MAP G4
74 rue des Martyrs Ⓜ Pigalle/Abbesses. ☎ 01 42 64 70 35.

Artfully distressed, high-ceilinged café-bar full of Parisian bobos sipping coffee and cocktails. Light meals available during the day. DJs at weekends.

MyTribe Social Hub

MAP P.124, POCKET MAP H1
33/35 Bd Jean Jaurès Ⓜ Mairie de Saint-Ouen. Ⓦ tribehotels.com/.

This new bold chain of hotels has set up near the flea market and its 24-hour hub has plenty of room to work, play, eat, meet, or just chill. There is a great al-fresco patio bar with a focus on high-quality cocktails and mocktails, courtesy of the chain's mixologist Matthias Giroud.

Clubs and music venues

Au Lapin Agile

MAP P.124, POCKET MAP G2
22 rue des Saules Ⓜ Lamarck–Caulaincourt. Ⓦ au-lapin-agile.com.

Les Trois Baudets

Painted and patronized by Picasso and other leading lights of the Montmartre scene, this legendary club – in a shuttered building hidden in a pretty garden – still hosts cabaret, poetry and *chanson* nights (€28, including one drink). Touristy crowd, but authentic musicians.

La Cigale

MAP P.124, POCKET MAP G4
120 bd de Rochechouart Ⓜ Pigalle.
Ⓦ lacigale.fr.
This historic 1,400-seater Pigalle theatre, which once played host to the likes of Mistinguett and Maurice Chevalier, is a leading venue for rock and indie acts from France and continental Europe.

Le Divan du Monde

MAP P.124, POCKET MAP G4
75 rue des Martyrs Ⓜ Anvers.
Ⓦ divandumonde.com.
A youthful venue in a former café whose regulars once included Toulouse-Lautrec, with an exciting programme ranging from poetry slams to swing nights to Congolese rumba.

La Machine du Moulin Rouge

MAP P.124, POCKET MAP F3
90 blvd de Clichy Ⓜ Blanche.
Ⓦ lamachinedumoulinrouge.com.
Next to the fabled Moulin Rouge, this club-live music venue has a concert space hosting international names, plus a basement club-music venue known as *La Chaufferie* and a funky bar with a garden.

New Morning

MAP P.124, POCKET MAP J5
7–9 rue des Petites-Ecuries Ⓜ Château d'Eau. Ⓦ newmorning.com.
One of the most exciting venues in Paris, mixed and buzzing, this is *the* place to catch international names in jazz and world music. It's usually standing room only.

Les Trois Baudets

MAP P.124, POCKET MAP F3
64 bd de Clichy Ⓜ Blanche/Pigalle.
Ⓦ lestroisbaudets.com.
This historic pocket theatre was refitted in 2009, and has found a proud place on the *chanson* scene. Specializes in young, upcoming French performers.

Northeastern Paris

Northeastern Paris, comprising the Canal St-Martin, Belleville, Ménilmontant and La Villette, is one of the most diverse and vibrant parts of the city, home to sizeable ethnic populations as well as students and artists. The area's most popular attractions are Père-Lachaise cemetery, the final resting place of numerous famous artists and writers; the leafy Canal St-Martin, with its trendy cafés and bars; and the vast, postmodern Parc de la Villette. Some of the city's best nightlife is concentrated on rues Oberkampf and Jean-Pierre Timbaud, while two attractive parks, the Buttes-Chaumont and Parc de Belleville, reward visitors with fine views over the city.

Place de la République

MAP P.136, POCKET MAP G13

Ⓦ République.

The **place de la République** (or Répu, as it's affectionately known by locals) is one of the city's largest squares, a paved expanse dotted with benches, trees and fountains. In the middle stands an enormous bronze statue of Marianne, the female symbol of the Republic, holding an olive branch in one hand, and a tablet inscribed with the words *Droits de l'Homme* in the other. By long-standing tradition, rallies and demonstrations often end at the place de la République. It was here in 2015 that huge crowds gathered to protest against the massacres carried out by Islamist extremists. The spirit of resilience shown by Parisians in the aftermath of these attacks is paid tribute to by the café at one end of the square, *Café Fluctuat*, a reference to the city's motto *Fluctuat nec Mergitur* ("it is battered but does not sink"). The café's terrace is the perfect place for people-watching. On the eastern side of the square an open-air "games kiosk", l'R de Jeux (Ⓦ aladressedujeu.fr; days and times vary – see website), offers some six hundred toys and games for both adults and children, including construction kits, scooters and board games, any of which you can borrow for free (bring ID).

Canal St-Martin

MAP P.136, POCKET MAP K4–6

Built in 1825 to enable river traffic to shortcut the great western loop of the Seine around Paris, the **Canal St-Martin** possesses a great deal of charm, especially along its southern reaches: plane trees line the cobbled *quais*, and elegant, high-arched footbridges punctuate the spaces between the locks, from where you can still watch the odd barge slowly rising or sinking to the next level. In the last decade or so the area has been colonized by the new arts and media intelligentsia, bringing in their wake trendy bars, cafés and boutiques. The area is particularly lively on Sundays when the *quais* are closed to traffic; pedestrians, cyclists and rollerbladers take over the streets, and people hang out along the canal's edge.

Rotonde de la Villette

MAP P.136, POCKET MAP K3

Ⓜ Stalingrad/Jaurès.

Ⓦ larotondestalingrad.com.

The Canal St-Martin goes underground at the busy **place de la Bataille de Stalingrad**, dominated by the Neoclassical **Rotonde de la Villette**, a handsome stone rotunda fronted with a portico, inspired by Palladio's Villa La Rotonda in Vicenza. This was one of the toll houses designed by the architect Ledoux as part of Louis XVI's scheme to tax all goods entering the city. At that time, every road out of Paris had a customs post, or *barrière*, linked by a 6m-high wall, known as "Le Mur des Fermiers-Généraux" – a major irritant in the run-up to the Revolution. Cleaned and restored, the *rotonde* is used for exhibitions and has a restaurant and bar (Ⓦ grandmarchestalingrad.com). Backing the toll house is an elegant aerial stretch of métro, supported by Neoclassical iron-and-stone pillars. Note that the area has a dodgy reputation at night, as it's a known haunt of drug dealers.

Canal St-Martin

Bassin de la Villette

MAP P.136, POCKET MAP L3

Ⓜ Stalingrad/Riquet/Laumière.

Beyond the Rotonde de la Villette the canal widens out into the **Bassin de la Villette**, built in 1808. The recobbled docks area bears few traces of its days as France's premier port, its dockside buildings now offering canal boat trips (see page 172) and housing a multiplex cinema, the **MK2** (see page 173), which has screens on both banks, linked by shuttle boat. On Sundays and public holidays people stroll along the *quais*, jog, cycle, play boules, fish or take a rowing boat out in the dock; in August, as part of the **Paris Plages** scheme (see page 177), you can rent canoes and pedaloes and even swim. Continuing regeneration has seen the arrival of new bars, restaurants and the *St Christopher's* hostel (see page 165), housed in a converted boat hangar.

Le 104

MAP P.136, POCKET MAP K2–L2

104 rue d'Aubervilliers Ⓜ Ricquet. Ⓦ 104. fr. Free entry to the main hall.

NORTHEASTERN PARIS

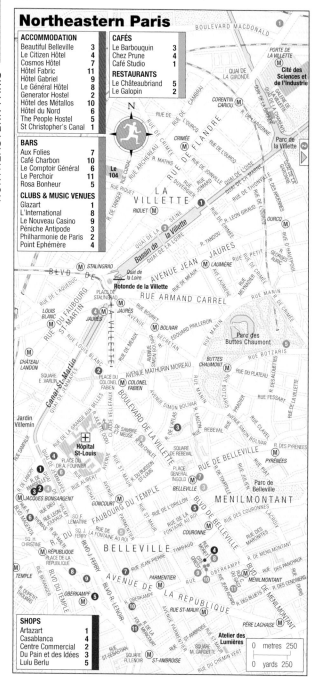

Located in one of the poorest parts of the 19e, in a former grand nineteenth-century funeral parlour, **Le 104** is a huge arts centre, with an impressive glass-roofed central hall (*nef curial*) and numerous artists' studios. It hosts exhibitions and installations, dance and theatre, with an emphasis on the experimental and cutting-edge. The complex also houses a good bookshop, a charity shop, a café and restaurant.

Parc de la Villette

MAP P.136, POCKET MAP M2
Ⓦ Porte-de-Pantin/Porte-de-la-Villette.
Ⓦ lavillette.com. Free.

Built in 1986 on the site of what was once Paris's largest abattoir and meat market, the **Parc de la Villette**'s landscaped grounds include a science museum, the Grande Halle arts centre, the Philharmonie concert hall, a superb music museum, a series of themed gardens and a number of jarring, bright red "follies". The effect of these disparate elements can be quite disorienting – all in line with the creators' aim of eschewing meaning and "deconstructing" the whole into its parts. All very well, but on a practical level you'll probably want to pick up a map at the information centre at the southern entrance to help you make sense of it all.

The extensive park grounds contain twelve themed gardens, aimed mainly at children. In the Jardin des Miroirs, for example, steel monoliths hidden among the trees and scrub cast strange reflections, while, predictably, dune-like shapes, sails and windmills make up the Jardin des Dunes (for under-13s and accompanying adults). Also popular with children is the eighty-metre-long Dragon Slide.

In front of the Cité des Sciences floats the Géode (Ⓦ lageode.fr), a bubble of reflecting steel that

The Géode in Parc de le Villette

looks as though it's been dropped from an intergalactic boules game into a pool of water. Inside is a screen for Omnimax films, not noted for their plots, but a great visual experience.

Cité des Sciences et de l'Industrie

MAP P.136, POCKET MAP M1
Parc de la Villette Ⓦ Porte-de-la-Villette.
Ⓦ cite-sciences.fr. Charge (includes access to planetarium). Planetarium shows hourly and shows take 35min. Cité des Enfants; check online for times of sessions. Charge.

The **Cité des Sciences et de l'Industrie** is one of the world's finest science museums, set in a huge building four times the size of the Centre Pompidou. An excellent programme of temporary exhibitions complements the permanent exhibition, called Explora, covering subjects such as sound, robotics, energy, light, ecology, maths, medicine, space and language. The Cité has a special section for children called the Cité des Enfants, with areas for 2- to 7-year-olds and 5- to

Parc des Buttes-Chaumont

12-year-olds; all children must be accompanied by an adult and a session lasts ninety minutes (book online). Among the engaging activities, children can play with water and construct buildings on a miniature construction site.

Musée de la Musique

POCKET MAP M3
Philharmonie 2, Parc de la Villette Ⓜ Porte-de-Pantin. Ⓦ philharmoniedeparis.fr. Charge; under-26s free.
The **Musée de la Musique** presents the history of music from the end of the Renaissance to the present day, exhibiting some 1,000 instruments and artefacts along with excellent audioguides (available in English, with special ones for children; free), which narrate the history of the instruments, accompanied by extracts of music. Among the exquisite instruments on display are ornately carved theorbos and viol da gambas, a piano that belonged to Chopin, and guitars once played by Jacques Brel and Django Reinhardt.

Pére-Lachaise cemetery

POCKET MAP A20/21–B20/21
Main entrance on bd de Ménilmontant Ⓜ Père-Lachaise/Philippe Auguste. Free.
Final resting place of a host of French and foreign notables, **Père-Lachaise** covers some 116 acres, making it one of the world's largest cemeteries. It's surely also one of the most atmospheric – an eerily beautiful haven, with terraced slopes and magnificent old trees spreading their branches over the moss-grown tombs. Free maps are available at the entrance, but it's worth buying a more detailed one, as some of the graves are tricky to track down; you can buy maps near the main entrance.

Among the most visited graves is that of Chopin (Division 11), often attended by Poles bearing red-and-white wreaths and flowers. Fans also flock to the grave of ex-Doors singer Jim Morrison (Division 6), who died in Paris aged 27.

One of the most impressive of the individual tombs is Oscar Wilde's (Division 89), topped with a sculpture by Jacob Epstein of a mysterious

Pharaonic winged messenger. *Femme fatale* Colette's tomb, close to the main entrance in Division 4, is very plain, though always covered in flowers, while Marcel Proust lies in his family's conventional black marble tomb (Division 85).

On a more sombre note, in Division 97 you'll find memorials to the victims of the Nazi concentration camps and to executed Resistance fighters.

Parc des Buttes-Chaumont

MAP P.136, POCKET MAP L5–M4
Ⓜ Buttes-Chaumont/Botzaris.

The **Parc des Buttes-Chaumont** was constructed under Haussmann in the 1860s to camouflage what until then had been a desolate warren of disused quarries, rubbish dumps and shacks. Out of this rather unlikely setting, a fairytale-like park was created – there's a grotto with a cascade and artificial stalactites, and a picturesque lake from which a huge rock rises up, topped with a delicate Corinthian temple. From the temple you get fine views of the Sacré-Coeur and beyond, and you can also go boating on the lake in summer.

Belleville

MAP P.136, POCKET MAP K6–L6
Ⓜ Belleville/Pyrénées.

Absorbed into Paris in the 1860s and subsequently built up with high-rise blocks to house migrants from rural areas and the ex-colonies, **Belleville** might not exactly be "belle", but it's worth seeing this side of the city. The main street, rue de Belleville, abounds with Vietnamese, Thai and Chinese shops and restaurants, which spill south along boulevard de Belleville and rue du Faubourg-du-Temple. African and Oriental fruits, spices, music and fabrics attract shoppers to the boulevard de Belleville market on Tuesday and Friday mornings. From the Parc de Belleville, with its terraces and waterfalls, you get great views across the city, especially at sunset.

Atelier des Lumieres

MAP P.136, POCKET MAP M7
38 rue Saint Maur Ⓜ Voltaire. Ⓦ atelier-lumieres.com. Charge; book online for entry after 4pm and weekends.

Since its opening in 2018, this digital museum of fine art has drawn widespread acclaim. Set in a former foundry, the centre is run by Culturespaces, an organization that specializes in immersive art displays. The huge walls, pillars and vast spaces are used to great effect, with every inch, including the floor, covered in large-scale projections of artworks. The images are accompanied by music, creating an enthralling multisensory experience. The first exhibition focused on the works of Gustav Klimt; in 2023, subjects include Chagall and Paul Klee.

Atelier des Lumières

Shops

Artazart

MAP P.136, POCKET MAP K5

83 quai de Valmy Ⓜ Jacques-Bonsergent.
Ⓦ artazart.com.

One of the many attractive shops on the Canal St-Martin, this one sells books, magazines and gifts devoted to contemporary graphic art, design and photography, and there are regular book signings, exhibitions and events too.

Casablanca

MAP P.136, POCKET MAP L6

17 rue Moret Ⓜ Ménilmontant.
Ⓦ casablanca-vintage.fr.

Cool vintage store, with lots of Thirties, Forties and mid-century gear and a particularly good line in natty men's suits. A visiting barber offers vintage-style haircuts.

Centre Commercial

MAP P.136, POCKET MAP K6

2 rue de Marseille Ⓜ Jacques-Bonsergent.
Ⓦ centrecommercial.cc.

This pioneering concept store is concerned with the environment and fair trade, stocking ecofriendly French designers such as Valentine Gauthier and Veja, plus a decent selection of lesser-known labels for both men and women.

Du Pain et des Idées

MAP P.136, POCKET MAP K6

34 rue Yves Toudic Ⓜ Jacques-Bonsergent.
Ⓦ dupainetdesidees.com.

This award-winning bakery set in a beautiful old shop creates heavenly baguettes, brioches and the signature *pain des amis*, a nutty flatbread.

Lulu Berlu

MAP P.136, POCKET MAP H14

2 rue Grand Prieuré Ⓜ Oberkampf. ☏ 01 43 55 12 52, Ⓦ lulu-berlu.com.

This shop is crammed with twentieth-century toys and curios, most with their original packaging. There's a particularly good collection of 1970–90s favourites, including *Doctor Who*, *Star Wars*, *Planet of the Apes* and *Batman* pieces, plus a good range of new toys.

Cafés

Le Barbouquin

MAP P.136, POCKET MAP L6

1 rue Denoyez, Ⓜ Belleville. ☏ 09 84 32 13 21.

Sitting on the corner of rue Dénoyez, a backstreet famous for its street art, *Le Barbouquin* is a welcoming bookshop-café where you can pluck one of the secondhand English or French books off the shelf, settle in an armchair and sip a coffee, mint-and-ginger tea or fresh juice; light food includes savoury tarts and wraps.

Chez Prune

MAP P.136, POCKET MAP K5

36 rue Beaurepaire Ⓜ Jacques-Bonsergent.
☏ 01 42 41 30 47.

Named after the owner's grandmother (a bust of whom can be found inside), *Chez Prune* is popular with an artsy crowd and is friendly and laidback, with pleasant outdoor seating overlooking the canal. Lunchtime dishes and evening snacks like platters of cheese or charcuterie.

Café Studio

MAP P.136, POCKET MAP K5

4 rue de Sambre et Meuse Ⓜ Colonel Fabien. Ⓦ cafestudio-paris.com/.

This café-boutique offers light bites, coffees and snacks, along with creative and upcycling workshops covering sewing, drawing and zero-waste vegetable dyeing. It's also a fashion and decoration boutique, a professional photo studio, and a friendly community space for local crafty types and creators.

Restaurants

Le Chateaubriand

MAP P.140, POCKET MAP H13
129 av Parmentier Ⓜ Goncourt.
Ⓦ lechateaubriand.net.

Innovative Basque chef, Inaki Aizpitarte, has helped change the face of the Paris dining scene with this avant-garde *bistrot*, one of the city's finest addresses. The multi-course tasting menu changes daily and is a culinary adventure, featuring the likes of mackerel ceviche with pear sorbet, and oyster soup with red fruits and beetroot. It's extremely good value for what you get. Book a few days in advance. €€€

Le Galopin

MAP P.136, POCKET MAP L5
34 rue Sainte-Marthe Ⓜ Belleville/ Goncourt. Ⓦ le-galopin.paris.fr.

With its pared-down decor of bare brick walls and simple wooden chairs, this neighbourhood place epitomizes the neo-*bistrot* scene, offering a seven-course no-choice dinner menu of small, delicate plates. At lunch there's a three-course set menu and mains might include cauliflower soup with salmon roe, squid with peppers and pork jus or seabass with celery and butternut squash. €€

Bars

Aux Folies

MAP P.136, POCKET MAP L5
8 rue de Belleville Ⓜ Belleville. Ⓦ aux-folies-belleville.fr.

Once a *café-théâtre* where Edith Piaf and Maurice Chevalier sang, *Aux Folies* offers a slice of Belleville life; its outside terrace

Chez Prune

and long brass bar, with mirrored tiles, pinball machine and broken window panes held together with sticking tape, are packed day and night with a cosmopolitan crowd, enjoying beer, cocktails and mint tea.

Café Charbon

MAP P.136, POCKET MAP L6
109 rue Oberkampf Ⓜ Saint-Maur/
Parmentier. Ⓦ lecafecharbon.fr.
The place that pioneered the rise of the Oberkampf bar scene in the mid-90s is still going strong and continues to draw in a fashionable crowd. Part of its allure is the attractively restored belle époque decor, with comfy booths and dangling lights. The three-hour happy hour helps, too.

Le Comptoir Géneral

MAP P.136, POCKET MAP K5
80 quai de Jemmapes Ⓜ Goncourt/
République. Ⓦ lecomptoirgeneral.com.
Tucked away like a secret off the Canal St-Martin, this is a super-cool bar with an exotic atmosphere and a quirky decor of chandeliers, red carpets, tropical plants and little nooks

full of African souvenirs and vintage objects. The great cocktails, friendly staff and impeccably cool playlist – from The Velvet Underground to soukous – keeps the lively, mixed crowd happy. Donation for entry requested.

Le Perchoir

MAP P.136, POCKET MAP M7
14 rue Crespin du Gast Ⓜ Ménilmontant.
Ⓦ leperchoir.fr.
The drinks may be pricey for the neighbourhood and you may have to queue to get in, but this popular seventh-floor cocktail bar has real pulling power – in summer you can languish on the huge rooftop terrace, enjoying amazing city views.

Rosa Bonheur

MAP P.136, POCKET MAP M4
Parc des Buttes-Chaumont, 2 av des Cascades Ⓜ Botzaris/Jourdain.
Ⓦ rosabonheur.fr.
Tucked away in the Parc des Buttes-Chaumont, the pretty Rosa Bonheur is set inside a former guinguette – an open-air café or dance hall. A very mixed crowd

Café Charbon

of Parisians of all ages comes to drink, dance and nibble on tapas here in a relaxed setting amid the birds and the trees. It gets packed in summer. Entrance to the park after closing is exclusively via 7 rue Botzaris.

Clubs

Glazart

MAP P.136, POCKET MAP M1
7–15 av de la Porte de la Villette ⓦ Porte de la Villette. ⓦ glazart.com.

An alternative-leaning venue, serious about its music, with live acts and DJ sets from punk to jungle. It's a trek from the city centre to get there, but it's comfortably spacious and in summer (June–Sept) there's a glorious outdoor "beach".

Le Nouveau Casino

MAP P.136, POCKET MAP L6
109 rue Oberkampf ⓦ Parmentier.
ⓦ nouveaucasino.fr.

Right behind *Café Charbon* (see page 142) lies this excellent venue. An experimental line-up of gigs earlier on makes way for a relaxed, dancey crowd later on, with music ranging from electro-pop or house to rock.

Music venues

L'International

MAP P.136, POCKET MAP L6
5 rue Moret ⓦ Ménilmontant.
ⓦ linternational.fr.

With two stages and at least two free gigs a night, this friendly *café-concert* is a staple on the Oberkampf scene, showcasing the best new, indie and edgy acts – mostly French, but not exclusively – in all genres, from rap to electro.

Péniche Antipode

MAP P.136, POCKET MAP L3
55 quai de La Seine ⓦ Riquet.

ⓦ penicheantipode.fr.
This popular venue, a barge moored on the Bassin de la Villette, puts on a lively programme of music (as well as a roster of plays, comedy nights and much else), including gypsy jazz, rock, reggae and chanson. It's also a lovely, inexpensive place to come for a drink or a meal. Nearby *Péniche Anako* (ⓦ penicheanako.org) is also worth checking out for its world music gigs.

Philharmonie de Paris

MAP P.136, POCKET MAP M2
221 av Jean-Jaurès ⓦ Porte-de-Pantin.
ⓦ philharmoniedeparis.fr.

Opened in 2015 and designed by Jean Nouvel, this state-of-the-art concert hall, seating up to 2,400, is a massive grey building with a ramp that zigzags its way up the facade and gives access to the panoramic rooftop. If the exterior is rather austere and angular, the interior is creamy-warm and soft, with curved balconies dipping down towards the stage. The acoustics are excellent and you never feel far away from the action, even when seated on the top level. The Orchestre de Paris and the Ensemble InterContemporain have taken up residence here with an exciting programme of music-making.

Point Ephémère

MAP P.136, POCKET MAP K4
200 quai de Valmy ⓦ Jaurès/Louis Blanc.
ⓦ pointephemere.org.

A great, energetic atmosphere pervades this creative space for music, dance and visual arts, set in a former canal boathouse. Bands play rock, indie, jazz and more, while the rotating art exhibitions run from the quotidian to the abstract. In the warmer months you can take your drinks outside and sit on the banks of the canal.

The Bois de Boulogne and western Paris

The Bois de Boulogne, with its trees, lakes, cycling trails and beautiful floral displays, is a favourite Parisian retreat from the city. It runs all the way down the west side of the well-manicured 16e arrondissement. The area is mainly residential with few specific sights, the chief exceptions being the Musée Marmottan with its dazzling collection of late Monets, and the spectacular Fondation Louis Vuitton contemporary art centre. The most rewarding areas for exploration are the old villages of Auteuil and Passy, which were incorporated into the city in the late nineteenth century. They soon became desirable districts, and well-to-do Parisians commissioned houses here. As a result, the area is rich in fine examples of architecture, notably by Hector Guimard and Le Corbusier. Further west bristle the gleaming skyscrapers of the purpose-built commercial district of La Défense, dominated by the enormous Grande Arche.

Bois de Boulogne

MAP P.146, POCKET MAP A5
Ⓜ Porte Maillot/Porte Dauphine.

The **Bois de Boulogne** was designed by Baron Haussmann and supposedly modelled on London's Hyde Park – though it's a very French interpretation. The "bois" of the name is somewhat deceptive, but the extensive parklands (just under nine square kilometres) do contain some remnants of the once great Forêt de Rouvray. As its location would suggest, the Bois was once the playground of the wealthy. It also gained a reputation as the site of the sex trade and its associated crime; the same holds true today and you should avoid it at night. By day, however, the park is an extremely pleasant spot for a stroll. The best, and wildest, part for walking is towards the southwest corner. Bikes are available for rent at the entrance to

the Jardin d'Acclimatation and you can go boating on the Lac Inférieur.

Parc de Bagatelle

MAP P.146
Bois de Boulogne Ⓜ Porte Maillot.

The **Parc de Bagatelle**, within the Bois de Boulogne, comprises a range of garden styles from French and English to Japanese. Its most famous feature is the stunning rose garden, at its best in June, while in other parts of the garden there are beautiful displays of tulips, hyacinths and daffodils in early April, irises in May, and waterlilies in early August. In June and July the park's orangery is the attractive setting for the prestigious Chopin Festival (Ⓦ frederic-chopin.com).

The Jardin d'Acclimatation

MAP P.146
Bois de Boulogne Ⓜ Porte Maillot.
Ⓦ jardindacclimatation.fr. Charge; see website for day pass and other deals.

The children's **Jardin d'Acclimatation**, which was given a major revamp in 2018, is an action-packed funfair, zoo and amusement park all rolled into one. The fun starts at the Porte-Maillot métro stop: a little train runs from here to the jardin (roughly every 15min). The park's many attractions include bumper cars, donkey rides, sea lions, bears and monkeys, a huge trampoline and a magical mini canal ride (*la rivière enchantée*).

Fondation Louis Vuitton

MAP P.146

Av du Mahatma Gandhi Ⓜ Porte Maillot/ Les Sablons. Ⓦ fondationlouisvuitton. fr. Charge (includes access to the Jardin d'Acclimatation).

The Frank Gehry-designed contemporary art centre, the **Fondation Louis Vuitton**, opened inside the Jardin d'Acclimatation a decade ago. Designed to house the collection of the richest man in France, Bernard Arnault, Gehry's huge, dramatic structure, dubbed "the cloud of glass", comprises twelve glass "sails" made up of 3,600 glass panels and sits surrounded by a moat of water. Evoking a ship buffeted by the wind (or possibly a giant insect), the glass sails jut out at odd angles, revealing the dazzling white inner walls.

Inside, escalators take you down to the moat level (or "grotto") with its striking Olafur Eliasson installation of coloured glass, mirror and sound, while stairways spiral up to roof terraces revealing unexpected vistas of the Eiffel Tower and La Défense. There are eleven galleries, an auditorium, a restaurant and a shop. The permanent collection, shown in themed exhibitions, includes choice works by Rothko, Jeff Koons, Takashi Murakami, Richard Serra and Jean-Michel Basquiat. Temporary exhibitions include the likes of Warhol and Basquat. A shuttle bus runs to the Fondation (every 20min) from avenue Friedland, just off place Charles de Gaulle.

Villa La Roche

POCKET MAP A7

Square du Dr-Blanche Ⓜ Jasmin. Ⓦ fondationlecorbusier.fr. Charge.

Jardin d'Acclimatation

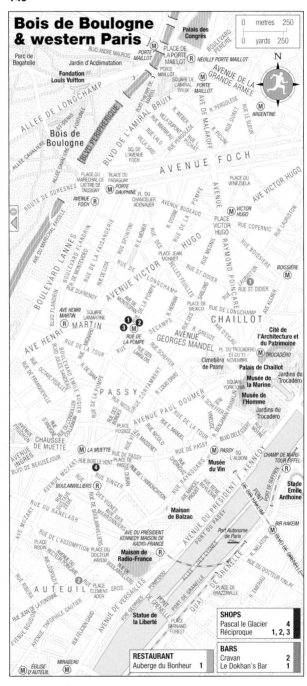

Bois de Boulogne & western Paris

Fondation Louis Vuitton

Le Corbusier's first private houses, dating to 1923, were the adjoining Villa Jeanneret and the **Villa La Roche**. The latter is in strictly cubist style, with windows in bands, the only extravagance being a curved frontage. It may look commonplace now from the outside, but at the time it was built it was in great contrast to anything that had gone before. The interior is appropriately decorated with Cubist paintings.

Maison de Balzac

MAP P.146

47 rue Raynouard Ⓜ Passy.
Ⓦ maisondebalzac.paris.fr. Free.
The **Maison de Balzac** is a summery little house with pale green shutters, tucked away down some steps that lead through a shady, rose-filled garden – a delightful place to dally on wrought-iron seats, surrounded by busts of the writer. Balzac wrote some of his best-known works here, including *La Cousine Bette* and *Le Cousin Pons*. The museum preserves his study, while other exhibits include a complex family tree of around a thousand of

the characters that feature in his *Comédie Humaine*. A new garden café should be open by the time you read this.

Auteuil

MAP P.146

Ⓜ Michel-Ange-Auteuil.
The **Auteuil** district has become an integral part of the city, and yet even now the atmosphere in its streets is decidedly village-like. You'll find a number of attractive *villas* (leafy lanes of old houses) in these parts, fronted with English-style gardens, not to mention some fine Art Nouveau buildings by Hector Guimard – there's a concentration on rue de la Fontaine, such as Castel Béranger at no. 14, with exuberant decoration and shapes in the windows, roofline and chimney.

Musée Marmottan

POCKET MAP A7

2 rue Louis-Boilly Ⓜ Muette. Ⓦ marmottan. fr. Charge.
The **Musée Marmottan** is best known for its excellent collection of Monet paintings. One of the highlights is *Impression, soleil levant*,

Grande Arche de la Défense

a canvas from 1872 of a misty Le Havre morning, and whose title the critics usurped to give the Impressionist movement its name. There's also a selection of works from Monet's last years at Giverny, including several *Nymphéas* (Waterlilies) and *Le Pont Japonais*. The collection also features some of his contemporaries – Manet, Renoir and Berthe Morisot – and a room full of beautiful medieval illuminated manuscripts.

La Défense

POCKET MAP A4
Ⓜ RER Grande-Arche-de-la-Défense/ Esplanade de la Défense.

An impressive complex of gleaming skyscrapers, **La Défense** is Paris's prestige business district. Its most popular attraction is the huge Grande Arche. Apartment blocks and big businesses loom between the arch and the river, while avant-garde sculptures by artists such as Joan Miró relieve the jungle of concrete and glass. Landmark buildings include the sleek Tour EDF, the Tour Majunga, with its radically "flowing" effect, and the Tour First, which, at

231m, is France's tallest skyscraper. The Cité de l'Histoire opened in 2023 (Ⓦ cite-histoire.com), a museum in which great events of the past and historical figures are revealed through shows, immersive experiences and the latest technology.

Grande Arche de la Défense

POCKET MAP A4
Ⓜ RER Grande-Arche-de-la-Défense. Ⓦ lagrandearche.fr. Charge.

The **Grande Arche de la Défense**, built in 1989 for the bicentenary of the Revolution, is an astounding 112-metre-high structure clad in white marble. Standing 6km out and at a slight angle from the Arc de Triomphe, it completes the western axis of this monumental east–west vista. There are excellent views of the city from the steps that lead up to the base of the arch and also from the roof, which is reached via a glass elevator. For the most dramatic approach to the arch get off the métro a stop early at Esplanade-de-la-Défense, and walk along Esplanade de Général de Gaulle.

Shops

Pascal le Glacier

MAP P.146, POCKET MAP A8

17 rue Bois-le-Vent Ⓜ Muette. ☎ 01 45 27 61 85.

Exquisite home-made sorbets – as well as delicious ice creams – made with Evian water and fresh fruits, in more than fifty seasonal flavours, such as sanguino orange, mango, white peach, raspberry, pear, and even rhubarb.

Réciproque

MAP P.146, POCKET MAP A7

89, 92, 93–97, 101 rue de la Pompe Ⓜ Pompe. ☎ 01 47 04 30 28.

Specialists in secondhand haute couture, with labels such as Christian Lacroix, Moschino and Manolo Blahnik. Women's design at nos. 93–95 and 101; suits, coats and accessories for men at no. 92; gifts and jewellery at no. 89.

Restaurant

Auberge du Bonheur

MAP P.146, POCKET MAP A5

All. de Longchamp Ⓜ Porte Maillot/Porte Dauphine. Ⓦ restaurantsparisiens.com/auberge-du-bonheur.

An oasis of calm in the capital, the *Auberge* has wonderful terraces and gardens for summer dining and then, in winter, the red-brick, heavily beamed building provides cosy respite from the weather. The food is traditional French cuisine with influences from the Thai chef who has made Paris her home. €€

Bars

Cravan

MAP P.146, POCKET MAP A8

17 rue Jean de la Fontaine Ⓜ Jasmin. ☎ 01 40 50 14 30.

Cocktails are the order of the day at this handsome café-bar, with its *belle époque* decor of mirrors and tiles. It's good for a light lunch (think croque monsieur, delicate finger sandwiches and grilled aubergine) or evening drinks on the *terrasse*.

Le Dokhan's Bar

MAP P.146, POCKET MAP A6

117 Rue Lauriston Ⓜ Boissiere. Ⓦ hotelledokhansparis.com.

An elegant wood-panelled champagne bar set within the *Dokhan's Hotel*. Sink into a velvet armchair and choose from over 200 champagnes. Live jazz once a week.

Réciproque

Day-trips

Even if you're on a weekend break, one or two major sights may tempt you beyond the city limits. It's worth making an effort to get out to the Château de Versailles, the ultimate French royal palace, awesome in its size and magnificence and boasting exquisite gardens that are free to visit. Also enchanting is the Château of Chantilly, with its gorgeous setting and wonderful art collection, while a trip to Monet's beautiful gardens at Giverny is equally enticing.

Versailles

Twenty kilometres southwest of Paris, the royal town of **Versailles** is renowned for Louis XIV's extraordinary **Château de Versailles**. With 700 rooms, 67 staircases and 352 fireplaces alone, Versailles is, without doubt, the apotheosis of French regal indulgence. It's not advisable, or indeed possible, to see the whole behemoth in one day – if you can, avoid the unbearable morning crowds by heading for the grounds and Marie Antoinette's estate first, moving

Château de Versailles

on to the palace proper in the relative peace of late afternoon.

Château de Versailles

🕿 01 30 83 78 00, ⓦ chateauversailles.fr. Tues–Sun: April–Oct 9am–6.30pm; Nov–March 9am–5.30pm.

Driven by envy of his finance minister's château at Vaux-le-Vicomte, the young Louis XIV recruited the same design team – architect Le Vau, painter Le Brun and gardener Le Nôtre – to create a **palace** a hundred times bigger. Construction began in 1664 and lasted virtually until Louis XIV's death in 1715. Second only to God, and the head of an immensely powerful state, Louis was an institution rather than a private individual. His risings and sittings, comings and goings, were minutely regulated and rigidly encased in ceremony, attendance at which was an honour much sought after by courtiers. Versailles was the headquarters of every arm of the state, and the entire court of around 3,500 nobles lived in the palace (in a state of squalor, according to contemporary accounts).

Following the king's death, the château was abandoned for a few years before being reoccupied by Louis XV in 1722. It remained a residence of the royal family until the Revolution of 1789, when

Versailles practicalities

To **get to Versailles**, take the RER line C5 from Champs de Mars or another Left Bank station to Versailles-Rive Gauche; it's a thirty-minute journey, and the palace is less than ten minutes' walk from the station.

Tickets for the **château** include an audioguide, and admission to the Domaine de Trianon is extra. Queues can be nightmarish, so by far the best option is to buy online; there's a price comparison table at ⓦ chateauversailles.fr so you can evaluate the best ticket for you. You can also buy tickets at the tourist office at Versailles (on the way to the palace). Ticket holders walk straight in through the gate marked "A".

Guided tours (charge), many of which are expertly conducted in English, take you into some of the wings and private apartments that you don't otherwise get to see. You can book online or just turn up on the day, but arrive early to guarantee a place; they're well worth it.

the furniture was sold and the pictures dispatched to the Louvre. Thereafter, Versailles fell into ruin until Louis-Philippe established his giant museum of French Glory here – it still exists, though most is mothballed. In 1871, during the Paris Commune, the château became the seat of the nationalist government, and the French parliament continued to meet in Louis XV's opera building until 1879.

Without a guide you can visit the **State Apartments**, used for the king's official business. A procession of gilded drawing rooms leads to the dazzling **Galerie des Glaces** (Hall of Mirrors), where the Treaty of Versailles was signed after World War I. More fabulously rich rooms, this time belonging to the **queen's apartments**, line the northern wing – beginning with the queen's bedchamber, which has been restored exactly as it was in its last refit of 1787 with hardly a surface free from gold leaf or pretty floral decoration.

In 2023, to celebrate the palace's 400th anniversary, Marie-Antoinette's private rooms have opened to the public. Expect two floors of private rooms which overlook an interior courtyard and include her boudoir, library and billiard room.

Domaine de Trianon

Hidden away in the northern reaches of the park is the **Domaine de Trianon**, Marie-Antoinette's country retreat, where she found relief from the stifling etiquette of the court. Here she commissioned some dozen or so buildings, sparing no expense and imposing her own style and tastes throughout (and gaining herself a reputation for extravagance that did her no favours).

The centrepiece is the elegant Neoclassical **Petit Trianon** palace, built by Gabriel in the 1760s for Louis XV's mistress, Mme de Pompadour, and given to Marie-Antoinette by her husband Louis XVI as a wedding gift. The airy, sunlit interior provides a lovely contrast to the stuffy pomp of the Versailles palace proper, and boasts an intriguing *cabinet des glaces montantes*, a pale-blue salon fitted with sliding mirrors that could be moved to conceal the windows, creating a more intimate space. West of the palace, in the formal Jardin français, is the Queen's Theatre where Marie-Antoinette would regularly perform, often as a maid or shepherdess, before the king and members of her inner circle.

On the other side of the palace lies the bucolic **Jardin anglais**, with its little winding stream, grassy banks and artificial grotto, and the enchanting, if bizarre, **Hameau de la Reine**, an olde-worlde play village and farm (now restocked with real animals) where the queen indulged her fashionable Rousseau-inspired fantasy of returning to the "natural" life.

The Italianate **Grand Trianon** palace, designed by Hardouin-Mansart in 1687 as a country retreat for Louis XIV, was refurbished in Empire style by Napoleon, who stayed here intermittently between 1805 and 1813.

Versailles Park & garden

You could spend a whole day exploring the lovely **park** (free, except when *spectacles* are on), with its symmetrical gardens, grand vistas, statuary, fountains and pools; trails of varying length are detailed on notice boards. Take a picnic, or stop at one of the tearooms, cafés or more formal restaurants dotted around the grounds. Baroque music is played in the garden (charge), and on weekends the fountains dance to the music (charge; Ⓦ chateauversailles-spectacles.fr).

Distances in the park are considerable. A *petit train* shuttles between the terrace in front of the château and the Trianons charge; every 10–20min). You could also rent a buggy (driving licence needed), a bike or a rowing boat.

Chantilly

People mostly visit **Chantilly**, a small town 40km north of Paris,

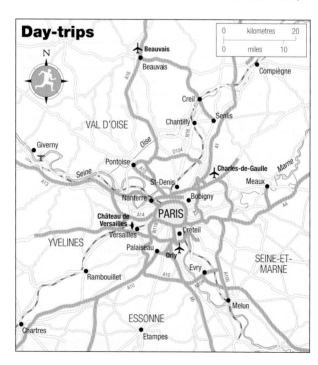

Day-trips

Beauvais · Beauvais · Compiègne · Creil · Chantilly · Senlis · VAL D'OISE · Giverny · Oise · Pontoise · Seine · St-Denis · Charles-de-Gaulle · Marne · Meaux · Nanterre · Bobigny · PARIS · Château de Versailles · Créteil · Versailles · YVELINES · Palaiseau · Orly · SEINE-ET-MARNE · Rambouillet · Evry · ESSONNE · Melun · Chartres · Etampes

0 kilometres 20

0 miles 10

to watch horses race and to see Italian art in the romantic château. The horses are hard to miss: scores of thoroughbreds can be seen thundering along the forest rides of a morning, and two of the season's classiest flat races are held here – the Jockey Club and the Prix de Diane.

Château de Chantilly

Ⓦ chateaudechantilly.fr. Charge for château, grounds, horse museum & horse show – see online for options.

Dating mostly from the late nineteenth century, the **Château de Chantilly** replaced a palace destroyed in the Revolution, which had been built for the Grand Condé, Louis XIV's famous general. It's a beautiful structure, surrounded by what's more a lake than a moat, looking out over formal gardens. Inside, in the **Musée Condé**, is a superb collection of Classical art, featuring works by Botticelli, Piero di Cosimo, Raphael, Delacroix, Poussin and Van Dyck.

Don't miss the **Cabinet des Livres**, which displays a perfect facsimile of the fabulous *Les Très Riches Heures du Duc de Berry*, the most celebrated of all the medieval Books of Hours, and the museum's single greatest treasure. The illuminated pages illustrating the months of the year with representative scenes from contemporary (early 1400s) rural life – such as harvesting and ploughing – are richly coloured and drawn.

You can also visit the **private apartments** of the Princes de Condé, with their superb furnishings and exquisite wood panelling, and take a separate guided tour (€3) of the apartments of the Petit Château, which belonged to the château's last private owners, the Duc and Duchess d'Aumale.

Just down the drive from the château is the colossal eighteenth-century stable block (Grandes Ecuries) housing the **Musée du Cheval**, which boasts fifteen rooms and more than two hundred objects and artworks devoted to the horse and its history. Check the website for the regular equestrian shows.

Trains run from the Gare du Nord to Chantilly every hour or so (25min). There are free buses to the town centre (DUC bus) from Chantilly station; get off by the Grandes Ecuries and walk 500m to the château gates. Alternatively, it's a 20min walk along a signposted path; turn right outside the station, then left along the avenue des Aigles.

Monet's gardens at Giverny

84 rue Claude Monet Ⓦ fondation-monet.com. Charge.

Claude Monet's gardens are in **Giverny**, Normandy – 65km from Paris, but well worth the trip. Monet lived in Giverny from 1883 till his death in 1926, painting and repainting the effects of the changing seasonal light on the gardens he laid out between his house and the river. Every month from spring to autumn has its own appeal, but May and June, when the rhododendrons flower round the lily pond and the wisteria bursts into colour over the famous Japanese bridge, are the prettiest months to visit.

Monet's house stands at the top of the gardens, an idyllic pastel-pink building with green shutters. Inside, the rooms are all painted different colours, exactly as they were when Monet lived here, and the painter's original collection of Japanese prints, including wonderful works by Hokusai and Hiroshige, still hangs on the walls.

Trains run to Vernon from Paris-St-Lazare (4–5 daily; 45min), from where there's a bus to Giverny (buses usually depart 15min after train arrival), or take a taxi, rent a bicycle or walk (7km).

ACCOMMODATION

Hôtel Pavillon de la Reine

Accommodation

Paris is extremely well supplied with hotels. The ones reviewed here are all classics, places that offer something special – a great location, unusually elegant décor, or a warm welcome. The grandest establishments are mostly found in the Champs-Elysées area, while the trendy Marais quarter is a good bet for something elegant but relatively relaxed. You'll find more homely, old-fashioned hotels around the Quartier Latin, St-Germain and the Eiffel Tower quarter. Most hotels offer two categories of room: at the bottom end of the scale this means choosing between an en-suite bathroom or shared facilities, while more expensive places may charge a premium rate for larger or more luxurious rooms. Prices aren't exorbitant, by European standards, but then rooms can be surprisingly small for the money. Many hotels offer lower rates than those publicly advertised; the reviews below show the lowest rate you're likely to get for a double room. Continental breakfast is normally an extra €7 to €14 per person.

The Islands

HÔTEL DU JEU DE PAUME MAP P.26, POCKET MAP F17. 54 rue St-Louis-en-l'Ile ⓦ Pont-Marie. ⓦ jeudepaumehotel.com. This quiet, charming boutique hotel occupies the site of a tennis court built for Louis XIII in 1634 ("jeu de paume" is "real tennis"). The wood-beam court is now a breakfast room, from which a glass lift whisks you up to the 28 rooms, decorated in contemporary style. €€

HÔTEL DE LUTECE MAP P.26, POCKET MAP E17. 65 rue St-Louis-en-l'Ile ⓦ Pont-Marie. ⓦ paris-hotel-lutece.com. This slender seventeenth-century townhouse, located on the most desirable island in France, has a cosy old-world charm and is run by helpful and friendly staff. The rooms are small, but comfy and characterful, with wood beams and fresh contemporary decor in shades of terracotta and cream. €

The Champs-Elysées and Tuileries

HÔTEL D'ALBION MAP P.36, POCKET MAP E5. 15 rue de Penthièvre ⓦ Miromesnil.

Booking accommodation

It's wise to reserve your accommodation as early as possible. All receptionists speak some English – but it's worth bearing in mind that most places offer online booking as well. If you book by phone you may be asked for just a credit card number, or sometimes for written or faxed confirmation. The tourist office can make bookings for you for free – either in person at one of their offices (see page 176 for addresses) or online at ⓦ parisinfo.com; many hotels on the site offer discounted rates.

Accommodation price codes

Throughout this guide we have given a price code to each accommodation review. The codes are for the lowest rack rate price for a standard double/twin room during high season. Single rooms, where available, usually cost between 60 and 80 percent of a double or twin, though many hotels do not offer discounts for single occupancy of double or triple-bed rooms. Prices in most hotels will include breakfast; private rooms and apartments will not.

€	under €100
€€	€100-150
€€€	€150-200

Ⓦ **hotelalbion.net.** This small, family-run hotel occupies a nineteenth-century townhouse set around a quiet courtyard garden. Just a 10min walk from the Champs-Elysées, it represents excellent value for the area. Most of the vibrantly decorated rooms have a view over the garden. **€**

HÔTEL ARIOSO MAP P.36, POCKET MAP E5. 7 rue d'Argenson Ⓜ Miromesnil., Ⓦ **hotelarioso.com.** About a 15min walk from the Champs-Elysées, this is a charming little hotel set in a solid Haussmann-era block, run by courteous and helpful staff. The 28 rooms are small, especially the cheaper ones, and some pick up a bit of street noise, but all are cosily decorated with quality furnishings and decorative fabrics. Some of the more expensive rooms have jasmine-strewn balconies looking onto a pretty little tiled interior courtyard. **€€**

HÔTEL LE BRISTOL MAP P.36, POCKET MAP D5. 112 rue du Faubourg St-Honoré Ⓜ Miromesnil. Ⓦ **oetkercollection.com.** Among the city's most iconic hotels, *Le Bristol* opened in 1925 and has maintained its reputation for discreet, warm luxury with superb service. The 188-odd rooms, all very spacious, come with authentic antiques – including Gobelins tapestries – and the most expensive have private roof gardens. There's also a spa, swimming pool and three gourmet restaurants to choose from. **€€€**

HÔTEL EKTA MAP P.36, POCKET MAP C5. 52 rue Galilée Ⓜ George-V. Ⓦ **hotelekta. com.** On a quiet side street, just off the Champs Élysées, a former office block houses this stylish hotel. A mirrored staircase takes you up to the striking reception and 25 rooms, sporting a decor of graphic black-and-white checks and zigzags with a shot of yellow, inspired by 60s and 70s fashion design. The rooms range from the small "Classic" to the larger balconied rooms on the top floor; all have phone chargers and Nespresso machines. **€**

HÔTEL LANCASTER MAP P.36, POCKET MAP C5. 7 rue de Berri Ⓜ George V. Ⓦ **hotel-lancaster.com.** Once the *pied-à-terre* for old-world celebs such as Greta Garbo and Marlene Dietrich, this elegantly restored nineteenth-century townhouse is still a favourite hideout for those fleeing the paparazzi. Rooms retain original features and are resplendent with Louis XVI and Rococo antiques, but with a touch of contemporary chic thrown in too. There's also a superlative restaurant and zen-style interior garden. **€€€**

LE PAVILLON DES LETTRES MAP P.36, POCKET MAP A13. 12 rue des Saussaies Ⓜ Champs-Élysées Clémenceau. Ⓦ **pavillondeslettres. com.** On a quiet road, yet very centrally located, this is an elegant, well-run four-star boutique hotel with a literary theme. Each of the 26 rooms is dedicated to a writer, from Andersen (Hans Christian) to Zola (Emile), with literary quotations decorating the walls; they're pretty small, but comfy and nicely furnished in soothing colours, with bigger-than-average bathrooms. **€€**

Eiffel Tower area

HÔTEL DU CHAMPS-DE-MARS MAP P.44, POCKET MAP C8. 7 rue du Champs-de-Mars Ⓜ École-Militaire. Ⓦ hotelduchampdemars.com. A well-run hotel with cosy, colourful and excellent-value rooms. The location – a nice neighbourhood lying just off the lively rue Cler market – is terrific. €

HÔTEL DU PALAIS BOURBON MAP P.44, POCKET MAP E8. 49 rue de Bourgogne Ⓜ Varenne. Ⓦ bourbon-paris-hotel.com. This handsome old building on a quiet street in the hushed, posh district near the Musée Rodin offers spacious, prettily furnished rooms, with plenty of period detail. Homely family rooms are also available. Breakfast is included in the price. €

The Grands Boulevards and passages

HÔTEL BRIGHTON MAP P.54, POCKET MAP A14. 218 rue de Rivoli Ⓜ Tuileries. Ⓦ paris-hotel-brighton.com. An elegant hotel dating back to the late nineteenth century. The "classic" rooms with internal views are fine, but the "superior" rooms are far preferable, particularly those that offer magnificent views down over the Tuileries gardens. €€

HÔTEL CHOPIN MAP P.54, POCKET MAP G5. 46 passage Jouffroy, entrance on bd Montmartre, near rue du Faubourg-Montmartre Ⓜ Grands-Boulevards. Ⓦ hotelchopin-paris-opera.com. A charming, quiet hotel set in an atmospheric period building hidden away at the end of a picturesque 1850s *passage*. Rooms are pleasantly furnished, though the cheaper ones are on the small side and a little dark. €

HÔTEL EDGAR MAP P.54, POCKET MAP A13. 31 rue d'Alexandrie Ⓜ Sentier. ⓣ Ⓦ edgaretachille.com. It doesn't get much more designer than this, with twelve small rooms conceived by artists, stylists and other creatives. It's all presented with great *joie de vivre*, and whether you want the soft greys of "Cocoon", the boudoir chic of "Ma Nuit" or the kooky-kiddy kitsch of "Dream", you'll find a niche. It's not all style over substance, either – the staff are friendly, rooms are comfy, with good bathrooms, and it's on a small, quiet square. It also has its own bar-restaurant, specializing in seafood. €

HÔTEL DES GRANDS BOULEVARDS MAP P.54, POCKET MAP A13. 17 blvd Poissonnière Ⓜ Grands Boulevards. Ⓦ grandsboulevardshotel.com. This four-star "lifestyle" hotel, opened in 2018, is set in a French Revolution-era building and has been given a glamorous makeover by celebrity designer Dorothée Meilichzon. The smallish rooms are decorated in muted colours, with many looking out onto the attractive courtyard. All have luxury canopy beds, coffee machines and mirror TVs. There's a restaurant in the courtyard, with retractable glass roof for summer dining, and two very cool bars, one on the roof. €€

HÔTEL MANSART MAP P.54, POCKET MAP A13. 5 rue des Capucines Ⓜ Opéra/Madeleine. Ⓦ paris-hotel-mansart.com. This gracious hotel is just a stone's throw from the *Ritz*, but offers rooms that are a fraction of the price; and while they're not quite in the luxury bracket, they're very agreeably decorated in Louis XIV style. It's worth asking to see a few rooms, as three in the standard class have balconies and some have huge bathrooms. The more expensive rooms look out onto place Vendôme. €€

HOTEL LE RELAIS ST HONORÉ MAP P.54, POCKET MAP B14. 308 rue St- Honoré Ⓜ Tuileries., Ⓦ hotel-relais-saint-honore.com. A snug little hotel run by friendly and obliging staff, and set in a stylishly renovated seventeenth-century townhouse. The pretty wood-beamed rooms are done out in warm colours and rich fabrics. Some have mezzanine areas and there's a suite suitable for families. €€

HÔTEL THERESE MAP P.54, POCKET MAP B14 5–7 Rue Thérèse Ⓜ Palais Royal-Musée du Louvre. Ⓦ hoteltherese.com. A very attractive boutique hotel, on a quiet street within easy walking distance of the Louvre. It offers more expensive "traditional" rooms, pared-down and stylish with dark wood fittings, and "classic" rooms, which are smaller but good value. Book in advance as it's very popular. €€

Beaubourg and Les Halles

HÔTEL DE ROUBAIX MAP P.64, POCKET MAP F16. 6 rue de Greneta Ⓜ Hôtel-de-Ville. ⓦ hdroubaix.fr. This family-run budget hotel has been around for years (and started to look like it), but it's been given a complete lift with a bright new refurb: vintage furniture and chandeliers are still dotted around the 53 small rooms, but the overall look is contemporary with a quirky touch lent by comic-book art on the walls. The staff are very welcoming and the location is pretty quiet, yet close to all the Marais action and the Pompidou Centre. €

HÔTEL TIQUETONNE MAP P.64, POCKET MAP B14. 6 rue Tiquetonne Ⓜ Etienne-Marcel. ⓦ hoteltiquetonne.fr. Located on a pedestrianized street a block away from lively rue Montorgueil, this excellent-value budget hotel in a 1920s building offers old-fashioned charm. Rooms have retro furnishings and are clean and well maintained: many are quite spacious, with larger-than-average bathrooms, though walls are thin. Non-en-suite rooms come with a sink and bidet, with use of a shower on the landing; but en-suites are available too. €

RELAIS DU LOUVRE MAP P.64, POCKET MAP C15. 19 rue des Prêtres St-Germain l'Auxerrois Ⓜ Palais Royal–Musée du Louvre. ⓦ relaisdulouvre.com. This discreet hotel is set on a quiet backstreet opposite the church of St-Germain l'Auxerrois. The decor is traditional, with rich fabrics, Turkish rugs and reassuringly solid furniture. The hotel's relaxed atmosphere and charming service attract a clientele who come back every year. €€

The Marais

HÔTEL DU BOURG TIBOURG MAP P.70, POCKET MAP F16. 19 rue du Bourg-Tibourg Ⓜ Hôtel-de-Ville. ⓦ bourgtibourg.com. Oriental meets medieval, with a dash of Second Empire, at this sumptuously designed, and perennially fashionable, boutique hotel. Tiny rooms are packed with

rich velvets, silks and drapes. The hotel makes a perfect romantic hideaway. €€€

HÔTEL DE LA BRETONNERIE MAP P.70, POCKET MAP F16. 22 rue Ste-Croix de la Bretonnerie Ⓜ Hôtel-de-Ville. ⓦ hotelparismaraisbretonnerie.com. A charming place on a lively Marais street; the rooms are decorated with quality fabrics, oak furniture, and, in some cases, four-poster beds. The beamed attic rooms on the fourth floor are particularly appealing. Front-facing rooms may suffer from street noise at night. €

HÔTEL CARON DE BEAUMARCHAIS MAP P.70, POCKET MAP F16. 12 rue Vieille-du-Temple Ⓜ Hôtel-de-Ville. ⓦ carondebeaumarchais.com. Named after the eighteenth-century French playwright Beaumarchais, this pretty hotel has only nineteen rooms. Everything – down to the original engravings and Louis XVI-style furniture, not to mention the pianoforte in the foyer – evokes the refined tastes of high-society pre-Revolutionary Paris. Rooms overlooking the courtyard are small but cosy while those on the street are more spacious, some with balconies, others with chandeliers. €

HÔTEL JEANNE D'ARC MAP P.70, POCKET MAP F16. 3 rue de Jarente Ⓜ St-Paul. ⓦ hoteljeannedarc.com. This popular and charming old hotel, just off lovely place du Marché Ste-Catherine, has been upgraded, but still remains a good-value choice, considering its central Marais location. The small rooms are elegant and modern, with wooden floors, some retaining original features such as exposed brick walls. The triple at the top has nice views over the rooftops, and corner rooms have more light. Staff are friendly and helpful. €€

HÔTEL JULES ET JIM MAP P.70, POCKET MAP F14. 11 rue des Gravilliers Ⓜ Arts-et-Métiers. ⓦ hoteljulesetjim.com. Very cool, contemporary hotel, with lots of hip design features – check out the reception desk made of books – and 23 quiet, swish rooms. There's a good bar opening onto the cobbled courtyard (it closes at 11pm to avoid disturbing guests in courtyard rooms), and really welcoming staff. €€

HÔTEL NATIONAL DES ARTS ET METIERS
MAP P.70, POCKET MAP F14. 243
rue Saint Martin Ⓜ Arts-et-Métiers.
Ⓦ hotelnational.paris. Opened in 2017 and
widely hailed the city's hippest hotel, this
stylish number sits in two Haussmann-era
buildings and has beautifully designed
contemporary rooms, many with their own
balcony or terrace. In addition, there's an
Italian restaurant, rooftop bar with fantastic
views, and ground-floor bar, *Herbarium*,
which specializes in unusual perfumed-
based cocktails. €€

HÔTEL DE NICE MAP P.70, POCKET MAP
F16. 42 bis rue de Rivoli Ⓜ Hôtel-de-
Ville. Ⓦ hoteldenice.com. A delightful
old-world charm pervades this six-storey
establishment, its pretty rooms hung with
old prints and furnished with deep-coloured
fabrics. Double-glazing helps to block out
the traffic on rue de Rivoli. €

HÔTEL PAVILLON DE LA REINE MAP
P.70, POCKET MAP G16. 28 pl des Vosges
Ⓜ Bastille. Ⓦ pavillon-de-la-reine.
com. A perfect honeymoon hideaway in
a beautiful ivy-covered mansion off the
adorable place des Vosges, it preserves
an intimate ambience. It also has a spa
and a fine restaurant, with seating outside
in the garden courtyard in the warmer
months. €€€

HÔTEL DU PETIT MOULIN MAP P.70,
POCKET MAP G15. 29–31 rue du Poitou
Ⓜ St-Sébastien- Froissart/Filles-du-
Calvaire. Ⓦ hoteldupetitmoulin.com. This
attractive boutique hotel is set in an old
bakery and was designed top to bottom by
Christian Lacroix. The designer's *joie de
vivre* reigns in the seventeen rooms, with
a fusion of styles from elegant Baroque to
Sixties kitsch: pinks and lime greens vie
with *toile de Jouy* prints, and pod chairs sit
by antique dressing tables. €€

Bastille

MAMA SHELTER MAP P.84, POCKET MAP
C21. 109 rue de Bagnolet Ⓜ Alexandre-
Dumas. Ⓦ mamashelter.com. The endless
focus on hip and cool branding – "Mama
says" this, "Mama says" that – can be
a bit wearing, but the youthful *Mama
Shelter*, owned by Club Med founders and
designed by Philippe Starck, actually offers
surprisingly good rates and can be a lot
of fun. Free in-room movies and iMacs are
standard, while a bar-restaurant (live music
at weekends), sun terrace and top-notch
service complete the package. €

HÔTEL MARAIS BASTILLE MAP P.84,
POCKET MAP H16. 36 bd Richard-
Lenoir Ⓜ Bréguet-Sabin/Bastille.
Ⓦ maraisbastille.com. Part of the Best
Western chain, this 37-room hotel has a
swish, contemporary interior. The public
spaces are a bit overdesigned, but the rooms,
while small, are comfy and clean, done out
in soothing hues with splashes of paintbox-
bright colour and modern bathrooms. €

HÔTEL PARIS BASTILLE BOUTET MAP
P.84, POCKET MAP C21. 22–24 rue
Faidherbe Ⓜ Faidherbe-Chaligny. Ⓦ all.
accor.com. The first five-star hotel in
eastern Paris opened in 2016 in a lovely
old Art Deco building, a former joinery
workshop and chocolate factory. It's been
stylishly restored to provide eighty sleek
decent-sized rooms in muted colours,
including eight rooftop suites with pretty
terraces. An added attraction is the spa,
hammam and beautiful indoor pool with its
blue-and-white glazed tiles. €€

HÔTEL DE LA PORTE DORÉE MAP P.84,
POCKET MAP M11. 273 av Daumesnil
Ⓜ Porte-Dorée. Ⓦ hoteldelaportedoree.
com. A welcoming, family-friendly hotel
tastefully refurbished by an American–
French family. Preserves period features
such as ceiling mouldings and fireplaces,
and many of the furnishings are antique,
but all rooms have private shower or bath,
TV and comfy beds. €

The Quartier Latin

HÔTEL DESIGN SORBONNE MAP P.92,
POCKET MAP E19. 6 rue Victor Cousin
Ⓜ Cluny La Sorbonne. Ⓦ hotelsorbonne.
com. Brilliantly situated hotel with designer
decor, eye-popping colour schemes and
iMacs in each room. Above all, though, the
rooms are cosy, comfortable and well-
equipped, the staff are friendly and prices
are good for this standard and location. €

ESMERALDA MAP P.92, POCKET MAP D17, 4 rue St-Julien-le-Pauvre ⓜ St-Michel/Maubert-Mutualité. ⓦ hotel-esmeralda.fr. Dozing in an ancient house on square Viviani, this rickety old hotel (no lift) offers a deeply old-fashioned feel, with cosily unmodernized en-suite rooms done up in worn red velvet or faded florals. A few rooms have superb views of Notre-Dame. €

FAMILIA HÔTEL MAP P.92, POCKET MAP E18. 11 rue des Écoles ⓜ Cardinal-Lemoine/Maubert-Mutualité/Jussieu. ☎ 01 43 54 55 27, ⓦ familiahotel.com. Friendly, family-run hotel in the heart of the *quartier*. Rooms are small but attractive, with beams and *toile de Jouy* wallpaper; some have views of Notre-Dame while others have balconies. €

HÔTEL DES GRANDES ÉCOLES MAP P.92, POCKET MAP E19. 75 rue du Cardinal-Lemoine ⓜ Cardinal-Lemoine. ⓦ hoteldesgrandesecoles.com. Follow the cobbled alleyway to a large, peaceful garden and this tranquil hotel, with its pretty, old-fashioned rooms. Reserve well in advance; it fills up fast. €€

HÔTEL MARIGNAN MAP P.92, POCKET MAP D18. 13 rue du Sommerard ⓜ Maubert-Mutualité. ⓦ hotel-marignan.com. Great-value place, totally sympathetic to the needs of rucksack-toting foreigners, with free wi-fi, laundry, ironing and kitchen facilities, a library of guidebooks – and rooms for up to five people. The cheapest rooms share bathrooms with one other room. €

HÔTEL RÉSIDENCE HENRI IV MAP P.92, POCKET MAP E18. 50 rue des Bernardins ⓜ Maubert-Mutualité. ⓦ residencehenri4.com. Set back from the busy rue des Écoles on a cul-de-sac, this hotel is discreet and elegant, featuring classically styled rooms. Some have period features like fireplaces, and all have miniature kitchenettes. €

SELECT HÔTEL MAP P.92, POCKET MAP C18. 51 place de la Sorbonne ⓜ Cluny-Sorbonne. ⓦ selecthotel.fr. Situated right on the *place*, this hotel has had the full designer makeover, with exposed stone walls, leather and recessed wood trim much in evidence. €€

St-Germain

HÔTEL DU DANUBE MAP P.102, POCKET MAP B16. 58 rue Jacob ⓜ St-Germain-des-Prés. ⓦ hoteldanube.fr. An elegant, very friendly hotel set right in the heart of St-Germain. The standard rooms are small and attractively decorated, but the *supérieures* are the ones to go for: unusually large, each with a pair of handsome, tall windows. It's very popular, so be sure to book well in advance. €€

GRAND HÔTEL DES BALCONS MAP P.102, POCKET MAP C18. 3 rue Casimir-Delavigne ⓜ Odéon. ⓦ balcons.com. Although it has been somewhat modernized, this appealing, comfortable hotel has retained a few Art Deco motifs in its rooms. It's fair value, and in a lovely location near the Odéon and Luxembourg gardens. Other than those on the fifth floor, the balconies in question are small, decorative affairs. €

L'HÔTEL MAP P.102, POCKET MAP B16. 13 rue des Beaux Arts ⓜ Mabillon., ⓦ l-hotel.com. A boutique hotel epitomizing louche Left Bank opulence, with twenty theatrical rooms, designed by Jacques Garcia, accessed by a spiral staircase. There's a hammam pool and steam room in the basement, a Michelin-starred restaurant and a stylish little bar. Oscar Wilde died here, "fighting a duel" with his wallpaper, and he's now remembered in a room with a "Wilde" theme. €€€

HÔTEL DES MARRONNIERS MAP P.102, POCKET MAP B16. 21 rue Jacob ⓜ St-Germain-des-Prés. ⓦ hoteldesmarronniers.com. A charming, old-fashioned hotel, with tiny rooms swathed in deep velvet curtains and expensive fabric wall-coverings. The breakfast room gives onto a pleasant pebbled courtyard garden. €€

HÔTEL MICHELET-ODÉON MAP P.102, POCKET MAP C18. 6 place de l'Odéon ⓜ Odéon. ⓦ hotelmicheletodeon.com. A bargain for a hotel so close to the Jardin du Luxembourg. Rooms are clean, quiet and unusually attractive (especially those facing onto the *place*) and some are unusually large for the price. €

HÔTEL DE NESLE MAP P.102, POCKET MAP C16. 7 rue de Nesle Ⓜ St-Michel. Ⓦ hoteldenesleparis.com. Eccentric and sometimes chaotic hotel whose rooms are decorated with cartoon historical murals that you'll either love or hate. Rooms are tiny, but inexpensive for the amazingly central location. Ideally, phone to reserve (it's best to have a little French). €

RELAIS CHRISTINE MAP P.102, POCKET MAP C17. 3 rue Christine Ⓜ Odéon/St Michel. Ⓦ relais-christine.com. Deeply elegant, romantic four-star in a sixteenth-century former convent set around a deliciously hidden courtyard. It's well worth paying the 20 percent premium for one of the *supérieure* rooms. €€€

RELAIS SAINT-SULPICE MAP P.102, POCKET MAP B18. 3 rue Garancière Ⓜ St-Sulpice/St-Germain-des-Prés. Ⓦ relais-saint-sulpice.com. Set in an aristocratic townhouse immediately behind St-Sulpice's apse, this is a discreetly classy small hotel with well-furnished rooms painted in cheerful Provençal colours. The sauna is a nice touch. €€

HÔTEL DE L'UNIVERSITÉ MAP P.102, Pocket map A16. 22 rue de l'Universite Ⓜ Rue-du-Bac. Ⓦ hoteluniversite.com. Cosy, quiet boutique three-star with antique details, including beamed ceilings and fireplaces in the larger, slightly pricier rooms. €€

Montparnasse and southern Paris

HÔTEL DELAMBRE MAP P.112, POCKET MAP F11. 35 rue Delambre Ⓜ Edgar-Quinet. Ⓦ delambre-paris-hotel.com. Beyond the appealing turquoise and gold exterior you'll find the odd colourful flourish in this reliable choice on the northern edge of Montparnasse towards St-Germain. Above all, though, the *Delambre* stands out for its friendly service and spotless, comfortable en-suite rooms, some of which have little balconies. €

HÔTEL HENRIETTE MAP P.114, POCKET MAP E19. 9 rue des Gobelins Ⓜ Les Gobelins. Ⓦ hotelhenriette.com. Gorgeous boutique hotel with an airy contemporary feel and impeccable attention to detail courtesy of the owner's experience in fashion styling. The 32 small rooms are each different and all lovely. Bonuses include the cute walled patio, the quiet location and the warm, friendly staff. €

LA MANUFACTURE MAP P.114, POCKET MAP J12. 8 rue Philippe de Champagne Ⓜ Place d'Italie. Ⓦ hotel-la-manufacture. com. Even the smallest rooms of the sixty-odd choices at this comfortable, welcoming hotel are attractive, trimmed in bright colours, with wood flooring; some have large bathrooms, some have balconies, and others look onto the handsome *mairie*. €

HÔTEL MISTRAL MAP P.112, POCKET MAP E12. 24 rue de Cels Ⓜ Pernety/Alésia. Ⓦ hotel-mistral-paris.com. Welcoming, cosy and pleasantly refurbished family-run hotel on a very quiet street, with a little courtyard garden, where breakfast is served in warmer weather. €€

SOLAR HÔTEL MAP P.112, POCKET MAP F12. 22 rue Boulard Ⓜ Denfert-Rochereau. Ⓦ solarhotel.fr. Set on an old-fashioned Montparnasse street, this budget hotel has an original and friendly spirit – there are paintings by local artists on the walls, cultural events in the back garden and the hotel strives to be ecological, with low-energy fittings, organic breakfasts and free bike rental. Don't be put off by the exterior: rooms are basic, but comfortable and bright, with a/c and TV. Wi-fi in the breakfast room only. Breakfast included in the price. €

Montmartre and northern Paris

HÔTEL DES ARTS MAP P.124, POCKET MAP G3. 5 rue Tholozé Ⓜ Abbesses/Blanche. Ⓦ arts-hotel-paris.com. Manages that rare combination of homeliness and efficiency, with courteous staff and a welcoming feel. Rooms are fairly small but well maintained, quiet and very comfortable, with dashes of colour and style – and the topmost "superior" ones have Eiffel Tower views. €€

HÔTEL BONSÉJOUR MONTMARTRE MAP P.124, POCKET MAP G3. 11 rue Burq ⓂAbbesses. ⓦ hotel-bonsejour.com. The location is a dream – on a quiet street on the slopes of Montmartre, footsteps away from great neighbourhood bars and restaurants – and the simple clean rooms (the cheaper ones with shared bathroom), renovated in 2018, are a bargain. Ask for the corner rooms 23, 33, 43 or 53, which have balconies. **€**

HÔTEL ELDORADO MAP P.124, POCKET MAP E3. 18 rue des Dames Ⓜ Place de Clichy. ☎01 45 22 35 21, ⓦ hoteleldoradoparis. com. Idiosyncratic hotel in the bohemian Batignolles village, with its own little restaurant and a flower-filled courtyard garden. The small rooms are worn in places, but charmingly decorated, with bright colours offsetting vintage furnishings and the old hotel fittings that are fast disappearing from Paris. The cheapest rooms have washbasin only and shared bathrooms. **€**

HÔTEL LANGLOIS MAP P.124, POCKET MAP F5. 63 rue St-Lazare Ⓜ Trinité. ☎01 48 74 78 24, ⓦ hotel-langlois.com. Despite having all the facilities of a three-star, this genteel hotel has barely changed in the last century, with antique furnishings and some handsome rooms. **€**

HÔTEL LORETTE OPERA MAP P.124, POCKET MAP G4. 36 rue Notre-Dame de Lorette Ⓜ St-Georges. ⓦ astotel.com. With its handsome location by elegant place Georges, this welcoming hotel feels refreshingly unlike a chain, though it is part of the Astotel group and staff are very professional. The warm, moderately stylish rooms are all a good size. **€**

Northeastern Paris

LE CITIZEN HÔTEL MAP P.136, POCKET MAP K5. 96 quai de Jemmapes Ⓜ Jacques Bonserpant. ⓦ lecitizenhotel.com. The *Citizen* is an ecofriendly design hotel with only twelve rooms. The Zen-style decor of light wood and pale tones makes for nice, airy rooms, all of which have windows overlooking the Canal St-Martin. The cheaper rooms are compact, the more expensive are twice as big. **€€**

COSMOS HÔTEL MAP P.136, POCKET MAP H14. 35 rue Jean-Pierre Timbaud Ⓜ Parmentier. ⓦ cosmos-hotel-paris. com. Contemporary budget hotel, excellently located for the bars and cafés of Oberkampf, offering clean, minimalist en-suite rooms. The styling is a little bland, the fittings occasionally a bit rough around the edges and the bathrooms are minuscule, but beds are super-comfortable and it's a welcoming base. The larger doubles (€82) are worth the extra for a longer stay. **€**

HÔTEL FABRIC MAP P.136, POCKET MAP E19. 31 rue de la Folie Méricourt Ⓜ Sainte-Ambroise/Oberkampf. ⓦ hotelfabric.com. A former fabric mill is the setting for this exceptionally welcoming and delightful boutique hotel, with colourful modern decor, high ceilings and exposed brick walls. Nice touches include complimentary coffee and cake and an honesty bar. **€€**

HÔTEL GABRIEL MAP P.136, POCKET MAP h14. 25 rue du Grand-Prieuré Ⓜ Oberkampf. ⓦ hotelgabrielparis.com. Beyond the unremarkable exterior is an elegant and tranquil hotel that combines an old-fashioned feel with modern design. Rooms are tiny but swish, with lots of cool contemporary furnishings and good bathrooms. Breakfast is included and can be eaten in your room. **€€**

LE GENERAL HÔTEL MAP P.136, POCKET MAP G14. 5–7 rue Rampon Ⓜ République. ⓦ legeneralhotel.com. This cool boutique hotel, run by helpful staff, is a lesson in restrained modern design. The bright rooms have spotless bathrooms and rosewood furnishings. Facilities include a sauna and fitness centre, and the breakfast area turns into a bar in the evenings. **€**

HÔTEL DES METALLOS MAP P.124, POCKET MAP H14. 50 rue de la Folie Mericourt Ⓜ Oberkampf. ⓦ hoteldesmetallos.com. While it might not quite live up to its description as a "design" hotel, the uncluttered, neutral decor of this modern, ecoconscious place has a certain simple appeal. There are excellent online discounts available too, making it very good value for the area. **€**

Hostels

Hostels are an obvious choice for a tight budget, but won't necessarily be cheaper than sharing a room in a budget hotel. Many take advance bookings, including the two main hostel groups: FUAJ (Ⓦ fuaj.org), which is part of Hostelling International; and MIJE (Ⓦ mije.com), which runs three excellent hostels in historic buildings in the Marais. Independent hostels tend to be noisier places, often with bars attached.

3 DUCKS HOSTEL MAP P.116, POCKET MAP B10. 6 place Etienne Pernet Ⓜ Commerce. Ⓦ 3ducks.fr. Lively, long-established and popular hostel in an eighteenth-century building offering homely and colourful mixed and female-only en-suite four- to eight-bed dorms and some en-suite twins/doubles. The interior decor is quite cool and the terrace and lively streetside bar are nice places to hang out. Rates include breakfast and there's a kitchen for guests' use. **Dorms from €**

BEAUTIFUL BELLEVILLE MAP P.136, POCKET MAP F17. 12 rue de l'Atlas Ⓜ Belleville. Ⓦ beautifulbelleville.fr. There are around thirty bright, clean rooms in this colourful, relatively quiet Belleville hotel-hostel, with three- and four-bed mixed dorms, as well as single, twin and double rooms. Rates include breakfast, and there's a simple kitchen with microwave for guests' use. **€**

BVJ OPERA MAP P.124, POCKET MAP F4. 1 rue de la Tour des Dames Ⓜ St-Georges. Ⓦ bvjhostelparis.com. This well-run hostel near SoPi is just about the best in the BJV group (there are others In the Latin Quarter, near the Louvre and in the 17e), attracting a young student crowd from around the world. The historic building is attractive, and though the clean ten-bed dorms have a somewhat institutional feel, the atmosphere is pretty peaceful. Breakfast is included, though wi-fi costs extra. From **€**

LE FAUCONNIER MAP P.70, POCKET MAP F17. 11 rue du Fauconnier Ⓜ St-Paul/Pont Marie. Ⓦ mije.com. MIJE hostel in a superbly renovated seventeenth-century building. Dorms sleep four to eight, and there are some single (€60) and double rooms too (€82), with en-suite showers. **Dorm beds €**

LE FOURCY MAP P.70, POCKET MAP F17. 6 rue de Fourcy Ⓜ St Paul. Another excellent MIJE hostel (same prices and deal as *Le Fauconnier*; see above). Housed in a beautiful mansion, this place has a small garden and an inexpensive restaurant. Doubles and triples also available. **Dorm beds €**

GENERATOR HOSTEL MAP P.136, POCKET MAP K4, 9–11 place du Colonel Fabien Ⓜ Colonel-Fabien. Ⓣ 01 70 98 84 00, Ⓦ staygenerator.com. A well-run and friendly party hostel right by the métro, with spotless dorms (four- to ten-bed, with one eight-bed women-only option) and private bathrooms. Facilities are excellent, with good bedding, lots of storage space, a rooftop bar, a handy café and a cellar club. **Dorm beds from €**

MAUBUISSON MAP P.70, POCKET MAP F16, 12 rue des Barres Ⓜ Pont Marie/Hôtel de Ville. A MIJE hostel in a magnificent medieval building on a quiet street. Shared use of the restaurant at Le Fourcy (see above). Dorms only, sleeping four. **Dorm beds €**

OOPS MAP P.114, POCKET MAP J12, 50 ave des Gobelins Ⓜ Gobelins. Ⓦ oops-paris.com. This "design hostel" is brightly decorated with funky patterns. All dorms are en suite, there's free wi-fi, a/c and a basic breakfast, and it's open 24 hours. Private doubles from €70. Unexceptional location, but it's just a couple of métro stops south of the Quartier Latin. **€**

THE PEOPLE HOSTEL MAP P.136, POCKET MAP L3, 59 blvd de Belleville Ⓜ Belleville. Ⓦ thepeoplehostel.com. Very cool and laidback hostel with a great bar serving good food and excellent coffee, with colourful communal spaces and a rooftop terrace. The dorms (four- to eight-bed) feature comfy bunks with blackout curtains, reading lights, storage space and power plugs. €

ST CHRISTOPHER'S INN MAP P.136, POCKET MAP L3, 68–74 Quai de la Seine Ⓜ Crimée/Laumière., Ⓦ st-christophers.co.uk/paris-hostels. Massive, slick hostel overlooking the waters of the Bassin de la Villette – a great spot, but some way from the centre. Rooms (some women-only) sleep four to twelve and feature curtained-off pod beds. There's a great bar, inexpensive restaurant and waterside terrace. As well as dorms, there are also twins and doubles available. There's another good St Christopher's near the Gare du Nord. €

LE VILLAGE HOSTEL MAP P.124, POCKET MAP H3, 20 rue d'Orsel Ⓜ Anvers. Ⓦ villagehostel.fr. Attractive independent hostel in a handsome building, with good facilities and a view of Sacré-Coeur from the terrace. Breakfast included. Small discounts in winter. €

YOUNG AND HAPPY HOSTEL MAP P.92, POCKET MAP H11, 80 rue Mouffetard Ⓜ Monge/Censier-Daubenton. Ⓦ youngandhappy.fr. Noisy, basic and studenty independent hostel in a lively, touristy location. Dorms (some women-only), with shower, sleep four to eight. There's also a kitchen and a bar. €

ESSENTIALS

Passage Choiseul, by Quatre-Septembre métro

Arrival

It's easy to get from both of Paris's main airports to the city centre using the efficient public transport links. The budget airline airport, Beauvais, is served by buses. If you're arriving by train, of course, it's easier still: the métro runs from all main railway stations.

By air

The two main Paris **airports** that deal with international flights are Roissy-Charles de Gaulle and Orly, both well connected to the centre. Information on them can be found on Ⓦ parisaeroport.fr. The website also allows you to book a number of services like airport hotels, car parking and the like.

Roissy-Charles de Gaulle Airport

Roissy-Charles de Gaulle Airport, usually referred to as Charles de Gaulle and abbreviated to CDG, is 26km northeast of the city. The airport has three terminals: CDG 1, CDG 2 and CDG 3.

The easiest and quickest way to reach the city centre is on RER line B, which takes thirty minutes (every 10–20min 5am–midnight). You can pick it up direct at CDG 2, but from CDG 1 you have to get a shuttle bus (*navette*) to the RER station first. The train is fast to Gare du Nord, then stops at Châtelet-Les Halles, St-Michel and Denfert-Rochereau, all of which have métro stations for onward travel. Ordinary commuter trains also run on this line, but make more stops and have fewer facilities for luggage storage.

Various **bus companies** provide services from the airport direct to a number of city-centre locations, though may take longer than the RER. The **Roissybus**, for instance, connects the three terminals with the Opéra-Garnier (corner of rues Auber and Scribe; Ⓦ Opéra/RER Auber); it runs every fifteen to twenty minutes from 6am to 12.30am and takes around 1hr.

A more useful alternative is the **minibus door-to-door service**, Paris Blue, which costs from €50 for two people, with no extra charge for luggage. It operates round-the-clock but bookings must be made at least 24 hours in advance on ☏ 01 30 11 13 00 or via Ⓦ paris-blue-airport-shuttle.fr.

Taxis into central Paris from CDG cost around €55 (Left Bank) or €50 (Right Bank) – a little extra if booked in advance and if passenger numbers exceed four – and should take between fifty minutes and an hour. If your flight gets in after 12.30am you could also use the Noctilien bus #N140 or 143, which links the airport to Gare de l'Est every 30min until 5.30am.

Orly Airport

Orly Airport (Ⓦ parisaeroport. fr), 14km south of Paris, has two terminals, Orly Sud (south; for international flights) and Orly Ouest (west; for domestic flights), linked by shuttle bus but easily walkable.

The easiest way into the centre is the **Orlyval**, a fast train shuttle link to RER station Antony, from where you can pick up RER line B trains to the central RER/métro stations Denfert-Rochereau, St-Michel and Châtelet-Les Halles; it runs every four to seven minutes from 6am to 11pm (30min to Châtelet; Ⓦ orlyval.com). Two other services are also worth considering: the **Orlybus**, which runs to Denfert-Rochereau RER/métro station in the 14e (every 15–20min 6am–12.30am; 30min); and tram T7, which runs to métro Villejuif-Louis-Aragon, on métro line 7 (every 8–15min 5.30am–12.30am; 40min).

Taxis take about 35 minutes to the city centre and cost around €30 for the Left Bank or €35 for the Right Bank.

Beauvais Airport

Beauvais Airport (☏ 08 92 68 20 66, ⊚ aeroportparisbeauvais.com) is a fair distance from Paris – some 80km northwest – and is used by Ryanair, Easyjet and WizzAir. Coaches shuttle between the airport and Porte Maillot, at the northwestern edge of Paris, where you can pick up métro line 1 to the centre. Coaches take about an hour and a quarter, and leave between fifteen and thirty minutes after the flight has arrived and about three hours before the flight departs on the way back. Tickets can be bought via the airport's website, at ⊚ busbeauvais.com

By rail

Eurostar (☏ 03432 186 186, ⊚ eurostar.com) trains terminate at the **Gare du Nord** in the northeast of the city – a bustling convergence of international, long-distance and suburban trains, the métro and several bus routes. Coming off the train, turn left for the métro and the RER. Turn immediately right and through the side door for licensed taxis (roughly €10–15 to the centre; ignore the touts who approach you directly and wait in line in the specified spot. The Eurostar offices and check-in point for departures are both located on the mezzanine level, above the main station entrance.

Gare du Nord is also the arrival point for trains from Calais and northern European countries, such as Belgium. Paris has five other mainline train stations, part of the national SNCF network: the **Gare de l'Est** serves eastern France and central and eastern Europe; the **Gare St-Lazare** serves the Normandy coast and Dieppe; the **Gare de Lyon** serves Italy, Switzerland and TGV trains to southeast France. South of the river, the **Gare Montparnasse** is the terminus for Chartres, Brittany, the Atlantic coast and TGV lines to southwest France and the Loire Valley; the **Gare d'Austerlitz** runs ordinary trains to the Loire Valley and the Dordogne.

By road

If arriving by bus – international or domestic – you'll almost certainly arrive at the main **Gare Routière**, at the eastern edge of the city; métro Gallieni (line 3) links it to the centre. If you're driving in yourself, don't travel straight across the city. Use the ring road – the **boulevard** périphérique – to get around to the nearest *porte*: it's quicker, except at rush hour, and easier to navigate.

Getting around

While walking is undoubtedly the best way to discover Paris, the city's integrated **public transport system** of bus, métro, tram and trains – the RATP (Régie Autonome des Transports Parisiens; ⊚ ratp. fr) – is reasonably priced, fast and meticulously signposted. The RATP is divided into **five zones**, and the métro system itself more or less fits into zones 1 and 2. You'll find a métro map at the front of this book; alternatively, free métro and bus maps of varying sizes and detail are available at most stations, bus terminals and tourist offices. You can also download a useful searchable interactive online version at ⊚ ratp.fr. If you have a smartphone it's worth downloading the RATP app, Next Stop Paris, useful for planning your journey across the city.

Tickets and passes

Unbelievably, you can still buy the classic paper métro tickets, in use since 1900, although you can also buy swipeable cards along the lines of the London Oyster card system. Buy the Navigo Easy rechargeable card and then load it with individual tickets, a carnet of ten tickets, or a day pass, the Navigo Jour). These are valid, in addition to the métro, on buses, trams and the RER express rail network. There is no refund for any credit remaining on the card at the end of your stay, but the card is valid indefinitely and can be passed on to others. Children under 4 travel free and from ages 4 to 10 at half-price.

Paris Visites, passes (ⓦ ratp. fr), one-, two-, three- and five-day visitors' passes covering either the central zones or extending as far as the suburbs and the airports are not as good value as the Navigo Jour pass, but they do give reductions on certain tourist attractions.

The métro and RER

The **métro**, combined with the **RER** (Réseau Express Régional) suburban express lines, is the simplest way of moving around the city. The métro and RER run from 5.30am to around 1.20am (the métro runs until 2.15am on Fridays and Saturdays). Stations (abbreviated: ⓜ Concorde, RER Luxembourg, etc) are evenly spaced and you'll rarely find yourself more than 500m from one in the centre, though the interchanges can involve a lot of legwork, including many stairs. Every station has a big plan of the network outside the entrance and several inside, as well as a map of the local area. The métro lines are colour-coded and designated by numbers for the métro and by letters for the RER, although they are signposted within the system with the names of

---

Touring Paris by public transport

A good way to take in the sights is to hop on a **bus**. Bus #20 (wheelchair accessible) from the Gare de Lyon follows the Grands Boulevards and does a loop through the 1er and 2e arrondissements. Bus #24 (also wheelchair accessible) between Porte de Bercy and Gare St-Lazare follows the left bank of the Seine. Bus #29 is one of the best routes for taking in the city: it ventures from the Gare St-Lazare past the Opéra Garnier, the Bourse and the Centre Pompidou, through the Marais and past Bastille to the Gare de Lyon. For La Voie Triomphale, take a trip on bus #73 between La Défense and the Musée d'Orsay, while bus #63 drives a scenic route along the Seine on the Rive Gauche, then crosses the river and heads up to Trocadéro, where there are wonderful views of the Eiffel Tower. Many more bus journeys – outside rush hours – are worthwhile trips in themselves: get hold of the *Grand Plan de Paris* from a métro station and check out the routes of buses #38, #48, #64, #67, #68, #69, #82, #87 and #95.

The **métro**, surprisingly, can also provide some scenery: the overground line on the southern route between Charles-de-Gaulle-Etoile and Nation (line 6) gives you views of the Eiffel Tower, the Ile des Cygnes, the Invalides, the new Bibliothèque Nationale and the Finance Ministry.

the terminus stations: for example, travelling from Montparnasse to Châtelet, you follow the sign "Direction Porte-de-Clignancourt"; from Gare d'Austerlitz to Grenelle on line 10 you follow "Direction Boulogne–Pont-de-St-Cloud". The numerous interchanges (*correspondances*) make it possible to travel all over the city in a more or less straight line. For RER journeys beyond the city, make sure that the station you want is illuminated on the platform display board.

Buses and trams

The city's **buses** (7am–8.30pm, with some continuing to 12.30am) are easy to use, and allow you to see much more than on the métro. However, many lines don't operate on Sundays and holidays – log onto ⓦratp.fr for a map of the most useful tourist routes.

Bus stops display the name of the stop, the numbers of the buses that stop there, a map showing all the stops on the route, and the times of the first and last services.

Night buses ply 47 routes at least every hour from 12.30am to 5.30am between place du Châtelet and the suburbs. Details of routes are available on the Vianavigo app.

Paris's **trams** are mostly concentrated in the outer reaches of the city; however, the T3a line, from Pont du Garigliano in the west to Porte de Vincennes in the east, is useful for getting from west to east in the south of the city (see ⓦratp.fr for maps and schedules). Tram stops are marked by a large "T".

Taxis

Taxi charges are fairly reasonable, though higher if you call one out as they add on a pick-up charge. There is also a minimum charge for a journey and they charge for waiting at a flat rate per hour. If the number of passengers exceeds four, drivers will charge more for each supplementary passenger. A **tip** of ten percent is expected.

Waiting at a **taxi rank** (*arrêt taxi*) is usually more effective than hailing one from the street. If the large green light on top of the vehicle is lit up, the taxi is free. Taxis can be rather thin on the ground at lunchtime and after 7pm, when you might prefer to call one out – the main firm is G7 and can be reached on ⓣ 01 47 39 47 39).

Cycling

Paris is becoming ever more cycle-friendly; it currently has 1,000km of cycle lanes, including lanes along the Champs Elysées and the major east–west artery, rue de Rivoli; in fact you can cycle all the way from the Bastille to the Arc de Triomphe. You can pick up a free map of the routes, Paris à Vélo, from the tourist office or bike-rental outlets, or download it from ⓦparisavelo.fr.

Renting a bike is easy in Paris thanks to the pioneering self-service Vélib' bike-rental scheme (ⓦvelib-metropole.fr), set up in 2007. Thousands of bicycles are stationed at around 1,400 locations around the city; you simply pick one up at one rack, or *borne*, ride to your destination, and drop it off again. It's best to check online for the latest information on fees and subscription options, but generally speaking you pay around €3 per 45 minutes. Helmets are not provided. There are between twelve and twenty bike stands at each *borne*, which are around 300m apart. Maps of the network are displayed at the *bornes*, and available to print in advance from their website. Incidentally, if you're caught running a red light while cycling in Paris, you'll be fined €100 on the spot.

Boat trips

Most tourists are keen to take a **boat trip** on the Seine. The faithful old Bateaux-Mouches (Ⓦ bateaux-mouches.fr) is the best-known operator. Leaving from the Embarcadère du Pont de l'Alma on the Right Bank in the 8e (ⓂAlma-Marceau), the rides last 1hr 10min and take you past the major Seine-side sights, such as Notre-Dame and the Louvre. From April to September boats leave every 30 minutes from 10am to 10.30pm; winter departures are around every 40 minutes from 11am to 9.20pm. Barge trips on Paris's canal are also possible and are a great way to discover a less well-known area of the city. Trips are run by Canauxrama (Ⓦ canauxrama.com) and Paris Canal (Ⓦ pariscanal.com).

Boats

One of the most enjoyable ways to get around Paris is on the **Batobus** (Ⓣ08 25 05 01 01, Ⓦ batobus.com), which operates all year round, apart from January, stopping at eight points along the Seine, including the Eiffel Tower and the Jardin des Plantes. Boats run every 25 to 40 minutes (Jan–March, Nov & Dec Mon–Thurs 10am–5pm, Fri–Sun 10am–7pm; March, April & Sept–Nov daily 10am–7pm; May–Aug daily 10am–9.30pm). The total journey time for a round-trip is around ninety minutes and you can hop on and off as many times as you like.

Driving

Travelling **by car** – in the daytime at least – is hardly worth it because of the difficulty of finding parking spaces. You're better off locating a motel-style place on the edge of the city and using public transport. If you're determined to use the pay-and-display parking system you'll pay per hour depending on location, for a maximum of six hours (with rates increasing after two hours). Payment can be made via the app P Mobile or with a credit card at the meter. If you're parking for more than two hours it's usually cheaper to park in an underground **car park**.

Directory A–Z

Accessible Travel

While the situation is improving, Paris has never had any special reputation for good access facilities. The narrow pavements make wheelchair travel stressful, and the métro system has endless flights of steps and not many stations with lifts. Museums and public transport, especially the bus network, however, are getting much better. Most Paris bus routes are wheelchair accessible; RATP indicates on their map when they are not accessible with a crossed-out wheelchair symbol (Ⓦ ratp.fr).

Addresses

Paris is divided into twenty districts, or arrondissements. The first arrondissement, or "1er", is centred on the Louvre, in the heart of the city. The rest wind outward in a clockwise direction like a snail's shell: the 2e, 3e and 4e are central; the 5e, 6e and 7e lie on the inner part of the left (south) bank, while the 8e–20e make up the outer districts. Parisian addresses often quote the arrondissement, along with the nearest métro station(s), too. The first four arrondissements have recently been regrouped into one administrative district that is called Paris Centre, but addresses will remain unchanged, with the arrondissement numbers being retained.

Banks and exchange

All **ATM**s – *distributeurs* or *points argent* – give instructions in French or English. You can also use credit cards for (interest-paying) cash advances at banks and ATMs. On the whole, the best **exchange rates** are offered by banks, though there's always a commission charge. Certainly be very wary of bureaux de change, as they can really rip you off. Standard banking hours are Monday to Friday from 9am to 4 or 5pm. A few banks close for lunch; some are open on Saturday 9am to noon; all are closed on Sunday and public holidays. Money-exchange bureaux stay open until 6 or 7pm, tend not to close for lunch and may even open on Sundays.

Cinemas

Paris has a world-renowned concentration of cinemas, and moviegoers can choose from around three hundred films showing in any one week. Tickets rarely need to be purchased in advance and are good value. Among the more interesting cinemas in the city are: **Le Louxor**, 170 bd de Magenta (Ⓜ Barbès-Rochechouart; Ⓦ cinemalouxor.fr), a 1920s cinema with wonderfully restored neo-Egyptian decor; **Le Grand Rex**, 1 bd Poissonnière (Ⓜ Bonne Nouvelle; Ⓦ legrandrex. com), a famously kitsch Art Deco cinema showing blockbusters (usually dubbed); **Max Linder Panorama**, 24 bd Poissonnière (Ⓜ Bonne Nouvelle; Ⓦ maxlinder.com), a 1930s cinema showing films in the original format, with state-of-the-art sound; the **MK2** cinema (Ⓜ Stalingrad; Ⓦ mk2. com), showing a mix of art-house and blockbuster films, but perhaps most

appealing for its setting on the banks of the Bassin de la Villette; and the cluster of inventive cinemas at the junction of rue Champollion and rue des Ecoles (Ⓜ Cluny-La Sorbonne), **Reflet Médicis** (Ⓦ ldulaccinemas. com), **La Filmothèque** (Ⓦ lafilm otheque.fr) and **Le Champo** (Ⓦ cinema-lechampo.com), which offer up rare screenings and classics. The **Cinémathèque Française**, 51 rue de Bercy (Ⓦ cinematheque.fr; Ⓜ Bercy), shows dozens of films every week, including lots of art-house fare. Film buffs might also like to check out the Fondation Jérôme Seydoux-Pathé at 73 avenue des Gobelins, 13e (Ⓦ fondation-jeromeseydoux-pathe. com); primarily a research centre, it also has an exhibition space, a small gallery of cinematographic equipment from 1896 onwards and a screening room showing silent movies with live piano accompaniment.

Crime

Petty theft sometimes occurs on the métro, at train stations and tourist hotspots such as Les Halles, and around rue de la Huchette, in the Quartier Latin. Serious crime against tourists is rare. To report thefts, you have to make your way to the *commissariat de police* in the arrondissement where the theft took place; you can find a list, organized by arrondissement, on Ⓦ prefecturedepolice.interieur.gouv.fr.

Embassies and consulates

Australia, 4 rue Jean-Rey, 15e (Ⓜ Bir-Hakeim) ☎ 01 40 59 33 00, Ⓦ france.embassy.gov.au; **Canada**, 35 av Montaigne, 8e (Ⓜ Franklin-D.-Roosevelt) ☎ 01 44 43 29 00, Ⓦ international.gc.ca; **Ireland**, 4 rue Rude, 16e (Ⓜ Charles-de-Gaulle-Etoile) ☎ 01 44 17 67 00, Ⓦ dfa.ie/irish-embassy/france; **New Zealand**, 103 rue de Grenelle, 7e (Ⓜ Solferino)

Emergency numbers
Ambulance ☎15; police ☎17; fire ☎18.

☎01 45 01 43 43; **South Africa**, 59 quai d'Orsay, 7e; (Ⓜ Invalides) ☎01 53 59 23 23, ⓦafriquesud.net; **UK**, 35 rue du Faubourg-St-Honoré, 8e (ⓂConcorde) ☎01 44 51 31 00, Wgov. uk/world/organisations/british-embassy-paris; **US**, 2 av Gabriel, 1er (ⓂConcorde) ☎01 43 12 22 22, ⓦfr. usembassy.gov.

Health
Pharmacies can give good advice on minor complaints, offer appropriate medicines and recommend a doctor. Most are open roughly 8am–8pm; details of the nearest one open at night are posted in all pharmacies. Pharmacies open at night include Dérhy/Pharmacie des Champs-Elysées, 84 avenue des Champs-Elysées, 8e (☎01 45 62 02 41, pharmaciedeschampselysees75. pharminfo.fr; 24hr; ⓂGeorge-V); Pharmacie Lafayette des Halles, 10 bd Sébastopol, 4e (☎01 42 72 03 23, pharmaciedeshalleslafayette. com; ⓂChâtelet). EU citizens with a European Health Insurance Card can take advantage of French health services. Non-EU citizens are strongly advised to take out travel insurance.

Internet
Though most hotels have free wi-fi, US and UK visitors will find that in general automatic free access in cafés and bars is not as widespread as in their home countries. Your best bet is to follow the *bobo* (bourgeois-bohemian) trail – to the Marais, Montmartre and the Canal St-Martin, for example, though note that some of the hipper coffee houses actively ban tablets and computers. More conveniently, you can connect to the city's free wi-fi network from 260 parks, museums and libraries; these are all clearly marked with a "Paris Wi-Fi" logo, and the municipal website, ⓦparis.fr/wifi, lists all the hotspots.

LGBTQ+ travellers
Paris has a vibrant, upfront gay community, and full-on prejudice or hostility is rare. Legally, France is liberal as regards homosexuality, with legal consent starting at 16 and laws protecting gay couples' rights. The Centre Gai Lesbien Bi et Trans, 63 rue Beaubourg, 3e, ☎01 43 57 21 47, ⓦcentrelgbtparis.org (Tues–Sat 3.30–8pm; ⓂArts-et-Métiers), is a useful port of call for information and advice. Useful contacts and listings can be found in the excellent glossy monthly magazine, *Têtu* (ⓦtetu.com).

Lost property
The **lost property office** (Bureau des Objets Trouvés Wobjetstrouvesprefecturedepolice.fr) is at the Préfecture de Police, 36 rue des Morillons, 15e; ☎08 21 00 25 25 (ⓂConvention). For property lost on public transport, contact RATP. If you lose your passport, report it at a police station, then your embassy.

Museum/monument passes
The cost of entrance tickets to **museums and monuments** can add up, but with a little pre-planning you can sightsee relatively cheaply. The permanent collections at all municipal museums are free all year round, while all national museums (including the Louvre and Musée d'Orsay) are free on the first Sunday of the month – see the tourist office website, ⓦparisinfo.com, for a full list – and to under-18s.

Elsewhere, the cut-off age for free admission varies between 18, 12 and 4. Reduced admission is often available for 18- to 26-year-olds and for those over 60 or 65 (regardless of whether you are still working or not); you'll need to carry your passport or ID card with you as proof of age. Some discounts (often around one-third off) are available for students with an ISIC Card (International Student Identity Card; ⦿isic.org); this is usually the only card accepted for student admissions.

If you're planning to visit a great many museums in a short time it might be worth buying the **Paris Museum Pass** (⦿parismuseumpass. com). Available online and from tourist offices and participating museums, it's valid for 35 or so of the most important museums and monuments. There is also the newer Paris Passlib' (Wparisjetaime.com/) which extends your options past just museums to various other tourist attractions, services and visits including bike hire, boat trips etc. There are several options on offer for both passes, depending on your length of stay and areas of interest.

Opening hours

Most shops, businesses, information services, museums and banks in Paris stay open all day. The exceptions are the smaller shops and enterprises, which may close for lunch sometime between 12.30pm and 2pm. Basic **hours of business** are from 8 or 9am to 6.30 or 7.30pm Monday to Saturday for the big shops, and Tuesday to Saturday for smaller shops (some of the smaller shops may open on Monday afternoon). You can always find boulangeries and food shops that stay open on days when others close – on Sunday normally until noon. Shops are also open on Sunday afternoons in the Marais, on the Champs-Elysées and in other major tourist zones.

Restaurants, **bars** and **cafés** often close on Sunday or Monday, and quite a few restaurants also close on Saturdays, especially at midday. It's common for bars and cafés to stay open to 2am, and even extend hours on a Friday and Saturday night, closing earlier on Sunday. Restaurants won't usually serve after 10pm, though some brasseries cater for night owls and serve meals till the early hours. Many restaurants and shops take a holiday between the middle of July and the end of August, and over Easter and Christmas.

Post

French post offices (la Poste) – look for bright yellow-and-blue signs – are generally open Mon–Fri 8am–7pm, Sat 8am–noon. However, Paris's main office, at 52 rue du Louvre (⦿Etienne-Marcel), reopened in 2019 after a five-year renovation, is open 24 hours for all postal

---

Eating out price codes

The restaurant prices quoted in this book are for a two-course meal for one including a glass of wine or similar. The following key has been applied throughout the guide based on these criteria and all prices are in Euro.

€	€25 or under
€€	€25-50
€€€	€50-100
€€€€	€100 and over

services (but not banking). The easiest place to buy ordinary stamps (*timbres*) is at a tobacconist (*tabac*). Send postcards (*cartes postales*) and letters (*lettres*) with normal stamps. For anything heavier, most post offices now have yellow *guichets automatiques* which weigh your letter or package and give you the correct stamps.

Racism

Paris has an unfortunate reputation for racism, but harassment of tourists is unlikely to be a problem. That said, there are reports of unpleasant incidents such as restaurants claiming to be fully booked, or shopkeepers with a suspicious eye, and travellers of North African or Arab appearance may be unlucky enough to encounter outright hostility or excessive police interest.

Telephones

Most foreign mobile/cell phones automatically connect to a local provider as soon as you reach France. Make sure you know what your provider's call charges are in advance, as things have changed since Brexit. Same applies to data roaming charges. France operates on the European GSM standard, so US cell phones won't work unless you've got a tri-band phone. For calling within Paris, you'll always need to dial the regional code first – ☏01. Beware that hotel phones might carry a significant mark-up. The number for French directory enquiries and operator assistance is ☏12.

Time

Paris, and all of France, is in the Central European Time Zone (GMT+1): one hour ahead of the UK, six hours ahead of Eastern Standard Time and nine hours ahead of Pacific Standard Time. In France, and all of the EU, Daylight Saving Time (+1hr) lasts from the last Sunday of March through to the last Sunday of October, so for one week in late March and/or early April North American clocks lag an extra hour behind.

Tipping

Service is almost always included in restaurant bills, so you don't need to leave more than small change. Taxi drivers and hairdressers expect around ten percent. You should tip only at the most expensive hotels; in other cases, you're probably tipping the proprietor.

Tourist information

Paris's main **tourist office** is at the Hôtel de Ville, 29 rue de Rivoli (daily: May–Oct 9am–7pm; Nov–April 10am–7pm; ☉ parisinfo.com; Ⓜ Hôtel de Ville), and there's a smaller welcome centre at the Gare du Nord (daily 8.30am–6.30pm). In addition to giving out general information and maps, you can book accommodation and buy travel passes or the Paris Museum Pass. The website has a hotel booking service and also allows you to buy tickets online for some of the most popular sites such as the Louvre and the Musée d'Orsay, enabling you to bypass long queues. Another useful information point is the Carrousel du Louvre, accessed from 99 rue de Rivoli (daily 10am–8pm; Ⓜ Palais Royal-Musée du Louvre; ☉ visitparisregion.com), which also has information on the Ile de France.

For detailed what's-on information check the weekly **listings magazine** *L'Officiel des Spectacles*, sold at newsagents and kiosks, or the online-only *Pariscope* (☉ pariscope.fr). In addition, a number of free independent pocket nightlife guides (*Lylo* is a good one; ☉ lylo.fr) can be picked up in bars and cafés.

Festivals and events

Paris hosts an impressive roster of festivals and events. In addition to the festivals listed below, France celebrates thirteen **national holidays**: January 1; Easter Sunday; Easter Monday; Ascension Day; Whitsun; Whit Monday; May 1; May 8; July 14; August 15; November 1; November 11; December 25.

Fete de la Musique

June 21 Ⓦ fetedelamusique.culture.gouv.fr
During the annual Fête de la Musique, buskers take to the streets and free concerts are held across the whole city in a fun day of music-making.

LGBTPride

Last Saturday of June Ⓦ inter-lgbt.com
The Marche des Fiertés LGBT, or gay pride march, is a flamboyant parade of floats and costumes making its way from Montparnasse to Bastille, followed by partying and club events.

Fete du Cinema

End June/early July Ⓦ feteducinema.com
A superb opportunity to view a wide range of films, from classics to the cutting-edge in French and foreign cinema. Buy one full-price ticket and you can see any number of films during the weekend-long festival for €4.

Bastille Day

July 14
The Big One: on Bastille Day the city celebrates the 1789 storming of the Bastille. The party starts the evening before, with dancing around place de la Bastille; in the morning there's a military march down the Champs-Elysées followed by fireworks.

Tour de France

July Ⓦ letour.fr
Paris stages the final romp home of the Tour de France, and thousands line the route to cheer cyclists to the finish line on the Champs-Elysées.

Paris Plages

Mid-July to mid-/late-August
Three sections of the Seine – from the Louvre to the Pont de Sully, at the foot of the Mitterand National Library near the Josephine Baker swimming pool, and at Bassin de la Villette – are transformed into "beaches", complete with real sand, deckchairs and palm trees. You can also swim in the Bassin de la Villette and muck about in boats. Various extras, from tai chi classes to lending libraries and cafés are available.

Journees du Patrimoine

3rd weekend in September
Ⓦ journeesdupatrimoine.culture communication.gouv.fr
Off-limits and private buildings throw open their doors to a curious public for this special weekend of "heritage days".

Festival d'Automne

Last week of September up to Christmas
Ⓦ festival-automne.com
The Festival d'Automne is an international festival of theatre and music, much of it avant-garde and exciting.

Nuit Blanche

Early October Ⓦ parisinfo.com
Nuit Blanche is a night-long festival of poetry readings, concerts and performance art, held in galleries, bars, restaurants and public buildings across the city.

Chronology

Third-century BC A tribe known as the Parisii begins to settle on the Ile de la Cité.

52 AD When Julius Caesar's conquering armies arrive they find a thriving settlement of some 8,000 people.

486 The city falls to Clovis the Frank. His dynasty, the feuding Merovingians, governs Paris for the next two hundred years or so.

768 Charlemagne is proclaimed king at St-Denis. Over the next forty years he conquers half of Europe – but spends little time in Paris.

987 Hugues Capet, one of the counts of Paris, is elected king of Francia and makes Paris his capital.

1200s Paris experiences an economic boom, its university becomes the centre of European learning and King Philippe-Auguste constructs a vast city wall.

1330s to 1430s The French and English nobility struggle for power in the Hundred Years' War.

1348 The Black Death kills some 800 Parisians a day, and over the next 140 years Paris's population falls by half.

1429 Joan of Arc attempts to drive the English out of Paris, but it is not until 1437 that Charles VII regains control of his capital.

1528 François I finally brings the royal court back from the Loire to his new palace at the Louvre. He sets about building the Tuileries palace.

1607 The triumphant monarch Henri IV builds the Pont-Neuf and sets about creating a worthy capital.

1661–1715 Louis XIV transfers the court to Versailles, but this doesn't stop the city growing in size, wealth and prestige.

1789 Long-standing tensions explode into revolution. Ordinary Parisians, the "sans-culottes", storm the Bastille prison on July 14.

1799 Army general Napoleon Bonaparte seizes control in a coup and, in 1804, crowns himself emperor in Notre-Dame.

1850s and 1860s Baron Haussmann literally bulldozes the city into the modern age, creating long, straight boulevards and squares.

1871 After a short Prussian occupation, workers rise up and proclaim the Paris Commune. It is speedily and bloodily suppressed by French troops.

1874 The first Impressionist exhibition is held in photographer Nadar's studio to mixed critical response.

1889 The all-new Eiffel Tower steals the show at the Exposition Universelle, or "great exhibition".

1900 The Métropolitain underground railway, or "métro", is unveiled.

1914 War with Germany calls time on the "belle époque". In September, the Kaiser's armies are just barely held off by French troops shuttled from Paris to the front line, just fifteen miles away.

1920s In the aftermath of war, the decadent *années folles* (or "mad years") of the 1920s rescue Paris's international reputation for hedonism.

1940 In May and June, the government flees Paris, and Nazi soldiers are soon marching down the Champs-Elysées. Four years of largely collaborative fascist rule ensue.

1973 Paris's first skyscraper, the Tour Montparnasse, tops out at 56 hideous storeys. The *périphérique* ring road is completed in April.

1981 Socialist François Mitterand becomes president but Paris remains firmly right wing, under Mayor Jacques Chirac.

1998 In July, a multiracial French team wins the World Cup at the new Stade de France.

2002 Parisians find themselves paying a little extra for their coffees and baguettes with the introduction of the euro, on January 1.

2007 As Nicolas Sarkozy becomes president, Mayor Delanoë continues his greening of Paris: bus and cycle lanes appear everywhere, as do the Velib' rental bikes.

2012 Socialist François Hollande is elected president but fails to tackle the country's economic woes, quickly becoming the least popular president in over fifty years.

2017 Emmanuel Macron comes from nowhere to become the youngest head of state since Napoleon.

2024 The Paris Olympics are scheduled to start at the end of July. It will be the third Olympics held in the capital.

French

Paris isn't the easiest place to learn French: many Parisians speak a hurried slang and will often reply to your carefully enunciated question in English. Despite this, it's worth making the effort, and knowing a few essentials can make all the difference. Even just saying "Bonjour monsieur/madame" will usually secure you a smile and helpful service.

BASICS

Yes Oui
No Non
Please S'il vous plaît
Thank you Merci
Excuse me Pardon/excusez-moi
Sorry Pardon/Je m'excuse
Hello Bonjour
Goodbye Au revoir
Good evening Bon soir
Good night Bonne nuit
How are you? Comment allez-vous?/Ça va?
Fine, thanks Très bien, merci
I don't know Je ne sais pas
Do you speak English? Parlez-vous anglais?
How do you say ...in French? Comment ça se dit...en français?
What's your name? Comment vous appelez-vous?
My name is... Je m'appelle...
I'm English/ Irish/Scottish/Welsh/ American Je suis anglais(e)/ irlandais(e)/ écossais(e)/ gallois(e)/ américain(e)
OK/agreed D'accord
I understand Je comprends
I don't understand Je ne comprends pas

Questions

Where? Où?
How? Comment?
How many Combien?
How much is it? C'est combien?
When? Quand?
Why? Pourquoi?
At what time? À quelle heure?
What is/Which is? Quel est?

FRENCH

Getting around

Which way is it to the Eiffel Tower? S'il vous plaît, pour aller à la Tour Eiffel?
Where is the nearest métro? Où est le métro le plus proche?
Bus stop Arrêt
Railway station Gare
Platform Quai
A ticket to... Un billet pour...
Single ticket Aller simple
Return ticket Aller retour
I'm going to... Je vais à...

Accommodation

A room for one/ two people Une chambre pour une/deux personnes
With a double bed Avec un grand lit
A room with a shower Une chambre avec douche
A room with a bath Une chambre avec salle de bains
For one/two/ three nights Pour une/deux/ trois nuit(s)

Eating out

I'd like to reserve Je voudrais réserver
...a table ...une table
...for two people ...pour deux personnes
at eight thirty à vingt heures et demie
I'm having the €30 menu Je prendrai le menu à trente euros
déjeuner lunch
dîner dinner
carte menu
entrées starters
les plats main courses
Waiter! Monsieur/madame! (never "garçon")
The bill, please L'addition, s'il vous plait

Drinks

eau minérale mineral water
eau gazeuse fizzy water
eau plate still water
carte des vins wine list
une pression a glass of beer
un café coffee (espresso)
un crème white coffee
bouteille bottle

verre glass
un quart/demi de rouge/blanc a quarter/ half-litre of red/white house wine
un (verre de) rouge/blanc a glass of red/ white wine

Days

Monday Lundi
Tuesday Mardi
Wednesday Mercredi
Thursday Jeudi
Friday Vendredi
Saturday Samedi
Sunday Dimanche

Numbers

1 un
2 deux
3 trois
4 quatre
5 cinq
6 six
7 sept
8 huit
9 neuf
10 dix
11 onze
12 douze
13 treize
14 quatorze
15 quinze
16 seize
17 dix-sept
18 dix-huit
19 dix-neuf
20 vingt
21 vingt-et-un
22 vingt-deux
30 trente
40 quarante
50 cinquante
60 soixante
70 soixante-dix
75 soixante-quinze
80 quatre-vingts
90 quatre-vingt-dix
95 quatre-vingt- quinze
100 cent

Publishing Information
Sixth Edition 2023

Distribution
UK, Ireland and Europe
Apa Publications (UK) Ltd; sales@roughguides.com
United States and Canada
Ingram Publisher Services; ips@ingramcontent.com
Australia and New Zealand
Booktopia; retailer@booktopia.com.au
Worldwide
Apa Publications (UK) Ltd; sales@roughguides.com

Special Sales, Content Licensing and CoPublishing
Rough Guides can be purchased in bulk quantities at discounted prices. We can
create special editions, personalised jackets and corporate imprints tailored to
your needs. sales@roughguides.com.
roughguides.com

Printed in Czech Republic

This book was produced using **Typefi** automated publishing software.

All rights reserved
© 2023 Apa Digital AG
Maps © 2023 Apa Digital AG
License edition © Apa Publications Ltd UK

No part of this publication may be reproduced, stored in or introduced into
a retrieval system, or transmitted in any form, or by any means (electronic,
mechanical, photocopying, recording or otherwise) without the prior written
permission of the copyright owner.

A catalogue record for this book is available from the British Library
The publishers and authors have done their best to ensure the accuracy and
currency of all the information in **Pocket Rough Guide Paris**, however, they can
accept no responsibility for any loss, injury, or inconvenience sustained by any
traveller as a result of information or advice contained in the guide.

Rough Guide Credits
Editor: Kate Drynan
Cartography: Katie Bennett
Picture editor: Tom Smyth
Layout: Greg Madejak

Original design: Richard Czapnik
Head of DTP and Pre-Press:
Rebeka Davies
Head of Publishing: Sarah Clark

Help us update

We've gone to a lot of effort to ensure that this edition of the **Pocket Rough Guide Paris** is accurate and up-to-date. However, things change – places get "discovered", opening hours are notoriously fickle, restaurants and rooms raise prices or lower standards. If you feel we've got it wrong or left something out, we'd like to know, and if you can remember the address, the price, the hours, the phone number, so much the better.

Please send your comments with the subject line "**Pocket Rough Guide Paris Update**" to mail@uk.roughguides.com. We'll credit all contributions and send a copy of the next edition (or any other Rough Guide if you prefer) for the very best emails.

Photo Credits

(Key: T-top; C-centre; B-bottom; L-left; R-right)

Atelier des Lumières 139
Alamy 6, 45, 69, 121, 149
Béatrice Hatala/Musée Picasso 12T
Castor Club 109
Dorchester Collection 59
Dreamstime.com 30, 61, 101
Four Seasons Hotels and Resorts 41
Francois Pasteau/L'Épi Dupin 108
Galerie Karsten Greve 81
Getty Images 80
Hôtel Pavillon de la Reine 154/155
iStock 4, 5, 10, 12/13B, 14B, 18T, 18C, 19T, 19B, 21T, 21C, 26, 28, 35, 62, 65, 94, 110, 113, 114, 118, 126, 148, 166/167
James McConnachie/Rough Guides 25, 38, 49, 53

La Veraison 120
Les Trois Baudets 132/133
Lydia Evans/Rough Guides 16/17B, 18B, 19C, 40, 57, 66, 73, 85, 87, 88, 91, 95, 97, 98, 104, 107, 123, 128, 130, 144/145
Ming Tang-Evans/Apa Publications 141, 142
Monsieur Bleu 20B, 51
Romain Buisson Photographe 78
Shutterstock 1, 2T, 2BL, 2C, 2BR, 11T, 11B, 12B, 13C, 14T, 15T, 15B, 16T, 16B, 17T, 20T, 20C, 22/23, 29, 32, 33, 34, 36, 43, 46, 56, 63, 74, 75, 77, 83, 100, 105, 111, 115, 116, 117, 119, 127, 129, 135, 137, 138, 147, 150

Cover: Sacre Coeur **Shutterstock**

Index

INDEX

NOTES

NOTES